Eng^d. by A. H. Ritchie.
From a Photo. by Bogardus.

H. Mattison

THE

IMMORTALITY OF THE SOUL,

CONSIDERED IN THE LIGHT OF THE

HOLY SCRIPTURES,

THE TESTIMONY OF

REASON AND NATURE,

AND THE VARIOUS PHENOMENA OF

LIFE AND DEATH.

"Immortality o'ersweeps
All pains, all tears, all time, all fears; and peals
Like the eternal thunders of the deep,
Into my heart this truth—THOU LIV'ST FOR EVER!"—BYRON.

BY

REV. HIRAM MATTISON, D. D.,

AUTHOR OF "DOCTRINE OF THE TRINITY," AND VARIOUS ASTRONOMICAL AND MUSICAL WORKS.

THIRD EDITION.

PHILADELPHIA:
PERKINPINE & HIGGINS,
No. 56 NORTH FOURTH STREET.
1867.

WESTCOTT & THOMSON, STEREOTYPERS.

CAXTON PRESS OF
SHERMAN & CO., PHILADELPHIA.

CONTENTS.

PART FIRST.

SCRIPTURE DOCTRINE OF IMMORTALITY.

PART SECOND.

RATIONAL EVIDENCES OF A FUTURE LIFE.

PREFACE.

THE work here presented to the public is the result of more or less reading, thought and preaching upon the subject for the last twenty-five years. At first the few facts and arguments in possession were embodied in a single discourse, upon what we have styled the Rational Evidences of a future life. As we still read and thought upon the subject, and preached upon it once or twice every year, revising with each delivery, the single sermon soon expanded into three; and finally into a course of Six Lectures, covering most of the ground traversed in the present volume. These Lectures were delivered in the several churches of which the writer was pastor, and elsewhere, with apparent interest and profit on the part of the people; and as their publication had been repeatedly called for, it was decided as early as 1856 to issue them in their present form, should it please God to spare the life of the writer till it could be accomplished.

After a delay of years, and amid the onerous duties of a city pastorate, we have at length embodied the *matter* of these Lectures in book form, committing our thoughts and illustrations to the enduring page, in hope that we may thus not only reach many whom we should never see face to face, but may thus still preach on when the living voice is hushed forever in death.

And yet, let it be distinctly understood, that the following chapters *are not sermons.* With the exception of the last two or three, no one would suspect from their form or style that their author was a clergyman, or that the matter of the book had ever been embodied in pulpit discourses. Every paragraph has been re-written; and, so far as we are aware, not a trace of their former sermonic aspect remains.

The *order* of the argument is different from that of any other work upon the subject with which we are acquainted. Believing with Mr. Watson, that without a revelation from God, either oral or written, we could have no knowledge of a future state, we have placed the Scripture argument in the foreground, where we think it logically and rightfully belongs; using the Rational argument only as a collateral support and elucidator of the grand and glorious revelation from God. Our reasons for this order are given at the commencement of Part Second.

The *style* of the work is designedly plain and simple. Although we trust it may repay perusal even by the student and the theologian, it was written for the farmer, the mechanic, the apprentice, the young Christian, and especially for the young minister whose opportunities for study have been limited, and to whom books upon the subject are seldom accessible. And yet we claim for the book a good degree of originality; not only in the arrangement of its matter, but also in its arguments and illustrations.

The *Poetic Quotations* embodied in the work, add greatly to its value. Many of them are exceedingly pertinent and beautiful, and will be new to most of our readers. They are the gatherings of thirty years, from a great variety of sources; and as we know not the authors of many of them, nor whence we obtained them, we have omitted all quotation marks and credits in the body of the work, now saying here, instead, that none of them are original with the writer. Most of them will be easily identified by persons familiar with the poets.

To the friends of our youth and early manhood—fellow Christians and fellow-laborers of other years—who, like the writer, begin to mark the lengthening shadows of life's fleeting day, and to look for the opening of the eternal gates—to all such we proffer here once more our Christian salutations. We shall meet but few of you again in this world; but hope to greet you finally in that "better country," where decay and death are unknown, and where,

> The dirge-like sound of parting words,
> Shall smite the soul no more.

The *plate* fronting the title is an excellent copy of a photograph taken in April, 1864. It is inserted in the belief that in the estimation of some it may add interest to the volume, and as a tribute of affection and remembrance to many cherished earthly friends, scattered here and there over the fields of our former itinerant labors, but whom we expect to meet no more in this world. It may not be an unwelcome souvenir to some while we yet live; and may be valued by others—kindred in the flesh and beloved brethren in Christ—as a memorial of our former earthly being, when we have left earth and time forever. For we would not be forgotten here, either while we live nor after our "departure." May we meet again in peace beyond the grave!

And now, grateful to Heaven that life and strength have been granted us to complete the work, and commending it to God in the language of the prayer with which it closes, we consecrate it to the future. May it cheer and encourage the Christian, establish the wavering, console the bereft and sorrowing, convince the unbeliever, awaken the thoughtless and unconcerned, and bring sinners to God, when the hand that wrote it has crumbled back to dust!

H. MATTISON.

NEW YORK, *Aug.* 5, 1864.

NOTE.—It is the author's purpose, should life and health permit, to prepare a similar volume upon *The Resurrection of the Dead*, to be followed by another upon *The Heavenly World*, and still another, upon the subject of *Future Punishment.* Should a gracious Providence favor this design, it is hoped that the entire four volumes may be issued, in uniform style, as early as January 1867 at the latest.

THE IMMORTALITY OF THE SOUL.

PART FIRST.

SCRIPTURE DOCTRINE OF IMMORTALITY.

CHAPTER I.

PHILOSOPHICAL DISTINCTION BETWEEN MATTER AND SPIRIT.

I. THE term *matter* is a generic term applied to all substances, of which we have knowledge by our natural senses. Whatever is visible or tangible, or has form or color, or odor, or may be heard, or smelled, or tasted, or which we may control or direct by material agencies, is justly denominated a *material substance.*

II. But our knowledge of matter is confined wholly to its *properties,* some of which are revealed to one of the senses, and some to another. We may have sensible evidence of the *form* and *color* of a substance, but of the ultimate particles of which it is composed, we know nothing beyond their qualities or attributes.

III. As a general rule, the peculiar properties of the various species of material objects adhere tenaciously to their original substances. We cannot change lead into gold, or silver into iron. This fact justifies the belief, that while each is alike material, there is an essential difference in the *ultimate particles* of which these substances are composed; or, in other words, that the properties of gold, &c., are due, not to the adventitious circumstances of arrangement or chemical combination, but to the very nature of their ultimate elements.

IV. As gold, and iron, and lead, and silver, are known by their distinguishing and peculiar properties, so *matter*, under whatever form, and with whatever special qualities, is known to possess certain *general* properties, which it possesses under every form, and under every circumstance of combination. These properties are termed *essential*, because, so far as we know, matter does not and cannot exist without them.

V. The fact that matter under certain forms has but one or two properties by which it can reveal itself to our senses, while in other cases it has many such properties; affords no ground for the presumption that matter ever exists without *any* such qualities. Such a presumption is not only contrary to all observation and experience, and to all the analogies of nature, but is both contradictory and absurd; in that it assumes the existence of a substance, of whose existence it is impossible, in the very nature of things, that we should ever have any knowledge.

VI. We have said that material substances are known only by their properties; and that the number of qualities revealed to the senses, varies in different substances. An orange, for instance, is *yellow* and *round* to the sight; *fragrant* to the smell; *smooth* and *soft* to the touch; *sweet* to the taste; and may be *heard* as it falls from the hand, or from the bough upon which it grew. It thus addresses all of our senses. But the atmosphere, which is as truly material as gold or marble, can only be *heard* and *felt*. We can neither *see* nor *taste* nor *smell* it. Those qualities, therefore, which appeal to these latter senses, cannot be essential properties of matter.

VII. Light, caloric, electricity and magnetism, find their appropriate classification, as material substances: for though they have but few of the qualities of matter, as generally found to exist, they are nevertheless more or less subject to mechanical laws, like the more gross and ponderable substances. *Light* may be evolved, reflected, refracted and analyzed, so as to separate its component rays. *Caloric* may be generated, transferred and divided. *Electricity* may be collected, transferred and divided; and *magnetism* can be divided and transferred. Thus, though in some respects as unlike solid matter on the one hand, as thought or spirit on the other, all these subtile essences, and all others of their class, bear the image and superscription of materiality. No one of them has consciousness or knowledge, will or memory; while, on the other hand, their subjugation to mechanical laws, proclaims them as belonging to the material world.

VIII. The same general law which enables us to identify a substance as *material*, enables us also to identify *each particular species* of material substances. For instance, we have learned by observation and experience, that a certain metallic substance is *yellow* and *very* heavy; that it melts at a certain temperature; is very malleable and ductile, and is not easily corroded. This substance we call *gold*. Whenever, therefore, we find a substance possessing all these qualities and none other, we pronounce it gold.

And so on through all the realm of nature. All classifications and all science are based upon this law of agreement, or disagreement in qualities. If we find a substance with all the properties of copper and no others, we are logically *obliged* to classify it as copper, unless we are prepared to unsettle the foundation of all science, and of all human knowledge.

IX. Ascending from species to genus, whenever we find a substance, however subtile or attenuated, that exhibits one or more of the properties of matter, and is evidently subject to one or more of the laws of the material world, we are constrained to pronounce it a *material substance;* however, it may differ in its qualities from matter in many other forms. We may not demand the hardness of steel, the weight of platinum, or the brilliancy of the diamond, before we pronounce it material. It is enough that it is known to possess *one* quality known to belong exclusively to material substances; or that it is subject to *one* law to which matter only renders obedience.

X. But if, for example, in the course of our investigations, we were to find a substance exhibiting all the properties of gold, with the additional quality of *transparency*, we have found a *new metal.* That one additional quality places it outside of all existing classifications, and calls for the recognition of a new species.

Such, then, is the great law which pervades the whole realm of nature, and lies at the foundation of all human knowledge. To ignore it, is to discard all physical science, and to shut our eyes to the light reflected, through the medium of science, from all the works of God.

XI. But we have come to know of a class of qualities, or attributes, or phenomena, that are not known to belong to matter in any of its existing forms. *Intelligence, reason, judgment, memory, consciousness, reflection and hope*, are not known to belong to matter; and upon the same principle that we create a new species in science, when we find in any substance or object, an assemblage of qualities before unknown; the development of intelligence, reason, &c., demands the recognition of a corresponding essence, different from matter, to which these attributes may be referred. For as all properties of matter imply a *basis* or *ultimate substance* to which they belong, and of which they are properties; so reason, memory and reflection, necessarily imply an ultimate essence to which they belong, and to which they may be referred. And if the difference in ultimate essences corresponds with the difference in their qualities, and phenomena, (as we have reason to believe,) then the difference between the essence which exhibits intelligence, memory and reason, and that which exhibits only extension, color and divisibility, must be as great as the difference in their properties respectively. The ultimate entity, therefore, which exhibits extension, color and form, must be essentially different *in its very nature*, from that which exhibits reason, hope and memory. There is a broad gulf between them—an immovable bonndary that neither can pass.

XII. To that ultimate essence, therefore, which exhibits consciousness, intelligence, memory, will, and reason, we give the name of SPIRIT. As we may not refer the properties of silver to a piece of iron; so we may not refer the properties of spirit to any material basis.

The properties of matter and spirit respectively, are essential characteristics of the respective essences, to which they belong. Copper cannot be iron, be cause it has not the peculiar properties of iron, and has a set of distinguishing properties of its own; and iron cannot be copper for the same reason. So of *matter* and *spirit:* matter cannot be spirit, because it exhibits none of the properties of spirit, and has its own distinguishing properties; and spirit cannot be matter, because it has none of the properties of matter, and has an assemblage of distinguishing attributes of its own.

Here, then, is the basis of the first grand division of the universe; namely, into MATTER and SPIRIT.* On the one side of this infinite boundary line, are GOD and angels, and the spirits of men; and on the other side, all things material, whether animal, vegetable, or mineral; organic, or inorganic; fluids, or solids; atoms, worlds, or systems. The former con-

*"So far as the researches of philosophy extend, there are but two primary substances in the universe, and these are MATTER and SPIRIT. All we know of these substances, is certain properties and phenomena which they exhibit. Matter is known to possess the properties of impenetrability, extension, figure, divisibility, indestructibility, attraction. Spirit is that which thinks, perceives, remembers, reasons, wills, and is susceptible of love, hatred, joy, and grief. The former of these properties are found in our bodies, in common with all other matter; the latter constitute the phenomena of the mind. It is not reasonable to suppose that properties so opposite to each other, inhere in the same substance, and the only rational conclusion is that matter is not mind, and that mind is not matter." *Lee's Theology,* p. 257.

stitute the spiritual and the latter, the material universe.

Such is the teaching of all true philosophy, and such we shall find to be the verdict of Divine Revelation.

CHAPTER II.

MATTER AND SPIRIT DISTINCT—SCRIPTURE TESTIMONY.

ASSUMING the Divine Inspiration and infallible authority of the Christian Scriptures, we shall now proceed to show that *they everywhere recognize the philosophical distinction between* MATTER *and* SPIRIT, *and the two-fold nature of man.*

I. "GOD *is a* SPIRIT." So taught the Great Teacher. John iv. 24. The same is taught 2 Cor. iii. 17, "Now the Lord is that Spirit"—and wherever the Spirit of God is spoken of throughout the Bible. Not that God *has* a spirit, as if his spiritual nature was united with another nature more gross and material; but that he is a spirit—immaterial, uncompounded, and indivisible; and unconnected with bodily form or organs.

The same is implied wherever we are taught that God exists in all places, at the same time, or fills immensity with his all-pervading presence. "Behold, heaven, and the heaven of heavens cannot contain thee." 1 Kings, viii. 27. "Whither shall I go from thy Spirit? or whither shall I flee from thy presence? If I ascend up into heaven, thou art there; if I make my bed in hell, behold, thou art there. If I take the wings of the morning, and dwell in the uttermost parts of the sea; even there shall thy hand lead me, and thy right hand shall hold me." Psa. cxxix. 7–10.

"Do not I fill heaven and earth, saith the Lord?" Jer. xxiii. 24. Now, unless a material being can have infinite extension, or universal presence, the omnipresence of God is impossible to him, as a material being. Hence, to assert his omnipresence, is virtually to assert his spirituality. On the other hand, to materialize the Deity, is not only to adopt a fundamental principle of Pantheism, but also to deny his omnipresence; either of which is equivalent to the denial of his existence.

Upon the authority of the Bible, then, we affirm that *in God himself we have a glorious specimen of purely spiritual existence*—an all-wise, all-powerful, everywhere present SPIRIT, without hody, or material organs. The existence, therefore, of at least *one* purely spiritual being, conscious, intelligent, and active, cannot be denied without denying the existence and spirituality of the Godhead.*

II. THE HOLY ANGELS ARE SPIRITS. This is taught Psa. civ. 4. "Who maketh his angels *spirits*," &c.,—and is cited by St. Paul, Heb. i. 7, as being spoken of "the angels of God." As God is a spirit, immaterial, invisible, and unembodied, so his angels, who stand in his presence, and do his pleasure, hearkening unto the voice of his word, are spirits also. Like Jehovah, the Father of spirits, they may have power to impress the natural senses,

*It is no valid objection to this argument that Jehovah has sometimes *manifested* himself to the bodily senses of man, as when he has been *seen* as a flame of fire, or a human form, or a cloud, or a dove; or *heard* as a human voice. Such manifestations furnish no ground for the assumption that God has a bodily form, or material existence; but simply that he has condescended to manifest himself to the senses of men, in a few instances, for wise and beneficent purposes.

for the purpose of communicating with mortals, as they have done in a few instances; but this in no way detracts from the idea of their pure spirituality. For even the Infinite Spirit has at times *seemed* to have form, and has spoken to man "face to face."*

III. THE FALLEN ANGELS OR DEVILS *are also* SPIRITS. They were once obedient and holy; but "they kept not their first estate." Jude 6. And though they "sinned," and were "cast down to hell," 2 Pet. ii. 4; and though Christ saw Satan fall as lightning from heaven, Luke x. 19; this dire fall did not change their essential nature as *spirits*. Hence, they are spirits still; and are merely characterized as "*evil* spirits," "unclean spirits,"&c., throughout the New Testament. And hence the facility with which they could come out of, and enter into human bodies, already the abode of one human spirit. Though no two drops of water, or particles of gas, can occupy precisely the same space at the same time, we have reason to think it is far different with spirits; for in the case of Mary Magdalene, out of whom the Redeemer cast seven devils, Mark xvi. 9; there were no less than *seven* of these "evil *spirits*," as Luke calls them, viii. 2; and one human soul in one body, at the same time. And in the case recorded, Luke viii. 26–36, one man had a "legion" of these "unclean spirits" in him at the same time; for "many devils were entered into him." If there was one for

* "Whatever is actually seen," says Archbishop Whately, "or presented to any of the senses, whether natural or supernatural, must of course be material: but a like *effect* may be produced on the *mind* (as we experience in the case of imagination and dreaming, and, as we read, in the case of visions,) without the presence (as far as we know) of any material object." *Future State*, p. 59.

each of the swine, into which they entered, there were not less than two thousand in one human body, Mark v. 13. And this was possible only because though devils, they were still spirits, like the unfallen Seraphim, and like God, their all-perfect Creator.*

The Holy Scriptures thus plainly teach us that there are in the universe these three classes of purely spiritual beings—GOD, who is a spirit; the *Holy Angels;* and the *Fallen Angels*, or *Devils*. And if one is material, so must the other be. They are all "SPIRITS;" and as such cannot be *bodies*.

* Mr. Geo. Storrs, a noted advocate of annihilationism, virtually admits that the fallen angels are spirits. When, speaking of their final annihilation, he says, "How indescribably tremendous must be that wrath which shall utterly consume A SPIRIT; a wrath so tremendous that even MIGHTY ANGELS utterly perish under it." *Six Sermons*, p. 34.

CHAPTER III.

TWO-FOLD NATURE OF MAN—A SPIRIT IN A BODY.

In the two previous chapters we have seen that matter and spirit are distinct essences; and that to deny the existence of pure and unembodied spirits, is not only to discard the very foundations of all true science, and contradict the plainest teaching of the Scriptures, but to materialize the Deity. We have also seen that the angels, both fallen and unfallen, are *spirits* also, like Jehovah himself. Thus we have not only proved the reality of the distinction between matter and spirit, but have adduced whole classes of specimens of purely spiritual existences. Leaving these points, therefore, as incontrovertibly established, we shall now proceed to show that *man, also, has a purely spiritual nature, distinct from the body in which it dwells, and therefore, capable of a separate and conscious existence, when the body is dissolved.*

By distinct, we mean of an entirely different nature. As electricity is distinct from the body in which it may exist, and light is distinct from the crystal through which it passes, and every part of which it pervades; so the spirit of man, though now in the body is distinct from it; and as capable of separate existence without a body, as electricity is without a conductor, or light without a telescope.

True philosophy and revelation are always in harmony. As we might expect, therefore, the Holy Scriptures every where recognize the philosophical distinction between *matter* and *spirit*, and the two-fold nature of man. The following passages may be taken as examples:—

I. Numbers xvi. 22, and xxii. 27; God is declared to be the "God of the *spirits* of all *flesh*." But what can this language mean, if "spirit" and "flesh" are the same? or, in other words, if man has no "spirit" or soul distinct from the material body?

II. Job iv. 18, 19. "Behold, he put no trust in his servants; and his angels he charged with folly. How much less *in* them that dwell in houses of clay, whose foundation *is* in the dust, *which* are crushed before the moth?" In this passage the soul is as clearly distinguished from the body, as the occupant of the house is distinguished from the house; and to confound the spirit with the body, would be to affirm that the house and he who dwells in it are essentially the same.

III. Job xiv. 22. "But his *flesh* upon him shall have pain, and his *soul* within him shall mourn." Here the "flesh" and "soul" are distinct—the flesh is "upon him," or envelops the soul; while the soul is "within him," or in the body. And these two, the "flesh" without, and the "soul" within, constitute the man.

IV. Job xxxii. 8. "But there is a spirit in man, and the inspiration of the Almighty giveth him understanding." Here the "spirit in man" is plainly distinguished from the physical man, in which it dwells. And "understanding" instead of being recognized as a result of mere animal organization, is expressly attributed to "the inspiration of the Almighty,"—the animating of a mortal body with its tenant spirit.

V. Isa. xxxi. 3. "Now the Egyptians are men, and not God; and their bones flesh and not spirit." Here the distinction between flesh and spirit is as plainly marked, as that between man and God; and we may quite as reasonably confound the creature man with his Creator, as to confound flesh with spirit.

VI. Zech. xii. 1. "The Lord stretcheth forth the heavens, and layeth the foundations of the earth, and formeth the spirit of man within him." Here the same doctrine is inculcated. The "spirit within man," and the "man" which the spirit is "within," are as distinct as the house, and the tenant within the house.

VII. Rom. viii. 16. "The Spirit itself beareth witness with our spirit, that we are the children of God." Here the term "spirit" is applied to both God and man in the same passage, as if, in one nature, man was as much a spirit as his Maker. If, then, this is not the case, what can such language mean?

VIII. 1 Cor. ii. 11. "For what man knoweth the things of a man, save the spirit of man which is in him? even so the things of God knoweth no man, but the Spirit of God."

As the seat of knowledge in man, is not in the flesh and bones, nor even in the brain, but in the "spirit" "which is in him;" so "the things of God" are confined to the infinite mind; and can no more be fully understood by man, spirit as he is, than "the things of a man," can be understood by his material body.

The distinction between the human body and soul is most obvious, and the parallelism of the text most striking.

IX. 1 Cor. vi. 20.—"For ye are bought with a price; therefore, glorify God in your *body*, and in your *spirit*, which are God's."

In this passage, the "body" and "spirit" are so clearly distinguished, that no comment can make it more plain.

X. 2 Cor. iv. 16.—"For which cause we faint not; but though our *outward man* perish, yet the *inward man* is renewed day by day." Now what could the apostle have meant by the "outward man," if it was not his body? and what by the "inward man," if it was not his soul? How can such scriptures be reconciled with the Materialists idea, that man has no soul distinct from his material body?

XI. "I knew a man in Christ above fourteen years ago, (whether in the body, I cannot tell; or whether out of the body, I cannot tell: God knoweth;) such an one caught up to the third heaven. And I knew such a man, (whether in the body, or out of the body, I cannot tell: God knoweth;) how that he was caught up into paradise, and heard unspeakable words, which it is not lawful for a man to utter." 2 Cor. xii. 4.

On the supposition that St. Paul was a Materialist, and did not believe in the existence of the human spirit, distinct from the body, what could he have meant in the above passage, by "*in the body*," and "*out of the body?*" He must certainly have known that he was not "out of the body," if such a thing was impossible. But he held to the true philosophy—that in his normal state he was a spirit "in the body;"

but there was yet another state, in which it was possible for him to exist; namely, that of separation from the body. In which of these two states he was caught up to the third heaven, he could not tell.

XII. The history of the creation of the first man, Genesis first and second chapters, shows conclusively, that he was created as a compound being, consisting of a material body and an immaterial soul. "And God said, Let us make man in our image, after our likeness: and let them have dominion over the fish of the sea, and over the fowl of the air, and over the cattle, and over all the earth, and over every creeping thing that creepeth upon the earth. So God created man in his own image, in the image of God created he him; male and female created he them." Here we have the general fact asserted, that the Infinite Spirit created man *in his own image.* He must therefore have had a *spiritual nature,* unless the offspring of "the Father of spirits" was simply a material being, and at the same time, "in the image" of that God who is a spirit. The order of events, or exact process of his creation, is more fully described in the second chapter, verse 7th. "And the Lord God formed man of the dust of the ground, and breathed into his nostrils the breath of life; and man became a living soul." Mark the order of events as here stated.

First, The Lord God "*formed man of the dust of the ground.*" This was of course a material nature—his *body.* There it lay, perfect in all its parts, but cold and motionless. The bones, and muscles, and tendons, and veins, and heart, and arteries, and brain, and nerves, and lungs, and eyes, and ears, were all in place and ready for action; but as yet, there was no consciousness, nor sensation, nor life, nor motion. The heart had never throbbed, nor the lungs respired. The brain could not think, nor the nerves feel. The eye could not see, the ear hear, nor the palate taste. And why not? Was not the animal organism perfect and complete? And if thought and reason are the result of animal organization alone, why could not the brain have thought, the nerves felt, and the eyes seen? What need of the "breath of life" to set this wonderful machinery in motion? But there was no life, no motion, no intelligence. The eye could no more see of itself than a refracting telescope. The ear could no more hear than a metallic ear trumpet. The quenchless fires of the immortal nature had not yet been kindled. The intelligent conscious *spirit* was not yet there. The "man" formed of "dust" was as yet a *mere human body*, inanimate and lifeless.

The second step in the process of creation, was the vivifying or animation of this man of dust. God "*breathed into his nostrils the breath of life.*" This act was plainly the infusion or inspiration of a spiritual nature into the material body. It was not the imparting of a merely animal life—it was more. Dr. Adam Clarke, like most other Hebrew critics, renders the passage, "*nishmath chaiyim*, the breath of LIVES, i. e., animal and intellectual." Benson renders the phrase, "*the soul of lives*," and the author of the "Literal Translation from the Hebrew," renders the passage, "and Jehovah Elohim formed a very man of dust of the ground, and *blew into his nostrils the* LIVING SPIRIT, and man was for a living creature."*

* For a somewhat elaborate discussion of this point, see Jewish Chronicle for 1852, p. 57.

Not only did animal life then begin, but also that higher life in which consisted, in a great measure, the image of his Maker. He was but a *body* before; but has now become "a living SOUL." Thus God "gave" man his spirit, Eccl. xii. 7, so that henceforth, "there is a spirit in man: and the inspiration of the Almighty giveth them understanding."* Job xxxviii. 8.

Thus the history of the creation of Adam shows as plainly as language can, that both his animal and intellectual "lives" began with the union of the spiritual nature with a material body. We thus learn synthetically what man is, by ascertaining his component essences, and the history and circumstances of their union. The same conclusions will be arrived at in a subsequent chapter, by what may be called the *analytical* method. But as all men are not created as were Adam and Eve, and as questions have arisen as to the *origin* of the souls of mankind in general—whether they pre-exist, are created from time to time, or are in some way transmitted; we must turn aside for a time to these side issues in the next chapter.

* "That the soul is immaterial," says Dr. Clarke, "and forms no part of the human body, is proved from the Scriptural account of the creation of Adam—his body being completely formed out of the dust of the earth, in all its organization, before the breath of lives was breathed into it by the Almighty, and in consequence of which Adam became a living soul, or animated being. Allowing the Scriptural account to be true, this argument is sovereignly conclusive." *Life, ed.* 1837, pp. 504, 505.

CHAPTER IV.

SOULS NOT PRE-EXISTENT, NOR SUPPLIED BY IMMEDIATE CREATION, BUT PROPAGATED.

AT the risk of breaking somewhat the connection between the preceding and the following chapter, we devote a few pages just here to a somewhat curious and not unimportant question in regard to the immediate origin of souls, in the case of individual human beings. If man is a compound being, consisting of a soul and body, and if the former is a distinct essence from the latter, and capable of existence independently of the body, may it not have lived *before* it became embodied? And if so, *when* is the soul united to the body? And if not pre-existent, are souls *created* one by one, as they are wanted for bodies conceived and in process of growth? or are they propagated with the body?

These we say are both curious and important questions—curious because among the deep things of God and of nature, and important because of their bearing upon the question of the separate existence of souls, and also upon the doctrine of transmitted depravity. Indeed these questions often take the form of objections to the doctrine of the distinct existence of human spirits.

There are four distinct hypotheses upon this subject: that souls are pro-created by the angels; that they are created by God, and pre-exist in another state before they appear here in the body; that they are created by the Deity, at the time of their union with the body; and that they are *propagated* or transmitted from parent to child in accordance with certain laws as yet unknown to man.*

Let us examine these hypotheses in order:

I. The idea of angelic pro-creation is founded solely upon the similitude which is supposed to exist between angels and the souls of men. But the more we study the subject in the light of the Scriptures, the more clearly shall we see that the vast difference between human souls and angels, utterly precludes the notion that the former are the offspring of the latter. "This fancy," says Flavel, "needs not any industry to overthrow it; for though it be certain there is a similitude and resemblance betwixt angels and souls, both being immaterial substances, yet angels neither propagate by generation, nor is it in their power to create the least fly or worm in the world, much less the soul of man, the highest, noblest, and most excellent being. Great power they have, but no creating power. That is God's incommunicable property. And pro-create our souls they did not, for they are spirits, yet are spirits of another species."†

II. The notion that all souls were created together and at once, as the angels are supposed to have been, and not one by one, as men are born into the world, has also had its advocates. The Brahmins believe in the pre-existence of souls, as well as in their transmigra-

* Bogue's Lectures. Vol. I. p. 258.

† Treatise of the Soul of Man. (Ed. 1789,) p. 79.

tion. "Of this opinion was Plato, who thought all human souls to be created together before their bodies, and placed in some glorious and suitable mansion, as the stars, till at last growing weary of heavenly, and falling in love with earthly things, for a punishment of that crime, they were cast into bodies, as into so many prisons."

"Origen imbibed this notion of the pre-existence of souls. And upon this supposition it was, that Porphyry tells us in the life of Plotinus, he blushed as often as he thought of his being in a body, as a man that had lived in reputation and honor blushes, when he is lodged in prison.

"The ground on which the stoics founded their opinion was, the great dignity and excellence of the soul, which inclined them to think they had never been degraded and abased as they are, by dwelling in such vile bodies, but for their faults; and that it was for some former sin of theirs, that they slid down into gross matter, and were caught into a vital union with it; whereas, had they not sinned, they had lived in celestial and splendid habitations, more suitable to their dignity."*

So far as pre-existence, and sinning in a previous state are concerned, Dr. Edward Beecher has recently advocated substantially the same view. In order, as he supposes, to vindicate the divine character and at the same time account for the origin of evil, and the fall and depravity of our first parents, he supposes that they had enjoyed a probationary existence, before entering their bodies in Eden; and that in this pre-

* Flavel, pp. 77–8.

existent state they had sinned and contracted a tendency to disobedience and a deep moral defilement. "By thus running back," says Dr. B., "to a previous state, we can mark a sphere in which those principles were observed toward new-created minds which consist with the character of God as revealed in the Bible; and, on those principles, we can account for all the native depravity and entire sinfulness of man; and, as no testimony of God confines us to this world for the origin of human depravity, then if these things are so, the character of God and the general principles and parts of the system prove that sin did not originate here, but that this dispensation is merely a step in the great system of exposure by which God is to be disclosed, truth and holiness vindicated, and error, unbelief, and sin to be exposed, paralyzed and punished forever.*

Of the general theory of the pre-existence of souls, Mr. Flavel further says: "But this is a pure creature of fancy: for, (1.) No soul in the world is conscious to itself of such a pre-existence, nor can remember when it was owner of any other habitation than that it now dwells in.† (2.) Nor doth the scripture give us the least hint of any such thing."‡

III. The hypothesis that souls are created from time to time, for each individual body, is also beset with numerous difficulties. (1.) It involves the idea,

* Conflict of Ages, p. 488. A brief but excellent review of this fanciful theory may be found in the *Ladies' Repository*, for January and February, 1857, pp, 53, 114.

† For a curious paper on the seeming recollections of scenes and events of a previous life, see *National Magazine* for Sept., 1857, pp. 268–271.

‡ Treatise of the Soul, p. 78.

of continuous creation, which has no foundation in scripture. (2.) It is incompatible with the doctrine of inherent moral corruption, which is clearly taught in the Bible. How a pure spirit fresh from the hands of its Creator could come into the world tainted by sin, as the scriptures teach us that human souls are born, is more than we can understand. It certainly involves the idea of physical depravity, a great absurdity, or of no depravity at all, unless souls go forth depraved from the hands of a holy God. (3.) It throws a shade over the divine character, by making God a partner in transgression, in the case of all illegitimate offspring; for if he creates a soul for every human body begotten, either at or before its birth; then even the profligate and the vile have power, while pursuing a course of sin, to control the creative acts of the Deity, and involve him as a party to their transgressions. An hypothesis which draws after it such terrible consequences, must, therefore, be abandoned as erroneous.

But notwithstanding these and many other difficulties, the more common opinion, probably, among all orders of Christians, is, that souls are created, one by one, immediately by God. Many wise and good men have advocated this doctrine. It is the view taken by Flavel in his elaborate and generally excellent treatise, who refers to Theodoret and Pemble as of the same opinion.* His theory of depravity is that "souls are neither pure nor impure as they come from the hand of the Creator. But if it [a question supposed] respect the condition and state in which

* Treatise, pp. 77, 79

God created them, I answer with Baronius," says he: "they are created neither morally pure nor impure: they receive neither purity nor impurity from him, but only their naked essence, and the natural powers and properties flowing therefrom. He inspires not any impurity into them, for he cannot be the author of sin who is the avenger of it. Nor doth he create them in their original purity and rectitude; for the sin of Adam lost that, and God justly withholds it from his posterity."*

We quote this passage not to endorse either the doctrine or the argument, but rather to show to what a strange theory the writer was obliged to resort, to maintain his doctrine of immediate creation, in connection with the doctrine of natural depravity. And, as if not satisfied with the first solution of the difficulty, he immediately proceeds to show, virtually, that after all, moral defilement is derived from the body—the oft exploded theory of physical depravity.

IV. The doctrine that souls are propagated by some mysterious, and yet natural laws of generation, seems more accordant with the Scriptures, and with the various physical and mental phenomena involved in the perpetuity of our species. It is an interesting fact, that although the creation of Eve was as much a miracle as that of Adam, no mention is made in history of the event of the inspiration or infusion of the "breath of life" or spirit into her body, as was the case with that of Adam. Here is the narrative:

"And the LORD God said, *It is* not good that the man should be alone; I will make him a help meet for him. And the LORD God caused a deep sleep to fall

* Treatise, p. 84.

upon Adam, and he slept; and he took one of his ribs, and closed up the flesh instead thereof. And the rib, which the LORD God had taken from man, made he a woman, and brought her unto the man. And Adam said, This *is* now bone of my bones, and flesh of my flesh: she shall be called Woman, because she was taken out of man. Therefore shall a man leave his father and his mother, and shall cleave unto his wife: and they shall be one flesh." Gen. ii. 18–24.

Would it be a forced construction of this passage, to say, that the omission of all reference to the infusion of a soul into the body of Eve, was designed to teach that her spirit was in some way propagated, in connection with the "rib," and that, after the first instance, souls were no more to be breathed into bodies by a direct act of the Almighty, than bodies were to be formed complete out of the dust of the earth.

The following pertinent remarks upon the general subject, are from the pen of Mr. Watson:—

"A question, as to the transmission of this corruption of nature from parents to children, has been debated among those who, nevertheless, admit the fact; some contending, that the soul is *ex traduce;* others, that it is by immediate creation. It is certain that, as to the metaphysical part of this question, we can come to no satisfactory conclusion. The Scriptures, however, appear to be more in favor of the doctrine of *traduction.* "Adam begat a son in his own likeness." "That which is born of the flesh, is flesh," which refers certainly to the soul as well as to the body.

"The fact also of certain dispositions and eminent

faculties of the mind, being often found in families, appears to favor this notion; though it may be plausibly said, that, as the mind operates by bodily instruments, there may be a family constitution of the body, as there is of likeness, which may be more favorable to the excitement and exertion of certain faculties than others.

"The usual argument against this traduction of the human spirit is, that the doctrine of its generation tends to materialism. But this arises from a mistaken view of that in which the pro-creation of a human being lies, which does not consist in the production out of nothing of either of the parts of which the compound being, man, is constituted, but in uniting them substantially with one another. The matter of the body is not, then, first made, but disposed, nor can it be supposed that the soul is by that act first produced.

"That belongs to a higher power; and then the only question is, whether all souls were created in Adam, and are transmitted by a law peculiar to themselves, which is always under the control of the will of that same watchful Providence, of whose constant agency in the production and ordering of the kinds sexes, and circumstances of the animal creation, we have abundant proof; or whether they are immediately created. The usual objection to the last notion is, that God cannot create an evil nature; but if our corruption is the result of privation, not of positive infection, the notion of the immediate creation of the soul is cleared of a great difficulty, though it is not wholly disentangled.

"But the tenet of the soul's *descent* appears to have

most countenance from the language of Scripture, and it is no small confirmation of it, that when God designed to incarnate his own Son, he stepped out of the ordinary course, and formed a sinless human nature immediately, by the power of the Holy Ghost."*

"Since the reformation," says Knapp, "this theory has been more approved than any other, not only by the philosophers and naturalists, but also by the Lutheran church. Luther himself appeared much inclined towards it, although he did not declare himself distinctly in favor of it. But in the "Formula Concordiæ," it was distinctly taught, that the soul, as well as the body, was propagated by parents in ordinary generation. The reason why this theory is so much preferred by theologians, is, that it affords the easiest solution of the doctrine of native depravity. If in the souls of our first progenitors, the souls of all their posterity existed potentially, and the souls of the former were polluted and sinful; those of the latter must be so too. This hypothesis is not however free from objections; and it is very difficult to reconcile it with some philosophical opinions which are universally received."†

Mr. Wesley once believed in the immediate creation of souls, and so explained Heb. xii. 9, in his Notes on the New Testament. But in his journal for Feb. 27, 1762, he says:—"I had a striking proof that God *can* teach by whom he *will* teach. A man full of words, but not of understanding, convinced me of what I could never see before, that *anima ex traduce;* [the soul is derived by propagation or traduction,] that

* Institutes, in one vol. pp. 362, 363.

† Lectures on Theology. Vol. I. p. 417.

all the souls of his posterity, as well as their bodies, were in our first parents."*

Under date of Oct. 25, 1763, he wrote as follows: "It may be of use to insert part of a letter I received about this time:—

"In reading your notes on Heb. xii., awhile since, I was struck with your exposition of the ninth verse: 'Perhaps these expressions, *fathers of our flesh, and Father of spirits*, intimate that our earthly fathers are only the parents of our bodies; our souls not being derived from them, but rather created by the immediate power of God, and infused into the body from age to age.'†

"But meeting with a curious old book, which asserts a contrary doctrine, I hope you will pardon my freedom in transcribing, and begging your thoughts upon it.

"'That souls are not immediately infused by God, but mediately propagated by the parent, is proved, 1. From the Divine rest; *And he rested on the seventh day from all the work which he had made;* Gen. ii. 1: 2. From the blessing mentioned Gen. i. 28; *And God blessed them, and said unto them, Be fruitful and multiply;* for this does not relate to a part, but to the whole of man: 3. From the generation of Seth; *And Adam begat a son in his own likeness, after his image;* Gen. v. 3; for this image principally consisted in the

* Works, Vol. IV. p. 115.

† After Mr. Wesley changed his opinions upon this subject, he struck this sentence from his Notes altogether, and substituting in its place the passage now standing in his Notes, which entirely evades the subject of the origin of human souls, except, so far as to say, that God is at some time, and in some way either directly or remotely, "the author, maintainer, and perfecter of our spiritual life."

soul: 4. From the procession of the soul from the parent, mentioned Gen. xlvi. 26; *All the souls which came out of his loins:* 5. From the very consideration of sin; for they are infused, (1.) Either pure, and then (I.) They will either be free from original sin, the primary seat of which is the soul; and so God will be cruel in condemning the soul for what it is not guilty of; or (II.) We must suppose the impure body to pollute the soul, which is absurd: or (2.) They are infused impure; and in that case, God will be the cause of impurity, which is impossible. This is further proved from the doctrine of regeneration; for that which is regenerated was also generated or begotten; but the whole man is regenerated, therefore, the whole man is generated. Compare John iii. 6. *That which is born of the flesh is flesh, and that which is born of the Spirit is spirit;* and Eph. iv. 23. *And be renewed in the spirit of your mind.*

"'That the human soul is propagated by the parents together with the body, is further proved, 1. By the creation of Eve, whose soul is not said to have been breathed into her by God; 2. From the confession of David; *Behold I was shapen in iniquity, and in sin did my mother conceive me;* Psalm li. 5; which words cannot possibly relate to the body only; 3. From our redemption: what Christ did not assume, he did not redeem; if, therefore, he did not assume his soul, together with his body, from the Virgin Mary, our souls are not redeemed by Christ; which is evidently false: 4. From similar expressions, Job. x. 8. *Thy hands have made and fashioned me;* and Psalm cxxxix. 13, *For thou hast possessed my reins: thou hast covered me in my mother's womb;* where God is said to have formed us with his own hands, which yet is no otherwise done than mediately by generation: 5. From the nature of the begetter and the begotten: they are of one species; but the man who begets consisting of a soul and body, and a body without a soul, are not one species.

"'Again, supposing the soul to be infused by the Deity, either, 1. It will be free from sin, and so God himself will be accused as guilty of injustice, in condemning a pure spirit, and infusing it into an impure body; or, 2. He will be accounted the author of the seul's pollution, by uniting it, a pure spirit, to an impure body, in order that it should be polluted:* 3. A double absurdity will follow upon the supposition; viz. (1.) The organical parts of man only will be slaves to sin: (2.) The immortal spirit would be corrupted by the mortal body: (3.) Or, if the soul, being thus infused, be polluted by sin, it will follow, that God is expressly assigned to be the cause of sin; which is the highest blasphemy.'"

The general doctrine of the above extract is more or less sustained by the analogies of vegetable reproduction. The seed consists not merely of the incipient organization of the plant or tree that shall be, but also of a mysterious *principle of life*, proceeding from the parent, and propagated in the seed. Of that vitalizing principle we know as little as of the essence of the soul itself; and can no more comprehend how that principle can be transmitted in a small and dry seed, detached from the parent bough, than we can

* We by no means endorse the doctrine of this passage, that the body itself can be the seat of moral pollution. Matter can have no moral character.

comprehend how souls may be propagated by natural generation. The one we know to be true, mysterious as it is; and the other is not to be doubted merely because it is incomprehensible.*

* One of the best papers we have ever read, on the question, *"Is the soul transmitted or created?"* may be found in the *Ladies' Repository* for March, 1857. That the soul is transmitted is thus argued. 1. From hereditary depravity. 2. From the completion of the work of creation prior to the Sabbath. 3. From the want of discrimination in the Scriptures between the origin of the soul, and that of the body. 4. From the creation of Eve. 5. From the transmission of psychical peculiarities. 6. From the analogies of the animal and vegetable kingdom. 7. From the Incarnation of Christ, and 8. From the fact of a common humanity. The curious reader will do well to look up and read the articles entire.

CHAPTER V.

THE NATURE OF DEATH.

LET us now return from the seeming digression of the last chapter.

Having shown in chapter third, that the natural life of Adam began with the *union* of his spiritual and material natures, we shall now proceed to show that it was to end with a *separation* of these two natures.

I. The original decree of death, Gen. iii. 19, implies only the death of the body. "In the sweat of thy face shalt thou eat thy bread, till thou return unto the ground; for out of it wast thou taken: for dust thou art, and unto dust shalt thou return." Here it is plain, that only so much of man as was "dust," and "taken out of the ground," was doomed to return to dust again. But the "breath of lives" breathed into Adam by his Creator, was *not* "dust," nor "taken out of the ground." It had therefore no affinity for the material clod, and was not doomed to return to the dust with the body at death.

> Life is real, life is earnest;
> And the grave is not its goal:
> "Dust thou art—to dust returnest,"
> Was not spoken of the soul.

II. Answering to the above view, we find that wherever the *fulfilment* of this decree is spoken of in the Scriptures, it is described as taking effect upon the "dust" or body only; while the spirit is released from the body and survives its dissolution. Take the following, as examples in point:—

Eccl. vii. 8. "There is no man that hath power over the spirit to retain the spirit; neither *hath he* power in the day of death: and *there is* no discharge in *that* war: neither shall wickedness deliver those that are given to it." This passage clearly refers to death; and the expression "to *retain* the spirit," clearly implies that in death the spirit departs from the body. It cannot be "retained" either by the burial of the body or by any other means.

Eccl. xii. 7. "Then shall the dust return to the earth as it was: and the spirit shall return to God who gave it." The decay of the mortal body had been traced step by step through its successive stages of decline. The eye had grown dim; the grinders had ceased because they were few; the voice had failed; and the almond tree had come to flourish; and at length the silver cord is loosed, and the golden bowl broken. But instead of saying, "then the aged man dies," the same idea is expressed in the language already cited—"then shall the dust return to the earth as it was." The allusion to Gen. iii. 19, is unmistakable; and it is a most lucid comment upon that passage. It shows us most clearly the scope and design of the decree, "dust thou art, and unto dust shalt thou return;" viz., that the "dust" or body only is to "return to the earth as it was," while "the *spirit* returns unto God who gave it."

III. To the same effect is Job xxxiv. 15. "If he set his heart upon man, if he gather into himself his spirit and his breath; all flesh shall perish together, and man shall turn again unto dust." Here observe, that contrary to the theory of our modern "Bible Deists," the "*spirit*" and "*breath*" of man are two distinct things; and when God "gathers these unto himself," man "turns again unto dust." Surely it is not the spirit, which God gathers unto himself, that returns to dust; but the *body*, and *that only*.

IV. In Eccl. iii. 19, 20, we are taught that death as inevitably awaits man, as it does the beasts which perish. "For that which befalleth the sons of men befalleth beasts; even one thing befalleth them: as the one dieth, so dieth the other; yea, they have all one breath; so that a man hath no pre-eminence above a beast: for all *is* vanity. All go unto one place; all are of the dust, and all turn to dust again." But lest it should be understood that the death of man is *in all respects* like the death of a beast, it is immediately added, "Who knoweth the spirit of man that *goeth upward*, and the spirit of the beast that *goeth downward* to the earth?" They do not die alike. Their *bodies* die thus: "as the one dieth so dieth the other." "All turn to dust again." But while "the spirit of the beast," like his body, "goeth downward to the earth," the spirit of the man "*goeth upward.*" It is not of earth, and may not perish with the mortal body.

V. The numerous scriptural descriptions of death as the "*giving up of the ghost,*" convey the idea of the *separation* of the ghost or spirit from the body. Abraham "gave up the ghost," Gen. xxv. 8; Isaac "gave up the ghost," Gen. xxxv. 29; Jacob "yielded up the ghost," Gen. xlix. 33; and "when Jesus had cried with a loud voice, he said, Father, into thy hands I commend my spirit: and having said this he gave up the ghost," Luke xxiii. 46. "But man dieth and wasteth away, yea, man giveth up the ghost, and where is he?" Job xiv. 10. Sapphira "fell down and yielded up the ghost," Acts v. 10; and so throughout the Scriptures; the giving up of the ghost is a common phrase to signify dying. Now whatever may be meant by the "ghost" or spirit, (a point that will be considered elsewhere,) it is evident from the above passages, that death is a "giving up" or departure of the spirit from the body.

VI. That death is a separation of the soul from the body, is clearly implied, 1 Kings xvii. 20–22, where Elijah prayed that the son of the widow of Zarephath might be restored to life. "And he cried unto the LORD, and said, O LORD my God, hast thou also brought evil upon the widow with whom I sojourn, by slaying her son? And he stretched himself upon the child three times, and cried unto the LORD, and said, O LORD my God, I pray thee, let this child's soul come into him again. And the LORD heard the voice of Elijah; and the soul of the child came into him again, and he revived."

Here instead of praying that the child's lungs might be inflated with air, the prophet prays that his "soul" might re-enter the lifeless body; and in answer to the prayer "the soul of the child came into him again, and he revived." Though he had once crossed the Jordan of death, and all its bitterness was past; though he had joined the blood-washed company in Paradise, and was now a companion of angels and glorified saints; yet, in answer to prayer he is remanded back to earth, to re-inhabit his mortal tenement. The race of probation is again renewed, and the home of immortals can only be regained, by passing a second time the dark gateway of eternity.

VII. When the ruler's daughter was raised to life, Luke viii. 49–55, it is said, "And her spirit [Gr. *pneuma*] *came again*, and she arose straightway, &c.;" implying that in dying her spirit had left the body, and must needs "come again" before she could again be restored to life.

VIII. When David learned that his beloved child was dead, 2 Sam. xii. 19–23, he ceased to weep and fast; and when questioned respecting his singular conduct, he said, "But now he is dead, wherefore should I fast? Can I bring him back again? I shall go to him, but he shall not return to me;"—language plainly indicating the belief that in some sense his child had *gone hence*, whence he could not return; and that the bereft father expected to depart also—to "go to him"—when this mortal life should terminate.

IX. The departure of the soul at death is compared to the escape of a bird from the hands of the fowler. Ps. xc. 10. "The days of our years *are* threescore years and ten; and if by reason of strength *they be* fourscore years, yet *is* their strength, labor and sorrow; for it is soon cut off, and we FLY AWAY "* A

* The opinions of the uninspired Jewish writers a few centuries before Christ, may be gathered from the following passage from the Apocrypha: "But the souls of the righteous are in the hand of God, and there shall no torment touch them. In the sight of the universe they seem to die: and their departure is taken for misery, and their going from us to be utter destruction: but they are in peace. For though they be punished in the sight of men, yet is their hope full of immortality." *Wisdom*, iii. 14.

very singular expression for a writer to use, who believed that man has no distinct spiritual nature, and that the soul becomes extinct with the dissolution of the body.

X. 2 Cor. v. 6–9. "Therefore *we are* always confident, knowing that, whilst we are at home in the body, we are absent from the Lord: for we walk by faith, not by sight; we are confident, *I say*, and willing rather to be absent from the body, and to be present with the Lord. Wherefore we labor, that, whether present or absent, we may be accepted of him." What does St. Paul here mean by "at home in the body," and "absent from the body," if the soul and body are not essentially distinct, and if death is not a separation of the one from the other? What Materialist would ever employ such language in reference to himself or the event of death? And in what sense was Paul "absent from the Lord" while "at home in the body?" How must he be "*absent* from the body" before he could be "present with the Lord? Is not this its obvious meaning; that previously to death he could not be with Christ, because he had "passed into the heavens;" but that at death his soul would leave the body, and ascend to Paradise, there to be "present" with Christ for ever?

XI. The inspired writers represent the human body as a "*tabernacle*," or frail dwelling-place; and death as the *putting off* of this tabernacle. Thus St. Paul, 2 Cor. v. 1–4: "For we know that, if our earthly house of *this* tabernacle were dissolved, we have a building of God, a house not made with hands, eternal in the heavens. For in this we groan, earnestly desiring to be clothed upon with our house which is from heaven: if so be that being clothed we shall not be found naked. For we that are in *this* tabernacle do groan, being burdened; not for that we would be unclothed, but clothed upon, that mortality might be swallowed up of life."

So also, St. Peter, 2d Epistle, i. 12–15. "Wherefore I will not be negligent to put you always in remembrance of these things, though ye know *them*, and be established in the present truth. Yea, I think it meet, as long as I am in this tabernacle, to stir you up by putting *you* in remembrance; knowing that shortly I must put off *this* my tabernacle, even as our Lord Jesus Christ hath showed me. Moreover I will endeavor that ye may be able after my decease to have these things always in remembrance."

The literal tabernacle here referred to, was the gorgeous tent in which was the ark of the covenant, and the symbol of the Divine presence, resting "between the cherubim." In the journeying of the Israelites, this tabernacle was often taken down, or "put off" from over the ark, while the ark of the covenant, the sacred heart and centre of the tabernacle, remaining unchanged, was borne on to the next station. To this practice the apostle alludes in the text, as illustrative of death—the putting off or decay of the body, while the soul, like the ark of God, moves on to the next stage of being, where the body, like the tabernacle, shall in due time clothe it again and for ever.

In these passages, then, the "tabernacle" to be "dissolved," and the dwellers in the tabernacle are as distinct as the house and its occupant. And that by the "putting off" his "tabernacle," (as Christ had shown him, John xxi. 18, 19;) Peter meant his "decease," is equally clear. But how can the use of such figures be justified upon the supposition that man has no immaterial spirit that will outlive the body? In what sense are we in a tabernacle, so that death is the putting off of our tabernacle, if it be not that death is the separation of soul and body?

XII. St. Paul was wont to describe death as a "*departure*," to occur when he should cease "to abide in the flesh," and without which he could not "be with Christ." Thus Phil. i. 21–24. "For to me to live *is* Christ, and to die *is* gain. But if I live in the flesh, this *is* the fruit of my labor: yet what I shall choose I wot not. For I am in a strait betwixt two, having a desire to depart, and to be with Christ; which is far better: nevertheless to abide in the flesh *is* more needful for you."

What does the apostle here mean by "abiding *in the flesh*," if it be not *living in the body?* And what by "departing," if it be not *dying* and ascending to heaven? Is he not obviously speaking of death? And how could he "be with Christ" after death, if his whole being went down together into the tomb, to dwell in silence and corruption to the general resurrection? Though "to live was Christ," yet "to die was gain;" not because he would find the oblivion of ages in the grave, but because he would ascend "to be with Christ" in the heavenly world, which is "far better" than the most intimate spiritual fellowship with him in this mortal life. It is scarcely possible for language more clearly to teach the doctrine that death is a separation of body and spirit, and a departure of the latter from this world.

The same doctrine is taught in numerous other

Scriptures, as, for instance 2 Tim. iv. 6, where the apostle says, "I am now ready to be offered, and the time of my *departure* is at hand," &c.

Also, Gen. xxxv. "And it came to pass as her soul was in *departing*, (for she died,) &c." It was revealed to Simeon that he should not see death till he had seen the Lord's Christ; and when he saw the infant Redeemer, he said, "Lord, now lettest thou thy servant *depart* in peace, according to thy word." To him, also, death was a *departure*, which could not be true in any sense if the soul died with the body, and was not separated from it.

XIII. Jacob is said to have been gathered unto his people at the moment of death, Gen. xlix. 33, though his body was not buried with the bodies of his ancestors till months afterward.

"And when Jacob had made an end of commanding his sons, he gathered up his feet into the bed, and yielded up the ghost, and was gathered unto his people."

Jacob died in Goshen in Egypt, but was buried in the land of Canaan. They were forty days embalming the body, and the mourning in Egypt continued thirty days longer. Joseph then obtained permission of Pharaoh to go and bury his father. Ch. l. 3–6. How long they were going is not stated; but they mourned seven days more at the threshing-floor of Atad, ch. l. 10, so that at least *eighty days* elapsed between the alleged gathering unto his people, and the burial of the body in the cave of Machpelah in Canaan. How, then, was he "*gathered unto his people*" at the time of his death, if it was not by the departure of his soul to Paradise, the home of Isaac, his father, and his grand-father Abraham?

The testimony that this place bears to the immortality of the soul, and to its existence *separate* from the body, should not be lightly regarded. In the same moment in which Jacob is said to have *gathered up his feet into the bed*, and to have expired, it is added, *and was gathered unto his people.* It is certain that his body was not then *gathered to his people*, nor till *seven weeks after;* and it is not likely that a circumstance so distant in point both of time and place, would have been thus *anticipated*, and associated with facts that took place at that moment. I cannot help, therefore, considering this an additional evidence for the *immateriality of the soul;* and that it was intended by the Holy Spirit to carry this grand and consolatory sentiment, that when a holy man ceases to live among his fellows, his soul becomes an inhabitant of another world and is joined to the spirits of just men made perfect."*

XIV. That death is a mere separation of soul and body, is further evident from James ii. 26.—"For as the body without the spirit is dead, so faith without works is dead also." Here the apostle refers for the illustration of his subject, to a fact acknowledged by all professing Christians of his day, viz: that the body was "dead" when it was "without the spirit;" or, in other words, that death is a *separation* of the soul and body of man.

Such, according to the infallible testimony of the word of God, is the nature of death. The original decree consigns "the dust" only to the dust; while "the spirit returns to God who gave it." Though "man shall turn again unto dust," like the beast, his

* Dr. A. Clarke's notes on the passage.

"spirit and his breath" shall his Maker "gather unto himself." Death is "the giving up of the ghost," and the dead are not restored to life, unless their "souls come into them again." We "fly away" at death, and must be "absent from the body" to be "present with the Lord." We are now dwelling in "earthly houses of this tabernacle" which we shall "put off" at death; to pass, if Christians, to "a house not made with hands eternal in the heavens." We now "abide in the flesh," but are destined to "depart and be with Christ; which is far better." Death will sever the mystic tie that binds the spirit to a material body; and these two essentially different natures will part company till the resurrection morning. Can we better conclude this chapter than by quoting the following beautiful lines from Mrs. Sigourney?

FAREWELL OF THE SOUL TO THE BODY.

Companion dear! the hour draws nigh
The sentence speeds—*to die, to die.*
So long in mystic union held,
So close with strong embrace compell'd,
How can'st thou bear the dread decree,
That strikes thy clasping nerves from me?
——To Him who on this mortal shore,
The same encircling vestment wore,
To Him I look, to Him I bend,
To Him thy shuddering frame commend.
——If I have ever caus'd thee pain,
The throbbing heart, the burning brain,
With cares and vigils turn'd thee pale,
And scorn'd thee when thy strength did fail—
Forgive! forgive!—thy task doth cease,
Friend! Lover!—let us part in peace.
If thou didst sometimes check my force,
Or, trifling, stay mine upward course,
Or lure from heaven my wavering trust,
Or bore my drooping wing to dust—

I blame thee not, the strife is done,
I know thou wert the weaker one,
The vase of earth, the trembling clod,
Constrained to hold the breath of God.
——Well hast thou in my service wrought,
Thy brow hath mirror'd forth my thought,
To wear my smile thy lips hath glow'd,
Thy tear, to speak my sorrow, flowed,
Thine ear hath borne me rich supplies
Of sweetly varied melodies,
Thy hands my prompted deeds have done,
Thy feet upon my errands run——
Yes, thou hast marked my bidding well,
Faithful and true! farewell, farewell.

* * * * * * * *

CHAPTER VI.

CONSCIOUS EXISTENCE OF SOULS BETWEEN DEATH AND THE RESURRECTION.

THE last chapter was devoted mainly to a single point—the nature of death;—the object being to show that according to the Scriptures, which are our only guide upon this subject, death is but the *separation* of the two natures of man, the body and the spirit. So far as this point is established, it goes also to establish the proposition argued in Chapter III., viz: *that man has a two-fold nature, a body and a spirit.* In like manner, whatever tends to prove that man has a conscious existence after death, will go equally to establish the doctrine of purely spiritual existence, and of the two-fold nature of man; as also, that death is but the *separation* of these two natures, and not the extinction of either.

Until quite recently, it has never been necessary to enter into a formal argument to prove the immortality of the soul from the Bible, with any who professed to believe its teachings. But within a few years past, certain persons who, by a system of literalism, had so interpreted the Bible as to prove, as they thought, that the world would end on a given day; by the same principles of interpretation applied to the subject of a future state, have demonstrated, as we think with equal uncertainty, that man has no soul distinct from the body, or capable of existence after the body dies. It would surprise no one to find this sentiment in the writings of Hobbs or Hume; but, to find men professing to be *Christians*, and yet attempting to prove this fundamental principle of Deism from the Bible, may well excite astonishment. It is in view of this theological monstrosity that we have thus far so carefully examined the Scriptures step by step, and adduced their unequivocal and overwhelming testimony in proof of the immortality of man.

But, before we proceed further in this examination, it may be well to call to mind the fact that the Jews, among whom Christ and his apostles taught, were in the main firm believers in the soul's immortality. They were divided into three principal sects—the *Pharisees*, the *Sadducees* and the *Essenes*.

The PHARISEES held to the immortality of the soul and the existence of angels. Hence when it is said, Acts xxiii. 8, that "the Sadducees say there is no resurrection, neither angel nor spirit," it is added, "but the Pharisees CONFESS BOTH." It is true that some of them held to the *transmigration* of souls from one body to another,* but this in no way affected the simple question of purely spiritual existence, and the soul's immortality. In his discourse to the Greeks concerning Hades, Josephus says, "This is the discourse concerning Hades, wherein the souls of all men are confined until a proper season which God hath determined, when he will make a resurrection of all men from the dead. * * * And to every body shall its own soul be restored." This was beyond all

* Horne's Introduction, Vol. I. p. 144.

question the prevailing belief among the Jews, at the time of our Lord and his apostles—a belief professedly drawn from their sacred writings. If, therefore, this doctrine was erroneous, our Saviour and his apostles ought so to have spoken and written as to have condemned it; or at least to have given it no countenance. But instead of this, we hear St. Paul exclaiming on one occasion, long after his conversion, "I am a Pharisee, the son of a Pharisee," Acts xxiii. 6.

The SADDUCEES denied the immortality of the soul, if not all purely spiritual existence. Josephus says, "the doctrine of the Sadducees is this, THAT SOULS DIE WITH THE BODIES."* "They take away the belief of the immortal existence of the soul, and the punishments and rewards of Hades."† St. Luke says, Acts xxiii. 8, that "the Sadducees say that there is no resurrection, *neither* ANGEL *nor* SPIRIT."‡ On this point, therefore, those who now teach that there is no "spirit" distinct from the animal nature, and that, consequently, the soul dies with the body, are only reproducing the oft refuted doctrines of the ancient Sadducees.

The ESSENES, like the Pharisees, "held, among other tenets, the immortality of the soul, (though they denied the resurrection of the body,) the existence of angels, and a state of future rewards and punishments;"§ so that the Sadducees excepted, who were

* Antiquities, b. xviii. § 4. † Wars, b. viii. § 14.

‡ "*Neither angel.* That there are no angels. They deny the existence of good or bad angels. '*Nor Spirit,*' or soul. They held that there was nothing but matter. They were materialists, and supposed that all the operations which we ascribe to mind, could be traced to some modification of matter." *Barnes' Notes.*

§ See Horne's Introduction, Vol. I. p. 146.

but an inconsiderable sect,* the whole Jewish nation, among whom Christ and his apostles went "preaching the kingdom of God," believed in the immortality of the soul, and in future rewards and punishments. This fact will enable us the better to understand the *design* of the New Testament writers, in the use of the language employed by them. Let us see, then, if they have not taught, and did not *design* to teach the doctrine of the soul's immortality.

I. All those scriptures cited in the preceding chapter to show that the death of man is a mere separation of the soul from the body, imply also the conscious existence of the soul in its disembodied state, and its immortality. If the spirit "returns to God who gave it," when "the dust returns to the earth;" if it "goeth upward," "flies away," "puts off" its "earthly house of this tabernacle;" and "departs to be with Christ," it has proved itself immortal by passing unhurt the vale of death, and extending its existence forward into a region where death is forever unknown. And unless we suppose it possible that the soul should live on forever in a state of unconsciousness, the idea of a future and immortal existence necessarily involves the idea that such existence will be one of conscious memory and reflection, and of endless joy or sorrow.

II. When the angel of the Lord appeared unto Moses in a flame of fire out of the midst of the bush, he said, "I am the God of Abraham, the God of Isaac, and the God of Jacob," Exodus iii. 2, 6; and when the Sadducees encountered our Lord, respecting the resur-

* "This doctrine is received but by a few." Josephus Ant. b. xviii. § 4.

rection, Luke xx. 27, 37, he said to them, "Now that the dead are raised, even Moses shewed at the bush, when he calleth the Lord the God of Abraham, and the God of Isaac, and the God of Jacob. For he is not a God of the dead, but of the living: for all live unto him."

Jehovah appeared to Moses in the bush 1491 years before Christ. Abraham died B. C. 1821; Isaac B. C. 1716; and Jacob B. C. 1689; consequently, at that time (B. C. 1491) Abraham had been dead 330 years, Isaac 225 years, and Jacob 198 years. And yet, God declared himself to be the God of these three persons who had long been dead.

The argument of our Lord based upon this passage is this: God "is not the God of the dead," or of those who are *extinct* or *annihilated*. But God was at that time the God of Abraham, and the God of Isaac, and the God of Jacob.

Therefore, Abraham, Isaac and Jacob must still have been alive. And this logical deduction from the premises laid down, is supported by the plain declaration of our Lord—"FOR ALL LIVE UNTO HIM." We talk of the death of man, because we see the "earthly house" dissolved; but it is only an illusion.

"There is no death; what seems such, is transition."

The body dies, but the soul survives death; so that he who is the God of the living only, is still the God of the departed, because "all live unto him."

The bearing of this quotation of our Lord upon the subject of the resurrection of the dead is obvious. The Sadducees denied all future existence. They held that when a man died all life both of soul and body became extinct together, and that neither would ever be reproduced. With them, therefore, the two doctrines—the immortality of the soul and the resurrection of the dead—stood or fell together; and to prove that the *souls* of men live after death, was effectually to overthrow the *system* of the Sadducees, and silence their objections to the resurrection of the body. If *any* life beyond the grave could be proved from the Pentateuch, the authority of which they professed to revere, their theory was in ruins, and the resurrection of the body was established.

III. It is said, Luke xxiii. 42, 43, that the dying thief upon the cross said to Jesus, "Lord, remember me when thou comest into thy kingdom. And Jesus said unto him, Verily, I say unto thee, to-day shalt thou be with me in Paradise." It is obvious that the thief expected soon to die. Indeed there was and could have been no hope of escape. It is equally certain that the prevailing belief among the Jews at this time was, that the soul left the body at death, and went to Hades or the world of spirits, to return again at the general resurrection. This was no doubt the belief of the thief when he said, "Lord, remember me, etc."

The term "*Paradise*" signifies *pleasure* or *delight*, and is used in the New Testament to signify the abode of the spirits of the righteous between death and the resurrection. St. Paul was caught up to Paradise, 2 Cor. xii. 4; and when the Spirit would incite believers to holy living by the promise of eternal life, he says, "To him that overcometh will I give to eat of the tree of life, which is in the midst of the Paradise of God;" Rev. ii. 7. Now, the promise of the Saviour was, that the thief should be with him in Paradise THAT DAY; and, as Paradise is the place of separate souls, to which Paul was caught up, where grows the tree of life, the purport of the whole is, that according to the prevailing belief of the separate existence of souls implied in the prayer of the dying but penitent thief, he should be with Christ that day in a place of happiness. If the Saviour meant simply to say that they would both soon be in the grave, it was no news to the thief, and no answer to his prayer. And if Paradise meant simply the place of the dead—a "paradise" of unconscious non-existence—what kind of a "remembrance" was that which the dying malfactor obtained? and what better off was he who repented and prayed, than he who railed and was forgotten? The passage can have but one meaning, therefore; and that is, that the soul of the dying thief should be saved; and should meet the human soul of Christ, which he was about to commend to his Father's hands, in the abode of forgiven and glorified spirits.

IV. The conscious existence of the soul after death, is clearly taught in the parable of the rich man, and Lazarus, Luke xvi. 19–31. We say *parable*, though the same doctrine is taught whether we regard the account as a parable, or as a veritable history. In either case, the souls of the dead are represented as living, talking and remembering, being "comforted" or "tormented" *after death*. The rich man "died, and was buried; and in hell he lifted up his eyes, being in torments." "The beggar died, and was carried by the angels to Abraham's bosom." Now what does this "comfort" and "torment" after death—this reference to the "life-time" of Dives as then past—the request that Lazarus be sent back to earth, and the plea that "if one went unto them *from the dead*, they will repent"—indeed, what does this whole narrative teach, if it be not that the soul lives after the body dies, and is happy or miserable in another world?

Let any one turn to this narrative, and read it carefully over, verse after verse, and if he does not find there the conscious existence of souls after death, he can find it in no creed, or essay, or argument whatever. Language could scarcely teach that doctrine more plainly; and the mind that can misinterpret or pervert such language, would pervert any language that could be employed.

Upon the subject of the locality of human spirits in the unseen state, Bishop Horsley has the following observations:—

"The soul existing after death, and separate from the body, though of a nature immaterial, must be in some place; for however metaphysicians may talk of space as one of the adjuncts of body, as if nothing but gross sensible body could be limited to a place, to exist without relation to space seems to be one of the incommunicable perfections of the Divine Being; and it is hardly to be conceived that any created spirit, of however high an order, can be without locality, or without such determination of its existence at any given time to some certain place; that it shall be true to say of it, 'Here it is, and not elsewhere.'"*

V. Our Saviour teaches, Matt. x. 28, that *the soul cannot be killed*—that though men can kill the body,

* Horsley's Sermons, Vol. II. pp. 89, 90

they cannot kill the soul. "And fear not them which kill the body, but are not able to kill the soul." The soul is not the body, nor the body the soul; so that while men are able to kill the one, they are not able to kill the other. But if the soul was a simple result of animal organization—the operations of the brain—as materialism teaches—then whoever killed the body, would, at the same time kill the soul. But so distinct are they, and so do they differ as to their mortality, that while men are "able to kill the body," they are "NOT ABLE TO KILL THE SOUL." That ethereal nature LIVES still, though the body dies. The poor material casket may be wasted, and wrecked, and smothered up in the dust from whence it came.

Yet not thus buried, or extinct,
The vital spark shall lie;
For in life's wreck that spark shall rise,
To seek its kindred sky.

And if those who are able to kill the body are not able to kill the soul, how say some among us that the body and soul are the same, and that to kill the one is, in all cases, to kill the other also?

VI. St. Paul teaches 1 Thess. v. 9, 10, that whether the righteous live or die, they are to live with Christ. "For God hath not appointed us unto wrath, but to obtain salvation by our Lord Jesus Christ, who died for us, that, whether we WAKE or SLEEP, [that is LIVE or DIE] we should LIVE TOGETHER WITH HIM." Even if they "*sleep*" they are nevertheless to "LIVE," and "to be with Christ, which is far better."

For there is no sleep, no grave so deep,
That can hold the human soul.

"Neither life nor DEATH" can separate the good man from his everlasting portion in Jesus Christ.

VII. In the account of Christ's transfiguration, Matt. xvii. 3, we are told that "there appeared unto him Moses and Elias talking unto him." Elias was translated without seeing death, nine hundred and twenty-eight years before, 2 Kings 2d chapter; and Moses DIED on Mount Nebo fourteen hundred and eighty-three years before. "So Moses, the servant of the Lord, died there, in the land of Moab—and he [Jehovah] buried him in a valley in the land of Moab, over against Beth-peor: but no man knoweth the place of his sepulchre unto this day." Deut. xxxiv. 5.

Here notice, first, that Moses was *dead* and *buried.* In the second place, it is certain that, at the time of the transfiguration his body had not been raised from the dead. St. Paul declares, Acts xxvi. 23, that "the prophets and Moses" had taught, "that Christ should suffer, and that he should be *the first that should rise from the dead.*" In the first epistle of Paul to the Corinthians, xv. 20, he declares that Christ had become "the first fruits of them that slept;" and Col. i. 18, he styles him "the first born from the dead; that in all things he might have the pre-eminence." The Revelator also styles him "the first-begotten of the dead," Rev. i. 5.

Though several had been restored from death to life prior to the crucifixion, no one of them was raised to immortality. Of the subjects of the resurrection proper it can be said, "neither shall they die any more;" but this was not the case with the widow's son raised by Elijah; nor with the son of the widow of Nain, nor with Lazarus. These all died again.

Never until Christ burst the bars of death, was a dead human body raised to life and immortality. And as the transfiguration was before the crucifixion and resurrection, it is certain that the body of Moses had not been raised from the dead.

What was it, then, that appeared on mount Tabor, and talked with Christ?—that which Matthew calls "Moses?" It was not the body of Moses, for that had not been raised from death, but still slept "in a valley in the land of Moab." It must, therefore, have been his *spirit*, unless he had some other nature beside body and spirit, that might with propriety be called "Moses."*

Here, then, we have the spirit of Moses, with Christ and Elias on the summit of Tabor, near fifteen centuries after his body died, and while it yet slumbered in its unknown resting-place, where it doubtless sleeps unto this day. It is certain, therefore, that the soul *can* and *does* survive the death of the body; and can *live*, and *think*, and even "*talk*" if necessary, ages after its "earthly house" has crumbled back to dust.

VIII. The Scriptures uniformly teach that the righteous enter upon at least an earnest of their eternal reward immediately after death. The heavenly Canaan, like the earthly, is but just beyond Jordan.

When the good man yields his breath,
(For the good man never dies,)
Bright beyond the vale of death,
Lo! the land of promise lies.

For his soul to "depart" is to "be with Christ." Phil. i. 23. Though he "sleep" or die, he lives

* See Macknight on Heb. xi. 40

together with Christ. 1 Thess. v. 10. Lazarus died, and was carried at once to Abraham's bosom. Luke xvi. 22. When the earthly house is dissolved, we enter that not made with hands, eternal in the heavens.

To be absent from the body is to be present with the Lord. 2 Cor. v. 7. "Blessed are the dead which die in the Lord FROM HENCEFORTH." Rev. xiv. 13. "Gr. *aparti. From this time; now, immediately.*"* They have not to sleep in the grave for perhaps thousands of years, a long and dreamless parenthesis of being,—before their heavenly joys begin; but enter at once upon their glorious reward.

> We know when the silver cord is loosed,
> And the veil is rent away,
> Not long and dark shall the passage be,
> To the realms of endless day.
>
> The eye that shuts in the mortal hour,
> Shall open the next in bliss;
> The welcome shall sound in the heavenly world,
> Ere the farewell is hushed in this.

"The transition is doubtless instantaneous. It is no tiresome walk down through a lonely, dark valley; it is no weary flight upward, as the eagle mounts, higher and higher; but no sooner is a believer's soul disembodied, than it is in Paradise. The partition once broken down, what shall hinder an immediate view of all beyond? And oh, what a morning is that day-break of glory! The sun of righteousness shines in all its brightness. It is the effulgence of Christ's person which lights up that whole far-stretching world, and sheds a quickening radiance on every resident

*Dr. A. Clarke.

there. If, two thousand years before Christ's coming on earth, Abraham rejoiced to see his day, what must be the joy of seeing him as he now is, at the right hand of majesty, in the heavens!

"Stray beams of his lustre often fall on the dying believer before his soul leaves its tenement. 'This is heaven begun,' said Rev. Thomas Scott; 'I have done with darkness, forever—forever. Satan is vanquished. Nothing now remains but salvation, with eternal glory—eternal glory.'

"Come to the veranda of a Braminic temple. In the last spasms of Asiatic cholera, Gordon Hall cries, 'Glory, glory, glory!' and he

'Passed through Glory's morning gate,
And walked in Paradise.'

"'Blessed are the dead that die in the Lord, *from henceforth!*' Blessed are the dead—not survivors, not the most favored of those who remain here, still sinning and repenting, and so imperfectly serving God—but blessed are the dead in Christ who have ceased from sin, are made perfect in holiness, and have passed into Paradise."*

"Life makes the soul dependent on the dust,
Death gives her wings to mount above the spheres.
* * * * * * * * * *
Death wounds to cure;—we fall,—we rise,—we reign!
Spring from our fetters, fasten in the skies,
Where blooming Eden withers in our sight.
Death gives us more than was in Eden lost;—
This king of terrors is the prince of Peace."

When Dr. Fisk was about to depart, he was heard

* Thompson's "Better Land."

to exclaim, "*from a chair to a throne.*"* To his fond wife whom he saw weeping, he said, "Do not suppose that your husband will be buried in the cold, dark earth of the college cemetery; this emaciated, suffering body may be laid there to sleep, but your husband cannot be buried. I shall be unspeakably happy with Christ in heaven."

The Rev. C. Love, minister at Lawrence Jewry, in London, was beheaded on Tower Hill, Aug. 22, 1651, in the time of Cromwell, for being suspected of plotting against the government. While standing on the scaffold he uttered the following most pathetic and weighty remarks:

"Although there be but little between me and death, yet this bears up my heart, there is little between me and heaven.

It comforted Dr. Taylor, the martyr, when he was going to execution, that there was but two stiles between him and his Father's house—but two steps between me and glory. It is but lying down upon that block and I shall ascend upon a throne. I am this day sailing toward the ocean of eternity—through a rough passage to my haven of rest; through a red sea to the promised land.

* * * * * * *

"Behold I am this day making a double exchange; I am changing a pulpit for a scaffold, and a scaffold for a throne; and I might add a third—I am changing the presence of this numerous multitude on Tower Hill for the innumerable company of saints and angels in heaven, the holy hill of Zion—and I am changing a guard of soldiers for a guard of angels,

* He was unable to lie down, and died sitting in a chair.

which will receive me and carry me to Abraham's bosom. This scaffold is the best pulpit that ever I preached in. In my church pulpit, God, through his grace, made me an instrument to bring others to heaven; but in this pulpit, he will bring me to heaven."

Such has been the hope of God's people in every age. In this hope they lived, and in it they died. And oh how disappointed if, instead of a convoy of angels, and the opening glories of the eternal day, they drank the lethean draught of annihilation, and sank down to non-existence; or found a long home amid unbroken silence and corruption! What a doctrine to teach as the gospel of Christ!

If this theory be true, how dreary is eternity! Its "whole family in heaven," Eph. iii. 15, consists of Enoch and Elijah who were translated, and Christ and those who arose after his resurrection. There is no "world of spirits bright;" and eternity is well nigh void. And the materialism that consigns the soul of man to the dust, implies the non-existence of angels as well; and, indeed, if carried out to its logical consequences, must blot out the Infinite Spirit himself!

This modern Sadduceeism denies all distinction between the righteous and the wicked till the general resurrection. Not only have the old saints, and patriarchs, and prophets been waiting for ages, without as yet a ray of light, or a gleam of conscious being; but they have yet to wait till the end of time. And the wicked are no worse off. With all the difference there is in the present life, and the difference that will exist hereafter, we are told that for ages between death and the resurrection, there is no differ ence whatever! Both are wrapped alike in the tran· quil slumbers of non-existence!

IX. In harmony with the preceding representation, that the souls of the righteous ascend at once to Paradise when the body dies, the book of Revelation represents the righteous dead as already "before the throne," singing and praising God in the land of life. They are a great multitude, of all nations, and kindreds, and people and tongues—are clothed with white robes, and have palms in their hands. "These are they which came out of great tribulation, and have washed their robes, and made them white in the blood of the Lamb. Therefore are they before the throne of God, and serve him day and night in his temple: and he that sitteth on the throne shall dwell among them. They shall hunger no more, neither thirst any more; neither shall the sun light on them, nor any heat. For the Lamb which is in the midst of the throne shall feed them, and shall lead them unto living fountains of waters: and God shall wipe away all tears from their eyes."

Happy dwellers in that "better country!"

Every tear is wiped away,
Sighs no more shall heave the breast;
Night is lost in endless day,
Sorrow in eternal rest.

Now all these Apocalyptic views of the heavenly world (of which there are many) are essentially wrong, and misleading, unless it be true that the souls of the righteous dead are now happy with Christ in heaven, though their bodies slumber in the grave. For let it not be forgotten, that the scene is laid beyond the region of sorrow, tears and death; consequently the descriptions can apply to no assembly this side the tomb. They are our happy brethren, who, like Moses, have crossed the flood, and entered Canaan, though their bodies still sleep in the vale of death.

No oppressive heat they feel,
From the sun's directer ray;
In a milder clime they dwell,
Region of eternal day.

X. Answering to the representation that the souls of the righteous are now happy with Christ in Paradise, we have the further representation that THEY ARE TO RETURN WITH HIM, when he comes to raise the dead and judge the world. Zechariah says, "And the Lord my God shall come, and ALL THE SAINTS WITH THEE," Ch. xiv. 5. St. Jude informs us that Enoch, the seventh from Adam, prophesied of these things, saying, "Behold the Lord cometh WITH TEN THOUSAND OF HIS SAINTS, to execute judgment upon all, etc.," Jude 14, 15, and St. Paul inculcates the same doctrine when he speaks of "the coming of our Lord Jesus Christ, WITH ALL HIS SAINTS," 1 Thess. iii. 13. Now what, we ask, are these "saints" that are to come with Christ at his second appearing, if they are not the *souls* of his people who have been with him in Paradise during the intermediate period between death and the resurrection? They cannot be the *bodies* of his saints, for they will not be raised till Christ arrives, and therefore cannot come with him. It is plain, therefore, that they are the *souls* of the righteous dead who have been in Paradise with him for ages, and who now return with him as he comes to raise their bodies to glory and immortality.

Hark! the Judgment trumpet calls!
Soul, rebuild thy house of clay,
Immortality thy walls,
And eternity thy day.

Abraham, Isaac and Jacob still lived in the time of Moses, though their bodies had long been dead. The penitent thief was with Christ in Paradise before the twelfth hour of the day of the crucifixion, though the bodies of both were on earth, under the dominion of death. Lazarus passed at once to Abraham's bosom, and the rich man to the torments of hell immediately after death. Men cannot kill the soul; for whether we sleep or wake we shall live together with Christ. Moses was with Christ on the mount, though his body still slumbered in the valley of Moab. The righteous depart at death to be with Christ; and the dead, who die in the Lord, are blessed *from henceforth.* A part of the family of God yet dwell on earth; but others are with Christ in glory. O blessed and glorious truth!

One family we dwell in Him,
One church above, beneath,
Though now divided by the stream,
The narrow stream of death.

The sainted dead are already before the throne, and serve God day and night in his temple; and when Christ shall appear in the clouds of heaven to raise the dead, and burn the world, and judge all men and angels, these "saints" shall attend him down his starry pathway, to re-enter their bodies, now made incorruptible and glorious, and for the redemption of which they have so long waited. Rom. viii. 23. Thus fully redeemed from death shall they ascend to the heaven of heavens, to be forever with the Lord. Then shall the gates lift up their heads, and the everlasting doors be lifted up; and the King of Glory, with his people shall enter in, to dwell in God's presence FOREVER! May both writer and reader be found in that glorious procession!

CHAPTER VII.

THE ALLEGED SLEEP OF THE SOUL BETWEEN DEATH AND THE RESURRECTION.

Besides adducing the direct Scripture proofs of the soul's immortality, it is proper to notice in this connection, certain new and peculiar views upon this subject, recently promulgated in this country and in England. Heretofore, Deism has usually denied both the immortality of the soul and the resurrection of the body; not because these doctrines were not taught in the Bible, but rather because they *were* therein taught. Denying the truth of the Scriptures, and spurning all their teachings, it claimed to follow *Reason* and *Nature*, and thence to derive proof that when a man dies that is his end forever.

But within a few years past an attempt has been made to unite the most pernicious features of Deism with one or two Bible truths; and to inculcate the whole as the veritable teachings of divine revelation. Thus we are told, by men professing to believe the Bible that man has no spiritual nature whatever distinct from his body; and that when that is dissolved by death, what is called the *soul* or *mind* goes out like an expiring lamp. Thus far they go hand in hand with the old Deists; and with these fatal errors they connect the doctrine of the resurrection of the body, when that which is called the "soul," say they, will be again evolved, and rewards and punishments will ensue. To this is added the notion that the punishment of the wicked will consist of their utter destruction of being, or annihilation, at the final judgment.

These are what we call *new* and *strange* doctrines —a sort of hybrid theology or cross between open infidelity and Bible Christianity. As the advocates of this mixed theory profess to respect the Scriptures, it is quite natural that they should attempt to press them into their service. It is altogether proper, then, in a treatise like this, to notice these anomalous attempts to prove the non-immortality, or literal death of the soul from the Sacred Writings. The present chapter, therefore, will be devoted to the alleged Scripture proofs that the soul or spirit of man is but a result of animal organization, and becomes extinct at the death of the body.

1. It is alleged that, as a general rule, we are to understand the Scriptures in their literal sense. It is also affirmed that the original terms rendered *soul*, *spirit*, and *ghost*, literally signify *wind* or *breath;* and that, therefore, when applied to man, they mean no more than the literal *breath* which leaves the body at death. In reply to this view we answer, that to give a literal interpretation to all the terms, and phrases, and figures of the Bible, is not only to understand it as we interpret no other book, but to turn it into nonsense. It is quite true that most of the terms employed to represent spiritual things were first used to represent material objects; but are they, therefore, to be taken in their literal and material sense? Take,

for example, the Greek term *pneuma*, which primarily signifies *wind* or *air;* must we, therefore, always adhere to this original meaning? "God is a Spirit" (*pneuma*) John iv. 24. Is he, therefore, mere *wind*, or *air*, or *breath?* In Acts v. 3, the term rendered Holy Ghost is *pneuma*. Rom. viii. 16, where it is said, "the Spirit itself beareth witness with our Spirit,"—*Auto to pneuma me to pneuma*,—the same term being employed to represent the human and Divine Spirit. 1 Cor. ii. 10, 11, the term *pneuma* is once used to denote "the spirit of a man," and thrice, in the same connection, to denote the Spirit of God—*pneuma tou Theou*. So, also, chapter 6, verse 20, the terms rendered Spirit of God are, *pneuma tou Theou*. Unless, therefore, the Spirit of God is mere *wind*, *air* or *breath*, the term *pneuma* must be understood to mean something more than this material substance. And, if it means a pure spirit, when applied to the Deity, must it not be taken in the same sense when, in the very same passage, it is applied to man? Would the Holy Ghost use the term *pneuma* in the sense of a pure spirit in one line, and in the sense of mere *wind* or *breath* in the next? Most certainly not.

There is another process by which we may test the correctness of the literalists' theory that the terms rendered *soul* and *spirit* mean simply the *breath*—a process which even the unlearned cannot fail to understand. If the original terms rendered "*soul*" and "spirit" in our English Scriptures mean simply the breath, then if we put the word "*breath*" in the place of the words "soul" and "spirit," wherever they occur, our "bad translation" (so called) will be rectified; and the texts cited will convey to us their true meaning. Let us translate a few passages according to this theory. And, first, a few samples in which the word SOUL occurs, putting the word BREATH, in the place of SOUL.

Psalm xix. 7:—"The law of the Lord is perfect, converting the BREATH." Psalm lxxxvi. 4:—"Rejoice the BREATH of thy servant: for unto thee, O Lord, do I lift up my BREATH." Psalm cvi. 15:—"And he gave them their request; but sent leanness into their BREATHS." Matt. x. 28:—"And fear not them which kill the body, but are not able to kill the BREATH: but rather fear him which is able to destroy both BREATH and body in hell." Matt. xxvi. 35:—"Then said he unto them, my BREATH is sorrowful even unto death." Luke xii. 19:—"And I will say to my BREATH, BREATH, thou hast much goods laid up for many years." 1 Thess. v. 23:—"And I pray God your whole spirit and BREATH and body be preserved blameless, etc." Heb. vi. 19:—"Which hope we have as an anchor to the BREATH." Heb. x. 39:—"But we are —— of them that believe to the saving of the BREATH." James v. 20:—"Let him know that he which converteth a sinner from the error of his way shall save a BREATH from death, etc." 2 Peter ii. 8:—"Lot dwelling in Sodom, vexed his righteous BREATH from day to day."

In the following specimens the word BREATH is put in the place of SPIRIT, with which it is said to be synonymous:—

Job xxxii. 18:—"For I am full of matter; the BREATH within me constraineth me." Eccl. iii. 21:—"Who knoweth the BREATH of man that goeth upward, and the BREATH of the beast that goeth downward to the earth." Acts xxiii. 8:—"For the Sadducees say there is no resurrection, neither angel, nor BREATH; but the Pharisees confess both." Also, verse 9:—"If a BREATH or an angel hath spoken to him." Rom. ii. 29:—"Circumcision is that of the heart, in the BREATH;" and viii. 16:—"The BREATH itself beareth witness with our BREATH that we are the children of God." 1 Cor. ii. 11:—"For what man knoweth the things of a man, save the BREATH of a man that is in him?" 1 Cor. v. 5:—"To deliver such a one unto Satan—that the BREATH may be saved in the day of the Lord Jesus." 1 Cor. vi. 5:—"For ye are bought with a price; therefore glorify God in your body and BREATH which are his." 2 Cor. vii. 1:—"Let us cleanse ourselves from all filthiness of the flesh and BREATH." Gal. vi. 15:—"Brethren, the grace of our Load Jesus Christ be with your BREATH. Amen."*

Such is the havoc which this wild and unscriptural theory makes with the word of God; for if the original terms rendered "*soul*" and "*spirit*" mean the literal breath, it is altogether proper and fair to put *breath* in their place; whereupon the Bible becomes one of the most unintelligible, not to say ridiculous productions, that ever was written. There is no alterna-

*Nothing would justify the exhibition of the Scriptures in so ridiculous a light, but a desire to explode one of the popular assumptions of the Annihilationists in the briefest possible space, by exposing the absurdity of their principles. If there be, therefore, a seeming want of dignity and reverence for the Scriptures in these illustrative examples, it is due to the false principles that we combat, and not to any unfairness or want of candor in their application. We have simply answered the Annihilationists according to their folly.

tive: we must either accept all this absurdity as the true meaning of the Scriptures, or reject the absurd principle of interpretation from which these consequences flow; and with the exploding of the principle, the whole argument falls to the ground.

II. It is argued that if the soul is a part of man, and men die, the soul must die as well as the body; otherwise the *man* does not die. This reasoning might appear sound, were it not for the fact that the Scriptures guard against such an error by teaching, as we have shown in chapter iv., that the death of a human being is but the *separation* of his two-fold nature,—the soul and body—and the extinction of his animal life. And even without this special instruction as to the nature of death, the above argument is fallacious on another account, insomuch as it assumes that whatever is affirmed of a human being, is affirmed of each and every part of that being. We affirm that a man is *asleep*, and yet his spirit may be awake in dreams, or somnambulism. So we may say he is *sick;* but we do not thereby affirm that his *soul* is sick. We habitually affirm that of *man*, which is true of *any part* of him. Man being a compound being, we can scarce avoid this mode of expression. As we affirm of Christ whatever is true of either of his natures, so of man;—we say he is *intelligent*, without affirming that his body is intelligent. In the same manner we affirm that he *dies*, without in the least implying that his *soul* dies. The dust may return to the earth as it was, but the spirit returns to God who gave it. Eccl. xii. 7.

III. It is affirmed that the numerous Scriptures in which death is spoken of as a *sleep*, convey the idea of the extinction of the soul at death. "The sleep of the soul after death," says Bishop Hobart, "in that sense which supposes it to be unconscious, is a modern invention, unknown to the ancient popular creed of both Jews and heathens, repugnant to reason, and contradicted by Scripture."*

The term *sleep*, when applied to death, must either be understood *literally* or *figuratively*. But it cannot be understood literally, because in literal sleep the animal life is not extinguished; the functions of but few of the bodily organs are suspended; the body does not tend to decay; and the subject may be easily roused again to wakefulness. None of these are true of the dead; consequently the sleep of death is not a literal sleep.

Again: If death were a literal sleep, it would by no means imply unconsciousness, much less the extinction of the soul; for in sleep we think, and reason, and hope, and fear, and enjoy, and suffer in our dreams, as really as when we are awake. Such a sleep, therefore, would fall far short of the materialists' idea of the sleep of the soul at death. For natural sleep is not only perfectly compatible with continued consciousness, but absolutely implies the perpetuity of our conscious being, under circumstances of renewed vigor and activity. "If he sleep," said the disciples of Lazarus, "he shall do well." Men sleep to increase and not to extinguish the mental and physical energies.

"The comparison between the state of the dead, and a state of sleep, is beautiful and appropriate. Sleep is that relaxation from the toils and afflictions

* State of the Departed, p. 48.

of life, that short suspension of the powers of corporeal sense and action, which are succeeded by a more vigorous exercise of the animal and intellectual faculties. And so death, releasing us entirely from our conflicts with the trials of this mortal existence, and suspending all the corporeal functions, is followed by a reviviscence of our whole nature, in the active delights and unalloyed glories of the heavenly state."*

It is safe, therefore, to affirm, that death cannot be a literal sleep; and that if it were it would rather support than conflict with the doctrine of the conscious existence of the soul after death.

But if death is not literally a sleep, it can only be so figuratively. In metaphorical language we call one thing by the name of another, on account of certain resemblances between the two. It is only a short way of making a comparison. Thus Christ is called a *lion*, a *lamb*, a *rock*, a *vine*, a *shepherd*, *bread*, &c. So as the death of a body in several respects resembles its falling asleep, the term "sleep" is employed metaphorically to represent death; without in the slightest degree implying the extinction of thought and consciousness.

"The expression *sleep*, or *sleeping*, so frequently applied in Scripture to the state of the dead, is evidently metaphorical; derived from the resemblance between a *dead* body, and the body of a person *asleep*. The body is said figuratively to "sleep in the dust of the earth;" expecting a resurrection at that day, when the dead, both small and great, shall be summoned to stand before God. Hence the word *cemetery*, and *dormitory*, from the Greek and Latin words

* State of the Departed, p. 45.

κοιμαω and *dormio*, to sleep, are applied to the receptacles of the dead."

"The term *sleep*, applied to the state of the dead, denotes not *unconsciousness*, but a freedom from the cares and labors of life; and, as it respects the righteous, expresses *comfortable enjoyment*, rest, security, and felicity. It is a phrase by which, in all languages, the state of the dead is denoted. And yet the popular belief among all nations, assigns consciousness and activity to the departed."*

IV. Psa. xxxvii. 9, 10:—"For evil doers shall be cut off: but those that wait upon the LORD, they shall inherit the earth. For yet a little while, and the wicked *shall* not *be:* yea, thou shalt diligently consider his place, and it *shall* not *be*."

From this passage it is argued that death is a cessation of conscious existence. But who does not see that the expression "*shall not be*," is the same as that the wicked shall be "cut off;" or shall not "inherit the earth?" The idea is, that the wicked shall not live out half their days, and shall soon disappear from the earth. And all that is said of him, is said of "his *place*." Of both alike it is said, they "shall not be." And it is still further evident that the whole relates to the present life, from what follows in the next verse:—"But the meek shall inherit the earth; and shall delight themselves in the abundance of peace." It would be quite as logical, therefore, to infer that the righteous shall live here forever, because it is said they shall inherit the earth; as to argue that the wicked shall cease to exist altogether,

* State of the Departed, p. 45.

because they are *not* to inherit the earth, but to be cut off.

V. Eccl. iii. 18–20, has often been quoted to show that man like the brute, has no soul that will outlive the body. "I said in mine heart concerning the estate of the sons of men, that God might manifest them, and that they might see that they themselves are beasts. For that which befalleth the sons of men befalleth beasts; even one thing befalleth them: as the one dieth, so dieth the other; yea, they have all one breath; so that a man hath no pre-eminence above a beast: for all *is* vanity. All go unto one place; all are of the dust, and all turn to dust again."

Two things are observable respecting this text. First, it purports to be but a *meditation* or *reflection* of the writer. "I said in mine heart, etc.;" and is more of the nature of a temptation to unbelief respecting a future state than any thing else. In the next place, lest it should be misunderstood, and used as it sometimes has been by modern materialists, it is added in the very next verse, "Who knoweth the spirit of man that goeth upward, and the spirit of the beast that goeth downward to the earth?"

It is thus shown that the deaths of the sons of men and of beasts are alike only so far as their *bodies* are concerned; while they are very unlike as to their spiritual natures. While one, like the bodies with which they are connected, "goeth downward to the earth," the other "goeth upward," or "returns to God who gave it." Ch. xii. 7.

VI. Psalm vi. 4:—"Return O Lord, deliver my soul: oh save me for thy mercies' sake. For in death *there is* no remembrance of thee: in the grave who shall give thee thanks?"

The prayer of the Psalmist that God would save him, is here urged upon the ground that it will be too late after death. This is the obvious import of the passage. The "remembrance" and "thanks" mentioned, are, therefore, such as are required *in this world*, as conditions of salvation. Such are not to be found in death or the grave; hence the earnest prayer for salvation while it might be found. There can be no *such* remembrance of God or thanksgiving to him in death or the grave.

VII. Psalm cxv. 17, 18:—"The dead praise not the Lord, neither any that go down into silence. But we will bless the Lord from this time forth and for evermore."

If the first of these passages teaches that the dead have no knowledge of God, the second certainly contradicts it, unless the Psalmist expected to live in this world "*for evermore;*" for such was to be the duration of his praise. It is plain, therefore, that in this passage, like the one preceding, the meaning is that none of the dead repent and turn to the Lord, and thus first *begin* to praise him; while the righteous, like David, can still say,

> My days of praise shall ne'er be past,
> While life, and thought, and being last,
> Or immortality endures.

VIII. Ecl. ix. 4–6:—"For to him that is joined to all the living there is hope: for a living dog is better than a dead lion. For the living know that they shall die: but the dead know not any thing, neither have they any more a reward; for the memory of them is forgotten. Also their love, and their hatred, and their envy, is now perished; neither have they any more a portion for ever in any *thing* that is done under the sun."

It requires very little effort to see that this text, like the two preceding, has reference solely to what the dead can know, or do, or receive, of any thing "under the sun;" that is *in this world.* The last two verses are simply explanatory of the statement of the first, that our hope and interest in all things earthly, are limited to this short and transitory life. The passage has no bearing, therefore, upon the question whether or not the soul is conscious after the body dies.

IX. Isaiah xxxviii. 17, 18:—"Behold, for peace I had great bitterness, but thou hast in love to my soul *delivered it* from the pit of corruption: for thou hast cast all my sins behind thy back. For the grave cannot praise thee, death cannot celebrate thee: they that go down into the pit cannot hope for thy truth. The living, the living, he shall praise thee, as I *do* this day: the father to the children shall make known thy truth."

The subject of this passage is the same as in the three preceding—the necessity of timely repentance and pardon. The Psalmist was grateful to God that though once in "great bitterness," his soul had been "delivered" by the pardon of his sins. And he magnifies the grace of God by the consideration that mercy came before it was too late. "The grave cannot praise thee," or turn to the service of God; the dead "*cannot hope for thy truth.*" It is too late then to hear the voice of warning. "The living," alone are thus privileged; and to them only can men "make known thy truth."

Acts ii. 34:—"For David is not yet ascended into the heavens, etc." The argument founded upon this passage is that as David's spirit had not ascended into the heavens, it must have been slumbering in the grave with his body; and, therefore, the doctrine of the immortality of the soul cannot be true. But unfortunately for the argument, the whole drift of the context shows that Peter was speaking of David's *body* and not of his soul. The subject under consideration is the resurrection of Christ; and the apostle affirms first, that Christ had been raised from the dead. "Whom God hath raised up, having loosed the pains of death: because it was not possible that he should be holden of it." Verse 24. In the second place, he shows *why* it was not possible that Christ should be holden of death. "For David speaketh concerning him, I foresaw the Lord always before my face; for he is on my right hand, that I should not be moved: therefore did my heart rejoice, and my tongue was glad; moreover also my flesh shall rest in hope: because thou wilt not leave my soul in hell, neither wilt thou suffer thine Holy One to see corruption. Thou hast made known to me the ways of life; thou shalt make me full of joy with thy countenance." Verses 25–28.

This prophecy, it is then urged, did not relate to David personally, but to Christ, the seed of David. "Men *and* brethren, let me freely speak unto you of the patriarch David, that he is both dead and buried, and his sepulchre is with us unto this day. Therefore being a prophet, and knowing that God had sworn with an oath to him, that of the fruit of his loins, according to the flesh, he would raise up Christ to sit on his throne; he, seeing this before, spake of the resurrection of Christ, that his soul was not left in hell, neither his flesh did see corruption. This Jesus hath God raised up, whereof we all are witnesses. Therefore being by the right hand of God exalted, and having received of the Father the promise of the Holy Ghost, he hath shed forth this, which ye now see and hear." Verses 29–33.

Then comes in the passage first cited. "For David is not ascended into the heavens: but he saith himself, The Lord said unto my Lord, Sit thou on my right hand, until I make thy foes thy footstool. Therefore let all the house of Israel know assuredly, that God hath made that same Jesus, whom ye have crucified, both Lord and Christ."

The argument of the apostle is, that the prophecy could not have related to David personally, because it was never fulfilled in him. He saw corruption, and his sepulchre was yet with them. "For David, after he had served his own generation by the will of God, fell on sleep, and was laid unto his fathers, and saw corruption: but he whom God raised again saw no corruption:"—Acts xiii. 36, 37. The prophecy spoke also of a "path of life," or way to immortality, and an ascension to the right hand of God, neither of which had been fulfilled in regard to the body of David. "For David is not passed into the heavens." He is neither raised nor enthroned; and yet such is the import of the prophecy. For "he saith himself, The Lord said unto my Lord, Sit thou on my right hand, until I make thy foes thy footstool." If, then, such are the prophecies, which were never fulfilled in David personally, it is plain that he "spoke of the resurrection of Christ," and not of himself. Nothing, therefore, could be more foreign to the subject than to understand the remark that David had not yet ascended into heaven, as relating to his *soul!* It is precisely like affirming that his soul had not gone to hades, or the world of spirits, because his *body* was yet in the grave.

XI. 1 Cor. xv. 16–18:—"For if the dead rise not, then is not Christ raised: and if Christ be not raised, your faith *is* vain; ye are yet in your sins. Then they also which are fallen asleep in Christ are perished."

The argument founded upon this passage, is, that if Christ is not risen, and there is no resurrection, there can be no future existence. This is true only in the sense intended by the apostle; and that is, that if Christ is not risen from the dead, the whole system which he taught, including the immortality of the soul as well as the resurrection of the body, falls to the ground. This the most firm believer in the immortality of the soul will readily admit. For if Christ be not risen, the whole Christian system is a cunningly devised fable; the hopes it inspires are delusive; and so far as we have any evidence to the contrary from any other and surer word of prophecy, the dead in Christ are perished. But even then, as we shall see hereafter, the word "*perished*" implies the loss of the soul only, or its failure to reach Paradise, rather than its having fallen into non-existence.

XII. 2 Tim. iv. 6–8:—"For I am now ready to be

offered, and the time of my departure is at hand. I have fought a good fight, I have finished *my* course, I have kept the faith: henceforth there is laid up for me a crown of righteousness, which the Lord, the righteous judge, shall give me at that day: and not to me only, but unto all them also that love his appearing."

From this passage it is argued that St. Paul did not expect his crown of righteousness till the second coming of Christ and the resurrection of the dead; and that consequently he had no reward, and indeed no conscious existence from death to that period. But the conclusion is not warranted by the premises. We are ready to admit that the "crown of righteousness"—the full and glorious reward of the righteous—will not be administered till the resurrection; but it by no means follows that there is *no* reward, nor happiness, nor existence, till the resurrected believer is fully crowned. And the fact that St. Paul looked forward with hope and joy to the resurrection of the dead, no more proves that he expected nothing *before* that event, than the same hope in a Christian now, proves that he believes in the death of the soul. In fact the firmer our belief in the immortality of the soul, the more ardent and joyful our hope of the resurrection of the body. So with St. Paul: he knew that to die was gain—to be with Christ which is far better—and yet he looked forward with rapturous joy, to the day when his salvation should be completed in the resurrection of his body. Such in fact is the true explanation of all those Scriptures in which the righteous seem to dwell upon the resurrection of the dead, as an object of hope and desire.

Not that they can have *no* happiness or conscious existence till the body is raised, but because the resurrection of their bodies incorruptible and glorious is the last and *crowning act* of their salvation from the power of sin and death. Is it at all strange, therefore, that they look forward to that glorious consummation, with holy joy and triumph?

XII. That the early Christians and martyrs for the word of God understood the Scriptures as we have explained them, and looked for conscious joy in Paradise immediately after death, might be shown to almost any extent from ecclesiastical history. But this would lead us too far aside from our purpose to confine ourself in this part of our inquiry, almost exclusively to the Sacred Writings. A few brief references, however, may not be out of place.

Of the thousands of Christian martyrs who sealed the truth with their blood during the first three centuries of the Christian era, not one of them gave expression in his last moments, so far as can be ascertained, to the idea that his soul would die or become unconscious when the body was dissolved. On the contrary they uniformly express the hope of immediate and conscious happiness after death. Take the following as examples:

POLYCARP was the companion of St. John, and often heard him preach. He suffered martyrdom, A. D. 166, in the eighty-seventh year of his age. When the Proconsul threatened him with wild beasts unless he recanted, he answered, "call them;" and when the proconsul threatened to burn him alive, he answered, "You threaten fire that burns for a moment and is soon extinguished, for you know nothing of the judgment to come, and the fire of *eternal punishment* reserved for the wicked." In his last prayer as he stood bound to the stake, after mentioning the blessed martyrs, he said, "Among whom may I be received in thy sight *this day*, &c."*

From these passages it is clear that Polycarp, the companion of St. John, not only believed in "eternal punishment," but looked for an immediate life with Christ in Paradise, when the pains of martyrdom were over. For him to die was to be introduced at once into the presence of God, and the society of the blessed who had gone before. And Eusebius, who wrote the account A. D. 324, concludes the narrative of his martyrdom by saying, he was "crowned with the crown of *immortality*." Neither the martyr nor the historian, therefore, believed in the doctrine of the death or sleep of souls.

LUCIUS perished under Urbicius about the time of Polycarp. When Urbicius commanded him to be led forth, Lucius thanked him, saying he was now "liberated from wicked masters, and was going to the good Father and King, even God."† To die was to go to God, and not to cease to exist.

BIBLIAS, while suffering the torture of martyrdom, was at the point to renounce Christ and escape, when "she was reminded," it is said, "by the punishment before her, of the ETERNAL PUNISHMENT OF HELL," and remained steadfast to the last.‡ She had no idea, therefore, that the death of a sinner placed him beyond the possibility of eternal punishment.

Again in the same book and chapter, Eusebius

* Eusebius' Eccl. Hist. bk. iv. Chap. xv.

† Ibid. b. iv. Ch. xviii.

‡ Ibid. b. v. Ch. i.

speaks of "those noble wrestlers," the martyrs, as having sustained a diversified contest; "come off with a glorious victory, and borne away the *crown of immortality.*"

BLANDINA was suspended on a stake, and exposed as food for wild beasts. She persuaded those who believed in Christ that "every one who suffers for Christ, will for ever enjoy communion with the living God." And yet, if annihilationism be true, she has *not yet* come to communion with God, and may not for a thousand years to come.

A little further on the historian says, "Thus she overcame the enemy in many trials, [the wild beasts refused to attack her,] and in the conflict received the crown of IMMORTALITY." On the next page it is said, "But the blessed Blandina, last of all, as a noble mother that had animated her children and SENT THEM AS VICTORS TO THE GREAT KING, herself retracing the ground of all the conflicts her children had endured, HASTENED at last, with joy and exultation at the issue, TO THEM, as if she were invited to a marriage feast, and not to be cast to wild beasts."*

Such was the testimony of the first martyrs—such the doctrine they learned from the Apostles, and from the Holy Scriptures. And I hesitate not to say that not the first instance can be cited in which, during the first three centuries, a Christian expressed any other hope in his last hours than that of entering AT ONCE upon the joys of an endless life.

XIII. I cannot refrain, in this connection, from adducing a few additional proofs of the views and hopes of the early martyrs. They are too striking

* Eusebius' Eccl. Hist. b. v. Ch. 1.

and conclusive to be omitted—monumental witnesses that stand unchanged by the lapse of ages, like the records of creation, written in the everlasting hills.

The Catacombs of Rome are a subterranean city of the dead, in which the bodies of the martyrs were buried during the first three centuries of the Christian era. The inscriptions upon these tombs throw no little light upon the faith of the early Christians. Take the following as examples: "Borne away by angels on the seventh Ides of January." "In Christ, Alexander is not dead, but lives above the stars—his body rests in this tomb." "Among the innocent ones." "One who lives with God." "Gone to dwell with Christ." "Snatched home eternally, etc." Other inscriptions speak of the day of their departure, as their "natal" or birth day; and what is still more significant, the word *death* is never used in reference to *one* of all that vast company of the departed!

Such is the testimony of these mute and incorruptible witnesses, to the separate and immortal existence of human souls when their bodies return to dust.*

The doctrine of the death or sleep of the soul from death to the resurrection, is liable to numerous and insuperable objections, a few of which may be briefly stated.

1. It is contrary to that large class of Scriptures cited in Chapter II., which go to show that matter and spirit are distinct essences.

2. It is contrary to a still larger list cited in Chapter III., which represent man as a two-fold being—a spirit in a body.

* National Magazine, Vol. v. pp. 123, 224, 227; or, Bishop Kip's Work upon the Catacombs.

3. It is contrary to all those Scriptures cited in Chapter IV., which go to prove that death is the *separation* of soul and body, and not the extinction of thought or consciousness.

4. It is contrary to a still larger and very explicit list of texts cited in Chapter V., which directly prove the conscious existence of the soul after death.

5. It is degrading to our species, in that it reduces man to a level with the brute; and so far as the effect of death upon him is concerned, gives him no preeminence over the beast.*

6. It represents the eternal world as an empty void, so far as human spirits are concerned—as upon this theory there are no human souls in heaven till the general resurrection; whereas, the Scriptures represent heaven as already peopled with a vast and joyful company which no man can number. See Rev. vii. 9–14.

7. It makes no distinction between the righteous and the wicked for long ages after death. Cain, and Abel, and Jeremiah, and Jezebel, and Judas, and St. John, and Payson, and Thomas Paine; and indeed, all sinners and saints, share precisely the same fate from death to the resurrection. It is to all alike a dreary unbroken parenthesis of being—a dark and yawning chasm in existence itself! In the case of the patriarchs and prophets a life of communion with God is followed by a worse than banishment of centuries; and the glory and bliss of heaven is preceded by ages of darkness and non-existence! Is this all that

* An infidel, who had been attempting to prove that men have no souls, asked a lady with an air of triumph what she thought of his philosophy. "It appears to me," she replied, "that you have been employing a good deal of talent to prove yourself a beast."

God has promised to his saints? Is this the best that he can do for his followers when the present life shall end? Is this "the hope of glory" which swelled the bosoms of the apostles and prophets, and emboldened the martyrs to meet death even with joy and triumph? Ah no! It is "another gospel!" The martyrs died with a different hope. With them it was death and immediate glory.

And so with modern Christian believers. Among the millions who have made the Bible their study during the last fifteen hundred years, how very few have understood it to teach any other doctrine. Not one in ten thousand. And yet they were not Infidels nor Papists, but devout Protestant Christians. They read the blessed Bible to learn the way to heaven, and they understood it to teach that death only separated the inner from the outer man, and introduced the souls of the righteous to eternal joys. In this faith they lived, and in this hope they died.

But were the primitive saints and martyrs all in error? Have nine hundred and ninety-nine out of every thousand of Christians who have ever lived, lived in error upon this vital point, and died with a false hope? Believe it, who can! Nay, rather; their's was the true gospel of the life to come, their's the well-grounded hope of immortality.

CHAPTER VIII.

THE "INTERMEDIATE STATE;" OR THE PLACE OF SOULS BETWEEN DEATH AND THE RESURRECTION.

IN the last three chapters we have shown, that death is but the separation of the soul from the body; and that the soul neither sleeps nor becomes unconscious between death and the resurrection. We have also shown incidentally that the souls of the righteous will be happy, and those of the wicked miserable immediately after death, and during this intermediate period. But an interesting question arises just here: *Where are the souls of men during this intermediate period from death to the resurrection?* Are they in the final heaven and hell that shall be after the resurrection and general judgment, or in intermediate abodes differing from their final allotment?

That the *state* of souls disembodied is, in some respects, different from that of souls embodied, is obvious; so that few will deny an intermediate *state*, who believe in a resurrection of the body. But the question here proposed relates, not to the *state* merely, but to the *place* of souls between the death of the body and its final resurrection.

Upon this question little has been said in modern

times, even by writers upon a future life.* For this there may have been two reasons—a foregone impression that the Scriptures shed but little light upon the subject; and a vague apprehension that in some way the doctrine of an intermediate place of souls, favors the doctrine of Purgatory, and of final and universal restoration. But this by no means follows. The doctrine of an intermediate place of souls may be true, and the idea of purification there and of final restoration a fiction.

That the place of souls between death and the resurrection is different from their final abode, was generally believed by the primitive church. It is a doctrine of the Church of England, and of the Protestant Episcopal church in this country, and was certainly believed by JOHN WESLEY and DR. ADAM CLARKE, two of the great lights of Methodism. It was also advocated by SCOTT, and MAGEE, and CAMPBELL, among the Presbyterians; as well as by scores of learned and pious men who were never suspected either of Popery or Universalism. We have, therefore, no reason to reject this doctrine, or to discuss it with prejudice, or fear, from any apprehension that its tendency is to favor the errors above alluded to.

That there is an intermediate *place* as well as a *state* of souls between death and the resurrection, seems highly probable from the following considerations:—

I. There must of necessity be a great difference between the intermediate state of souls, and

* The best treatise we have seen is that on "*The State of the Departed*," by Bishop Hobart.

their final condition after the resurrection of their bodies.

Man is a compound being consisting of body and soul. Death is a separation of these two natures. The soul of the good man goes to "Paradise," and the body goes back to corruption.

Now it must be obvious that just so far as the want of an immortal and glorified body is an *imperfection* in man, (not moral, perhaps, but physical,) he is in an *imperfect state* till his body is raised from the dead. And if no imperfection can enter the final abode of the righteous, man is not *prepared* to enter his final dwelling-place, till after the general resurrection. And if so there is an analogical necessity for an intermediate *place* of souls between death and the resurrection, answering somewhat to the peculiar *state* of disembodied spirits.

Again: It should be remembered, not only that man's normal condition is soul and body in union, while a state of separation and dissolution is an abnormal state;—a sort of parenthesis in his being;—but that this abnormal condition is a *result of sin;* and one of the victories achieved by it, from which even the righteous are not yet delivered. No man is or can be fully "saved," therefore, while his body is yet in the grave, under the dominion of death. When that is raised in incorruption, and power, and glory; aud re-inhabited by the soul which was dislodged from it at death, then, and not till then, will any be "saved" in the highest and fullest sense; and death be swallowed up of victory. Why, then, should souls go up beforehand to the heavenly mansions, to which they are admitted when made perfect and complete by the general resurrection? Is not an intermediate place of souls more in harmony with this imperfect and abnormal state, than the highest exaltation in the heavenly world?

II. There are intimations in the Scriptures of an *established order*, on the part of God to introduce all his saints to their final and glorious reward *at one and the same time.* Mark, we say the "*final*" reward. Take the following passages as samples.

1. 1 Thess. iv. 15–17:—"For this we say unto you by the word of the Lord, that we which are alive *and* remain unto the coming of the Lord shall not prevent them which are asleep. For the Lord himself shall descend from heaven with a shout, with the voice of the archangel, and with the trump of God: and the dead in Christ shall rise first: then we which are alive *and* remain shall be caught up together with them in the clouds, to meet the Lord in the air: and so shall we ever be with the Lord."

In the 15th verse the word "prevent" is used in its old English sense of to *go before* or *anticipate.* The living Christian, who hears the sound of the resurrection trumpet, and is changed from mortal to immortality in a moment, shall not *go before* or *outstrip* his brother Christian, whose body has been dissolved by death, and whose inanimate dust sleeps in the grave. "The dead in Christ shall rise first." Not, as some understand it, before the *wicked* rise, but before the *righteous* who "are alive and remain," ascend. "*Then*,"—after the righteous dead have arisen—both shall be caught up *together*, to meet the Lord in the air, and to be forever with the Lord. This established order, therefore, seems to imply that the righteous do not enter the final heaven at death, that there must be an intermediate abode, where their souls are in joy and felicity.

2. Heb. xi. 39, 40, speaking of the Old Testament saints, the apostle says:—"And these all, having obtained a good report through faith, received not the promise: God having provided some better thing for us, *that they without us should not be made perfect.*"

This last clause is generally understood to teach that the saints of former ages are not "made perfect," that is, do not enter upon their eternal reward, till those of the later dispensation enter also upon their final glory. MR. WESLEY in his notes says, "*that they might not be perfected without us.* That is, that we might all be perfected together in heaven." DR. CLARKE says,—"The preceding believers cannot be consummated even in glory, till the gospel church arrives in the heaven of heavens."

Upon this passage DR. MACKNIGHT observes: "*Made perfect,*" here signifies *made complete*, by receiving the whole of the blessings promised to believers, the expectation of which animated the ancients, whose great actions are celebrated in the preceding part of the chapter. These blessings are the resurrection of the body, the everlasting possession of the heavenly country, and the full enjoyment of God as their exceeding great reward. The apostle's doctrine that believers are all to be rewarded together, and at the same time, is agreeable to Christ's declaration, who told his disciples that they were not to come to the place he was going away to prepare for them, till he returned from heaven to carry them to it. * * This determination, not to reward the ancients without us, is highly proper; because the power and veracity of God will be more illustriously displayed in the view of angels and men, by raising the whole of Abraham's seed from the dead at once, and by introducing them into the heavenly country in a body, after a public acquittal at the day of judgment, than if each were made perfect separately at their death.*

Now if such be the order of God in reference to his people, how say some among us that Abel, and Noah, and Job, and the prophets ascended at once to their final heaven the moment they dropped their earthly tabernacles? If the saints who are alive at Christ's second coming cannot ascend till the saints who "sleep in the dust of the earth" are raised, to go with them; and if none of God's people of former ages are made perfect without or before the saints of the last days, is not their present state an imperfect one, so far as their fulness of joy is concerned? And does not that imperfection of *state*, imply a corresponding imperfection of *place*, or an intermediate Paradise, other than our final home after the resurrection?

III. The same general idea is more directly conveyed in a numerous class of Scriptures, which teach that men are not to be fully rewarded or punished till Christ's second coming and the resurrection.

Matt. xiii. 39–43:—"The harvest is the end of the world. * * * * The Son of man shall send forth his angels, and they shall gather out of his kingdom all things that offend, and them which do iniquity; and shall cast them into a furnace of fire: there shall be wailing and gnashing of teeth. Then shall the right-

* See Commentary and Notes.

eous shine forth as the sun in the kingdom of their Father."

2 Thess. i. 7–10:—"And to you, who are troubled, rest with us, when the Lord Jesus shall be revealed from heaven with his mighty angels, in flaming fire taking vengeance on them that know not God, and that obey not the gospel of our Lord Jesus Christ: who shall be punished with everlasting destruction from the presence of the Lord, and from the glory of his power; when he shall come to be glorified in his saints, and to be admired in all them that believe (because our testimony among you was believed) in that day."

2 Pet. iii. 7:—"But the heavens and the earth, which are now, by the same word are kept in store, reserved unto fire against the day of judgment and perdition of ungodly men." These passages relate to the wicked, and clearly teach that they are not to be "cast into a furnace of fire;" to "be punished with everlasting destruction," and to experience their complete "perdition," till the second coming of Christ and the resurrection. Take also another still more extended class that speak only of the righteous:—

Luke xiv. 13, 14:—"But when thou makest a feast, call the poor, the maimed, the lame, the blind; and thou shalt be blessed: for they cannot recompense thee: *for thou shalt be recompensed at the resurrection of the just.*"

1 Pet. i. 5, 7, 13:—"Who are kept by the power of God through faith unto salvation, *ready to be revealed in the last time.* That the trial of your faith, being much more precious than of gold that perisheth, though it be tried with fire, might be found unto

praise, and honor, and glory, *at the appearing of Jesus Christ.* Wherefore gird up the loins of your mind, be sober, and hope to the end for the grace that is to be brought unto you *at the revelation of Jesus Christ.*"

1 Pet. iv. 13:—"But rejoice, inasmuch as ye are partakers of Christ's sufferings; that, *when his glory shall be revealed,* ye may be glad also with exceeding joy."

1 Pet. v. 4:—"And *when the chief Shepherd shall appear,* ye shall receive a crown of glory that fadeth not away."

2 Tim. iv. 8:—"Henceforth there is laid up for me a crown of righteousness, which the Lord, the righteous Judge, shall give me *at that day:* and not to me only, but unto all them also that love his appearing."

1 John iii. 2:—"Beloved, now are we the sons of God, and it doth not yet appear what we shall be: but we know that *when he shall appear,* we shall be like him; for we shall see him as he is."

John xiv. 2, 3:—"In my Father's house are many mansions: if *it were* not *so,* I would have told you. I go to prepare a place for you. And if I go and prepare a place for you, I will come again and receive you unto myself; that where I am, *there* ye may be also."

In this last passage the reception of the righteous to the heavenly mansions prepared for them is represented as to occur *when Christ comes* again, and *not* at the hour of death. And so in the other passages cited—they all clearly teach that the righteous are not to "shine forth as the sun" in the kingdom of

God; to be "recompensed;" to "be glad with exceeding joy;" to receive their "crowns of glory, etc.," till Christ descends again from heaven, raises the dead, and distributes to all men their eternal rewards. How, then, can it be true that the heaven to which the spirits of the righteous ascend, and where they now are, is the very heaven to which they shall return after the general resurrection and final judgment?

IV. Still more strikingly, if possible, is the doctrine of an intermediate place of souls implied in every description of the final judgment. Matt. xxv. 31, and onward is one of the most unequivocal and imposing of these descriptions. The Son of God descends from heaven, with his holy angels; all nations are summoned before him. He then proceeds to separate the righteous from the wicked, as a shepherd divideth his sheep from the goats. To the righteous he says, "Come, ye blessed of my Father, inherit the kingdom prepared for you from the foundation of the world;" and to the wicked, "Depart from me, ye cursed, into everlasting fire, prepared for the devil and his angels." "And these shall go away into everlasting punishment; but the righteous into life eternal." Whatever that fulness of joy or misery may be to which men are thus finally adjudged, unless the Scriptures are utterly misleading, it is plain that the righteous do not "inherit the kingdom" of their complete and eternal glory till after the resurrection and final judgment. Neither do the wicked depart to their final and everlasting doom before that time.

The same doctrine is taught in the parable of the talents, Matt. xxiv. 14–30:—It is not till "the Lord of those servants cometh," that he saith to the "good and faithful," "Enter thou into the joy of thy Lord;" or of the wicked, "Cast ye the unprofitable servant into outer darkness." So in the parable of the wise and foolish virgin, in the same chapter—it is not till "the bridegroom cometh," that the wise "go in unto the marriage," and the door is shut against the foolish.

Upon the hypothesis of no intermediate place of souls, and their introduction to the final heaven or hell, immediately after death, both have entered on their respective rewards, in their eternal abodes, *before they are judged,* and without their immortal bodies. They are then each to be called subsequently, from their respective abodes, judged and sent back *to the very places from whence they came!* Does not such a theory destroy much of the *consistency* (we speak with reverence) much of the *reasonableness* of and sublimity of the grand and solemn procedure? If men are to be publicly judged and rewarded or punished, at the resurrection, why should they be rewarded or punished in the same manner, and the same place, *before* the resurrection and final judgment? And what can be the force of the sentence, "*Come*, ye blessed, *inherit the kingdom;*" "*Depart*, ye cursed into everlasting fire;" if the former has been inheriting the "kingdom," and the latter enduring the "fire" for long ages before?

We know it has been replied that there will be other degrees of joy or sorrow after the resurrection and final judgment, sufficient to warrant the language of the preceding descriptions. But it is not so much of new *degrees* of joy or sorrow that shall follow the day of judgment, of which the Scriptures seem to speak, as of new *abodes* both for the righteous and the wicked. Then the righteous are to come to their heavenly Zion, with songs, and everlasting joy upon their heads; and *then* the wicked are to "go away into everlasting punishment." Surely, then, they have not entered upon either already; but the souls of each are in *Hades*—the place of souls, happy or miserable as their works have been, but awaiting the coming of the Son of man; the resurrection of their bodies; the final judgment; and the final heaven or hell that are to follow.

The doctrine of an intermediate state is, therefore, the only doctrine that can be reconciled with the Scripture doctrine of a general judgment; and by losing sight of it many have been perplexed with those Scriptures which connect rewards and punishments with the resurrection. And some have thus been led even to countenance the doctrine of the sleep or extinction of the soul, during the death of the body, to the support of which these Scriptures are perverted.

V. We have several descriptions of the resurrection of the dead, both in the Old and New Testament, in all of which it is implied that souls do not return after the resurrection and general judgment, to the places from which they come forth to be judged. We cite a few specimens.

Hosea xiii. 14, is one of these descriptions. "I will ransom them from the power of the grave; I will redeem them from death: O death, I will be thy plagues; O grave, I will be thy destruction: repentance shall be hid from mine eyes." That this passage is a prophecy of the resurrection is certain from the use made of it by St. Paul, 1 Cor. xv. 54, 55.

We have first the announcement, "I will ransom them from the power of the grave, I will redeem them from death;" and then the triumphant double apostrophe to death and the grave, "O death, I will be thy plagues; O grave, I will be thy destruction: repentance shall be hid from mine eyes."

Fully to appreciate this sublime prophecy, we must remember what man is; what death does to him; and what the resurrection is to effect. As man, he consists of a material and mortal body, and an immaterial and immortal spirit. Death separates the soul from the body, consigning the latter to the dust, and the former to *hades*—the abode of departed souls. In the resurrection the body is raised from death to life and immortality, and the soul leaves its intermediate abode, to re-enter its deathless body, and to dwell in it forever.

Answering to all this a triumphant apostrophe is addressed, in the above passage, as well to the place of souls, as to the grave. "O death, [Hebrew *maveth* —*the principle of corruption*, the grave,] I will be thy plagues. O grave, [Hebrew *sheol*—the place of the dead,] I will be thy destruction." "*Sheol*," says Clarke, "shall be destroyed, for it must deliver up its dead,"—the souls of men. "*Maveth* shall be annihilated, for the *body shall be raised incorruptible*."

The import, then, of this prophetic description is not that *sheol* or the present abode of souls shall continue after the resurrection, any more than *maveth*, the present abode of dead bodies shall continue. Both are alike to pass away, to be succeeded by the everlasting habitations to which men will be assigned after the general resurrection.

In the xvth chapter of first Corinthians, St. Paul cites this same passage, with slight modification. His subject is the resurrection of the dead. He has just constructed one of the most sublime arguments ever put forth upon any subject, and thus crowns the glorious structure:—

"For this corruptible must put on incorruption, and this mortal *must* put on immortality. So when this corruptible shall have put on incorruption, and this mortal shall have put on immortality, then shall be brought to pass the saying that is written, Death is swallowed up in victory. O death, where *is* thy sting? O grave, where *is* thy victory? The sting of death *is* sin; and the strength of sin *is* the law. But thanks *be* to God, which giveth us the victory through our Lord Jesus Christ."

Here the believer's victory is consummated in the resurrection, "through our Lord Jesus Christ:" and in that glorious consummation "the saying that is written" by the prophet "shall be brought to pass."

But observe that here also the present abode of souls and the grave are each separately addressed, and both are to be alike abolished in the resurrection. "O death, [Gr. *thanate,*] where is thy sting?" Thy *power to harm* is gone—thy prey set free! "O grave, [Gr. *hades*—the place of souls,] where is thy victory?" "Hades," says CLARKE, "which we translate grave, is generally understood to be *the place of separate spirits.*" "O *hades,*" says MR. WESLEY, "the receptacle of separate souls—*where is thy victory? Hades* literally relates to the invisible world, and relates to souls; *death* to the body." And so DR. BARNES, "O *hades*—the place of the dead." And mark, that *hades* no more retains the *souls* of men after the resurrection, than the grave does their bodies. They come each from their respective temporary abodes, and re-unite. Hades and the grave are thus superseded and abolished, and immortal man then enters upon his eternal dwelling-place.

Finally, in the twentieth chapter of Revelation, we have still another prophecy and a more sublime and minute description of the general resurrection:

"And I saw a great white throne, and him that sat on it, from whose face the earth and the heaven fled away; and there was found no place for them. And I saw the dead, small and great, stand before God; and the books were opened: and another book was opened, which is *the book* of life: and the dead were judged out of those things which were written in the books, according to their works. And the sea gave up the dead which were in it; and death and hell delivered up the dead which were in them: and they were judged every man according to their works. And death and hell were cast into the lake of fire. This is the second death."

Here, in the thirteenth verse, as in the prophecy of Hosea, and the quotation of St. Paul, there is a two-fold yielding up in the resurrection; the one relating to *souls* and the other to *bodies*. Both death, (the grave,) and Hades, the place of souls, delivered up their dead, the one the souls, and the other the bodies. "*Hades*, the place of separate spirits," says CLARKE. "The *sea* and *death* have the *bodies* of all human beings; *Hades* their *spirits*." "Death gave up all the *bodies* of men," says MR. WESLEY, "and *Hades*, the receptacle of separate souls, gave them up to be re-united to their bodies."

Then death or the grave and Hades are both abolished. "And death and hell were cast into the lake of fire;" that is, says Mr. Wesley, "were abolished for ever. For neither the righteous nor the wicked were to die any more: their souls and bodies were no more to be separated. Consequently, neither death nor hades could any more have a being." Thus each of these inspired descriptions of the resurrection, strongly implies, to say the least, that in that future consummation the souls of men will come from a place to which they will not return, but which will be superseded by other and different abodes, which shall be unalterable and eternal. Their present abodes must therefore be only intermediate and temporary, and not the final heaven or hell that shall be, beyond the day of judgment.

VI. The same doctrine seems also to be taught by our Saviour in the parable of the rich man and Lazarus, Luke xvi. 19. To understand this parable fully it should be borne in mind that the Jews, to whom our Lord was speaking, or at least, the chief sect of that people, held to the doctrine of an intermediate state. This is evident from Josephus' discourse to the Greeks upon that very subject. Josephus was a learned Jewish historian, who wrote about A. D. 80. In his discourse to the Greeks concerning Hades, he says:—

"Now, as to Hades, wherein the souls of the righteous and unrighteous are detained, it is necessary to speak of it. * * This region is allotted as a place of custody for souls, in which angels are appointed as guardians to them, who distribute to them temporary punishments, agreeable to every one's behavior and manners.

"In this region there is a certain place set apart, as a lake of unquenchable fire, whereinto we suppose no one hath hitherto been cast, but it is prepared for a day afore determined by God, in which one righteous sentence shall deservedly be passed upon all men; when the unjust, and those that have been disobedient to God, and have given honor to such idols as have been the vain operations of the hands of men, as to God himself, shall be adjudged to this everlasting punishment, as having been the cause of defilement; while the just shall obtain an incorruptible and never-fading kingdom. These are now, indeed, confined in hades, but not in the same place wherein the unjust are confined."

This passage clearly sets forth the *Jewish* idea of the nature of hades, as a receptacle of souls, both good and bad; and we cite it solely for this purpose, and not to settle anything directly as to the existence or non-existence of an intermediate state.

Still further on he gives the current belief that in the resurrection the souls in hades will be united with their former bodies made immortal.

"This is the discourse concerning hades, wherein the souls of all men are confined until a proper season which God hath determined, when he will make a resurrection of all men from the dead. * * * * And to every body shall its own soul be restored."

He then proceeds to give an account of the general judgment, which he describes as following the resurrection, and the re-union of the souls of men with their bodies; and to be followed by everlasting happiness to the righteous, and eternal misery to the wicked. It is certain, therefore, from this discourse, as well as from other testimony that in connection with the doctrines of the immortality of the soul, the resurrection of the body, and a day of judgment, the Jews generally held to that of an intermediate state, or abode of spirits, between death and the resurrection. This place they called *sheol* in Hebrew, and *hades* in Greek; and described it as the common receptacle of both the righteous and the wicked, having separate apartments for each, viz., Abraham's bosom for the righteous, and Tartarus or Gehenna for the wicked.

Now such being the current theology upon the subject among the Jews—the Pharisees at least—how must they have understood the parable of the rich man and Lazarus? Who can read it now, in the light of the known belief of those to whom it was addressed, and not perceive that it is built upon their acknowledged doctrine of an intermediate state; and is a virtual endorsement of it? Take for instance the part of the parable from the 22d to the 26th verses inclusive.

"And it came to pass, that the beggar died, and was carried by the angels into Abraham's bosom: the rich man also died, and was buried; and in hell he lifted up his eyes, being in torments, and seeth Abraham afar off, and Lazarus in his bosom. And he cried and said, Father Abraham, have mercy on me, and send Lazarus, that he may dip the tip of his finger in water, and cool my tongue; for I am tormented in this flame. But Abraham said, Son, remember that thou in thy lifetime receivedst thy good things, and likewise Lazarus evil things: but now he is comforted, and thou art tormented. And beside all this, between us and you there is a great gulf fixed: so that they which would pass from hence to you cannot; neither can they pass to us, that *would come* from thence."

After describing the abode of the righteous in hades, Josephus says, "This place we call the bosom of Abraham." So in the parable, and according to the Jewish belief as described by Josephus, as soon as Lazarus dies he is taken in charge by good angels, and conveyed to Abraham's bosom.

"The Jews from whom the phrase is borrowed, spoke of *all* true believers as going to Abraham, as being in his bosom. To be in Abraham's bosom was equivalent with them to the being 'in the garden of Eden,' or 'under the throne of glory,' the being gathered unto the general receptacle of happy but waiting souls. The expression already existing among them, received here the sanction and seal of Christ, and has come thus to be accepted by the church, which has understood by it in like manner the state of painless expectation, of blissful repose, which should intervene between the death of the faithful in Christ Jesus, and their perfect consummation and bliss at his coming in his glorious kingdom. It is the 'Paradise' of Luke xxiii. 43, the place of the souls under the altar, Rev. vi. 9; it is, as some distinguish it, blessedness, but not glory."*

The rich man also dies, but in hell (*hades*) he lifts up his eyes, not being in "Abraham's bosom," but "in torment." Abraham's bosom was just as much

* Trench's Notes on the Parables, pp. 376, 377.

in hell, (that is, in *hades*, or the place of departed spirits,) as was the place of "torment." Mark, also, that they are represented as within *sight* and *hearing* of each other, though there is an impassable gulf between them; and that the time for alleviating each other's sufferings, and for exerting an influence on earth is forever past.

"Abraham's bosom is not heaven, though it will issue in heaven, neither is hades '*hell*,' though to issue in it when death and hades shall be cast into the lake of fire, which is the proper hell. Rev. xx. 14. It is a place of restraint where the souls of the wicked are reserved to the judgment of the great day, &c."*

So fully then do the leading features of this parable answer to the Jewish theology concerning an intermediate state, that when we consider to whom it was addressed, we conclude, not only that it was *based* upon that doctrine, but that our Lord intended thereby to *endorse* the doctrine of an intermediate state, upon which the parable is so obviously founded.

VII. The words of our Lord to the penitent thief, "To-day shalt thou be with me in Paradise," Luke xxiii. 43, seem also to imply an intermediate state. That this penitent was a Jew and not a Pagan, is evident from his words to the other thief, "Dost not thou fear GOD, seeing thou art in the same condemnation?" He must, therefore, have understood the word *Paradise*, as used by our Lord in its ordinary Jewish acceptation. Primarily it denoted the garden of Eden,† from which it came to be used for any place

* Trench's Notes on the Parables, p. 379.

† Josephus' Antiquities of the Jews, book I. Chap. I.

of "pleasure or delight;" and it is obviously here used by the Saviour to denote the abode of happy souls after death. It was then "about the ninth hour," or near three o'clock, P. M., and the promise, "To-day shalt thou be with me in Paradise," imported that before that Jewish day, which would end at six o'clock, was closed, the soul of the praying penitent should be with the soul of the Redeemer, in the abode of departed spirits.

That this promise was literally fulfilled is certain. The only remaining question, is, *Where is Paradise?* Does it here mean *heaven*, in the final sense of that term, or simply the abode of happy souls in hades, the place of the departed?

Whatever will help to determine where the soul of Christ was while his body lay in the grave, will tend in the same measure, to determine where the soul of the penitent thief was, and whether there is or is not an intermediate place of souls, distinct from heaven and hell, where they remain till after the final judgment. Let us inquire, then, what light the Scriptures throw upon the first of these questions.

1. In the sixteenth Psalm we have the following prophecy of the resurrection of Christ:—

"I have set the LORD always before me: because *he is* at my right hand, I shall not be moved. Therefore my heart is glad, and my glory rejoiceth: my flesh also shall rest in hope. For thou wilt not leave my soul in hell; neither wilt thou suffer thine Holy One to see corruption."

2. In the second chapter of the Acts of the Apostles, St. Peter distinctly applies this passage to Christ and his resurrection:—

"For David speaketh concerning him, I foresaw the Lord always before my face; for he is on my right hand, that I should not be moved: therefore did my heart rejoice, and my tongue was glad; moreover also my flesh shall rest in hope: because thou wilt not leave my soul in hell, neither wilt thou suffer thine Holy One to see corruption. Thou hast made known to me the ways of life; thou shalt make me full of joy with thy countenance. Men *and* brethren, let me freely speak unto you of the patriarch David, that he is both dead and buried, and his sepulchre is with us unto this day. Therefore being a prophet, and knowing that God had sworn with an oath to him, that of the fruit of his loins, according to the flesh, he would raise up Christ to sit on his throne; he, seeing this before, spake of the resurrection of Christ, that *his soul was not left in hell*, neither his flesh did see corruption. This Jesus hath God raised up, whereof we all are witnesses."

The soul of Christ, then, was in *hades*—the place of departed spirits—while his body lay in the grave; and as Paradise, according to the Jewish idea, was a department of hades, the promise to the penitent thief and the remark of the apostle ("his soul was not left in hell"—hades,) are in perfect keeping with the idea that the Paradise to which Christ went, and where he met the soul of the penitent thief, was in *hades*, or the separate place of souls, and not in the final abode of the righteous after the resurrection.*

3. In the seventeenth Psalm the Hebrew word translated "hell" is *sheol*, which simply means the state or place of the dead, without reference to their happiness

* See Pearson on the Creed, American edition, page 346 and onward.

or misery; and in Acts ii. 27, 31, the Greek word *hades*, also rendered "hell," has the same general meaning. The soul of Christ was not left in *sheol* or *hades*, whither it had gone, but came back to re-enter the body it had left, which was not suffered to see corruption. It is clear then, that the "Paradise" where the soul of the penitent thief met that of Christ, was in *hades*, where the soul of Christ was, but from which it came at his resurrection. "Thou wilt not leave my soul in hades."

4. Although the expression "I am not yet ascended," John xx. 17, probably relates to the ascension of the *body* of Christ to heaven, it seems hardly compatible with the idea that his soul ascended thither while his body lay in the grave. It appears much more in harmony with the ancient confession that his soul "descended into hell," or hades, the place of departed souls, and did not ascend to the heaven of glory where the righteous shall dwell forever.

5. So also of the expression, "For David is not yet ascended into the heavens," no doubt relates mainly to his *body;* that is to say, it is a denial that the prophecy just cited had been fulfilled in David by his resurrection. And yet the statement seems hardly consistent with the popular idea that the soul of David had at that time been in the heaven of heavens more than a thousand years. But upon the hypothesis of an intermediate state all is clear. He was in "Paradise" or "Abraham's" bosom, as was the soul of Christ while his body lay in the grave; but yet, he "is not ascended into heaven," and will not so ascend till his body is raised in glory. Then, like their glorious "forerunner," the saints of God shall ascend far above

all heavens, to the eternal mansions prepared for them. All these considerations go to show that the words of Christ to the penitent thief imply what is called an "Intermediate State."

VIII. Despite the plausibility of the popular theory that souls go either to heaven or hell as soon as the body dies, the Holy Scriptures certainly seem to teach the doctrine of an intermediate place of souls, called *sheol* and *hades*, distinct from heaven and hell, and where souls remain from death to the resurrection—that this intermediate place embraces *Paradise* and *Tartarus*, the separate abodes of the spirits of the righteous and the wicked—that *hades* is but a temporary abode of souls, from which all shall come forth in the resurrection, when hades and the grave shall both be abolished;—and that following the abolition of hades, and the grave, will come the general judgment, when the wicked will be cast into *Tartarus* or *Gehenna*, (hell itself,) and the righteous exalted to the heaven of heavens, to be forever with the Lord.

This view not only explains such Scriptures as "no man hath ascended up to heaven," etc.; but it seems to harmonize the order of events at the end of time, and to vindicate the reasonableness and moral grandeur of the Day of Judgment. It also greatly exalts our ideas of the final rewards of the blessed, to conceive that none enter upon them till the last traces of the effects of sin are wiped away by raising even the bodies of the saints to glory and immortality.

But that even this theory has its difficulties, we are free to admit; though they seem to us less formidable than those which beset the prevailing popular theology

To the common objection that this view dims the believer's hope, and dampens the ardor of his celestial longings, by obscuring his immediate prospects after death; and deferring the bestowment of his "crown of life," till the resurrection, we answer; that it can only be the case where the theory of an intermediate state is misunderstood. The believer's conceptions of his future rest are derived from the descriptions of the Bible—the robes of white—the palms of victory—the harps of gold—the crowns of life, and songs of everlasting joy. But suppose all this is but a description of *Paradise,* and not of the final and eternal mansions? Suppose it should turn out that eye hath not seen, nor ear heard but little as yet even in the Scriptures, of that "far more exceeding and eternal weight of glory," which lies beyond the resurrection morning?

In the viith chapter of Revelation we have a description of the great multitude who stand before the throne, and before the Lamb, clothed in white robes, and with palms in their hands.

In the xxth chapter, verses 12–15, we have a description of the resurrection and judgment. The former, therefore, if descriptive of the happiness of the righteous in another life, must be understood to relate only to the intermediate state, and not to the heaven that shall follow the Day of Judgment. This last seems to be more especially described in Chapter xxi.; for immediately after the description of the resurrection and general judgment, Chapter xx., we have an account of "a new heaven and a new earth," the first heaven, as well as the first earth having passed away. Then follows a description of "the holy city, New Jerusalem," the everlasting home of all whose names are written in the Lamb's Book of Life. Now, what are we to understand by the idea that the first heaven is to pass away, to be succeeded by the New Jerusalem, if it be not that "Paradise" or "Abraham's bosom," is to be abolished after the resurrection, to be followed by a more glorious mansion, as the final abode of the saints? May not what we see in Rev. vii., be only as the porter's lodge, down by the gates of immortality, while the glorious, heavenly mansion is as yet hidden or but dimly seen amid the unrevealed glory beyond?

Not a shadow is thrown across the flowery plains of Paradise, by the idea of another and more perfect rest hereafter. Oh no! Let the Christian still gaze in rapture upon the white-robed company who triumph there. Let him listen to their immortal rejoicings. Let him know that to all this his freed spirit shall be exalted the moment it leaves the earthly tabernacle. Let him hope and long for this rest, as he may, and he shall not be disappointed. But let him also know, that when Christ shall descend from heaven to raise the dead, and judge all men—when their salvation shall thus be perfected, and he shall say to the righteous, "inherit the kingdom;" *then* shall he enter a world of beauty and splendor to which Paradise, with all its joys, has been but a faint and imperfect shadow; and then shall he know "the far more exceeding and eternal weight of glory." And having entered upon this his glorious dwelling-place, he shall go out no more; but shall be forever with the Lord.

And so of the sinner. The "torments" of *hades* are but the beginning of his sorrow. For when his body has been raised as Christ has said "unto the resurrection of damnation," John v. 29, *then* and not till then shall he be punished with "everlasting destruction;"—and depart into "everlasting fire, prepared for the devil and his angels."

From all these considerations, then, we believe the doctrine of an "Intermediate State;" or separate abode of souls between death and the resurrection, to be a doctrine of the Bible; and to be taught and received as such. It explains all those Scriptures which speak of the rewarding of the saints at the resurrection, without implying that they have no conscious existence till then; and is in other respects a most "wholesome doctrine and very full of comfort."*

* For a more extended treatment of the subject the reader is referred to Bishop Hobart's "State of the Departed," and to Pierson on the Creed. See also *Watson's Theological Institutes*, Part Second, Ch. xxix.; Wesley's works, Vol. ii. pp. 466, 7, and notes on Luke, xxiii. 43.

CHAPTER IX.

IMMORTAL EXISTENCE NOT A RESULT OF FAITH IN CHRIST.

UNLIKE the open Deism of the past, the modern theory of annihilation rests largely upon the assumption that the penalty of sin is extinction of being. The idea that the wicked will be annihilated at the day of judgment is especially dependent upon the former assumption. The theory is that the penalty of sin, in the first instance, and onward, is "death," in the sense of *annihilation;* and that, consequently, all who fail of salvation through faith in Christ, will finally go out of existence.

Mr. Dobney, an able English writer, and the apostle of this school of theologians, is thus clear and explicit upon the first part of this theory. Commenting upon Gen. ii. 17, "In the day that thou eatest thereof thou shalt surely die," he says:—

"The very words would seem to shut us up to the idea that utter destruction, cessation of existence, return to that nothingness out of which the divine power had called him, was the death threatened to our first father in case of transgression."

Again:—"We find ourselves imperatively compelled to believe that the sentence pronounced in case of transgression, considered in itself, and as it must have been understood by Adam, and as it was expounded by the Judge himself, and was illustrated in the banishment from the life-sustaining tree, * * * conveyed the sole idea of cessation of existence—a return to that blank nothingness out of which he was brought—and that unless a remedial system had mercifully intervened, when Adam died there would have been an utter and everlasting extinction of his conscious being."

Still again:—"The death threatened to Adam was the death of the entire man, the cessation of all conscious existence, etc."*

Mr. Ellis, an American advocate of annihilation, reiterates the same view:—"The penalty threatened, was to end in death; and God's interpretation of it plainly declared, that it would result in death, a gradual *returning* to the primitive elements of his being, *the dust;* and the facts show that it did result in death, in the *entire extinction of his being.*"†

Mr. Hudson, another American advocate of the future annihilation of the wicked, seems to adopt the same views, though he has nowhere stated them with equal clearness.

But there are two classes of theorists in this country, who, while they unite in denying the immortality of man, differ widely as to the grounds of this denial. One class, like Messrs. Storrs, and Ellis, and Hastings regard the soul as a *material essence*—in fact as *part of the body*—and as having no existence whatever when the animal organism is dissolved.

* Dobney on Future Punishment, pp. 128, 134, 135.

† Bible *vs.* Tradition, p. 62.

One of Mr. Ellis' chapters is entitled, "Proof from the Bible of the corporeal nature and mortality of the soul of man, etc." "The very highest nature," says he, "that man has, irrespective of Christ and the resurrection, is flesh, an evanescent wind."* When the body is raised again, say they, the soul also will live again; and not before; and when at the judgment the wicked are "burned up," their souls will go out of being as they did at the first or natural death of the body; and will live no more forever. Now, if the first assumption were true, viz.: the materiality of the spirit of man, all else might follow. The soul might cease to live when the body died, and only live again when the body was raised; and if the body was again dissolved, by fire or any other means, the soul might perish with it. But the main point being an erroneous assumption, all that is built upon it must be without foundation.

But there are other annihilationists who cannot quite adopt the idea that the soul is material, and are, therefore, compelled to admit its conscious existence separate from and independent of the body; but who nevertheless hold that the wicked will be annihilated at the Day of Judgment. Of this class is Mr. C. F. Hudson. "The writer," says he, "with many others, regards the soul not as a mere result of the physical organism, nor as dying with the body. By reason of the Redemption, or in some other divine economy, the entire sentence of death is divided in the case of those who incur it, the soul finally perishing in the so-called 'second death.'"†

This theory is, if possible, more absurd than that

* Treatise, pp. 15, 20.

† Christ our Life, p. 3.

of Mr. Storrs; for if, as Mr. Hudson admits, the soul is to such an extent indestructible as to survive the dissolution of the body, and live for ages independent of it, that fact of itself furnishes a strong presumption against its subsequent annihilation, by any catastrophe that may overtake it.

Besides, the theory of "dividing" the penalty is, to say the least, a theological novelty, an invention to give a show of consistency to a discordant theological system. The original decree was "IN THE DAY that thou eatest thereof thou shalt surely die." Orthodox Christians believe the death threatened to have been *spiritual*, a loss of God's favour and falling under the curse of his broken law, and that it fell upon Adam and Eve *that day*, as God had threatened. But those who, like Mr. Hudson, make the death threatened to consist of *annihilation*, are obliged either to deny that the penalty ever visited the transgressors, or to defer its execution till the body dies; and then, if they find the soul outliving the body, must follow that up to the last day, and thus complete their work of annihilation! Thus "the sentence is divided" by all the years that lie between the natural death of the first sinner, when his body perished, and the day of Judgment, when his "death" is completed by the annihilation of his soul!

Upon this theory the meaning of the passage "in the day that thou eatest thereof thou shalt surely die," would be, "thou shalt surely die sooner or later, thy body at the end of near a thousand years, (Gen. v. 4,) and the soul after some six thousand years more, *i. e.* at the day of Judgment." Surely, this is not only "dividing," but *deferring*, and as we think strangely *distorting* "the sentence of death."

But to come to the particular subject of this chapter. It is admitted that the everlasting life promised the righteous, and the "death" with which the finally impenitent are threatened, are conditional. "He that believeth in the Son of God shall not perish, but have everlasting life." Christ is, indeed, "our life,"—the living bread that came down from heaven, of which if we eat we shall live forever. And so, on the other hand, "the wages of sin is death;" and he that believeth not the Son, shall not see life, but the wrath of God abideth on him.

But the question is, what do "life" and "death" mean, when used to denote the results of faith in Christ on the one hand, and of unbelief on the other? The whole controversy turns upon the settlement of this question. If "everlasting life," means continued existence merely, and "death" means annihilation, the question is settled. Immortality is not a destiny but a privilege, to be secured by faith. But if the terms "life" and "death" as thus employed, are used metaphorically, to indicate *salvation*, or deliverance from spiritual death on the one hand, and "damnation," or the "second death" on the other, then the hypothesis of a conditional immortality finds no support from the doctrine of conditional life and death.

That the terms above referred to, are used metaphorically, to indicate *conditions* of being, and not existence or non-existence, is obvious from the following considerations.

I. In metaphorical language we call one object or quality or event by the name of another, on account of the resemblance between the two. Thus Christ is a "rock" a "vine," a "lamb," &c. And as the elements of language are derived from things terrestrial and visible, all ideas in regard to the spiritual and unseen world must needs be conveyed to us in terms first employed in reference to things temporal and material. Hence it is that heaven itself is described as a "city" and "country," and even the soul of man can find no more etherial word with which to clothe itself, than that which represents the intangible and invisible atmosphere.

And so in regard to the terms "life" and "death," when used to indicate rewards and punishments. As *life* is the most precious boon known to mortals here, it is employed in the Scriptures to represent the inestimable blessings which God has in reserve for the righteous; and as *death* is regarded as the most dreaded of all earthly calamities to the body, it is employed to represent the great calamity to the soul in a coming life—its banishment from God's presence for ever.

II. If the term "life," when employed as above stated, means simple *existence*, and "death" non-existence, then the Scriptures should never employ any terms or phrases, when speaking of the results of faith or unbelief in this life, other than such as convey this meaning, and may be substituted by the term immortal on the one hand and annihilation on the other. But such is not the fact. "He that believeth not, shall be damned," said Christ. Now who will affirm that the damnation here spoken of is not the *final* reward of unbelief, or that it does not distinctly import a malediction resting upon a still living soul?

Will it do to render the sentence, "He that believeth and is baptized shall be immortal, and he that believeth not, shall be annihilated?" Every one can see, by this experiment, that the words "saved" and "damned" are not used in the sense of made immortal and annihilated; and consequently that such do not constitute the reward and penalty of unbelief, or of a life of sin.

III. If the final "death" of the sinner were annihilation, then every description of that death should indicate not only freedom from all suffering for ever, but the termination of all existence. It would be as misleading to employ terms and figures and parables conveying an idea of suffering beyond the day of judgment, as it would to speak of our suffering ages *before* we had existence. But what are the facts? When the righteous enter "life eternal" the wicked "go away into everlasting punishment." Can that mean annihilation? And if so, how is it "everlasting?" How is it, if the wicked go out of being, that "their worm dieth not and the fire is not quenched?" How is it that we hear the voice of weeping and wailing and gnashing of teeth from souls that have been stricken out of existence?

IV. If it had been the design of Christ and his apostles to teach that the penalty of sin is annihilation, while continued being was the reward of piety, a doctrine of so much importance would not have been confined to the use of the terms *life* and *death*, (which have never been understood to imply simple existence and non-existence, except by the Deist and the unenlightened heathen) but would have been expressed in other words, as the true sense of these terms now is.

The righteous are to "inherit the kingdom"—to "sit down in the kingdom of God"—to walk with Christ in white, etc., all as elements of salvation and results of saving faith in Christ; but by no terms or figures is the idea ever conveyed that their salvation consists either wholly or in part in deliverance from annihilation. They praise God that their robes have been washed, and made white in the blood of the Lamb; that is, that they have been fitted for a blissful eternity; but never for release from utter extinction. No such danger ever threatened them, and they praise God and the Lamb for no *such* deliverance.

And aside from the terms "*die*" and "*death*," neither of which imply annihilation, there is not a warning or admonition in all the Bible that enforces faith in Christ by the threat of annihilation. The appeal is always to the more terrible and consequently more potent consideration of endless banishment from God, and from the glory of his power.

V. Those who insist that the term "*death*" as applied to the sinner in a future state, implies annihilation, ought to be able to show that such is its meaning when applied to man in this world; that is, that when a wicked man, at least, *dies* in this world he ceases to exist. But instead of this Mr. Hudson admits that his soul lives on for ages, though in the language of earth he is dead. If, then, the term does not imply non-existence in its original application, by what stretch of interpretation is it made to signify extinction of being in another life?

Even the materialist, who holds to the future resurrection and annihilation of the wicked, does not regard natural death as an annihilation. Though their theory might logically compel them to regard it in this light, nevertheless, they *keep up the personal identity* in some way, from death to the resurrection;—a supposition utterly irreconcilable with the idea that natural death is annihilation. To such also we may ask with equal propriety, why do you understand the terms "*death*" and "*die*" to imply cessation of being? Is it not a meaning foreign to their original import even according to your own admissions?

From age to age and from pole to pole the term "*death*" when applied to man here has been understood to mean a certain *condition* of being, and not non-existence. And so you still understand it. Why, then, do you not understand it in the same sense when applied to man in a future state; that is, as imparting a *circumstance* or *quality* of existence, rather than annihilation?

Such is beyond all question the sense in which the term is employed in the Bible; so that when "life" is promised to such as believe in Christ, it does not mean immortal *existence* merely, but *eternal* HAPPINESS. Hence, *future* HAPPINESS alone is conditioned upon faith in Christ, and not our future being. Consequently the future non-existence of the wicked cannot follow for lack of a vital connection with Christ, by faith in him. He is "our life" in that he restores the soul to spiritual life by his Spirit, raises our bodies from the dead, and finally crowns the righteous with glory in heaven. But our immortal existence is not made dependent upon the reception or rejection of salvation through his name. We shall exist forever, whether in happiness through faith in Christ and a holy life, or in misery through a life of sin, and the rejection of offered mercy through Him, the only Saviour.

But there are yet other views of the doctrine of annihilation which will require to be considered in a distinct chapter.

CHAPTER X.

SUPPOSED ANNIHILATION OF THE WICKED AT THE DAY OF JUDGMENT.

THOUGH the particular subject of this chapter is not necessarily connected with the question whether or not the soul survives the death of the body, still as the doctrine of the annihilation of the wicked is often taught in connection with that of the sleep or death of souls, and is directly opposed to the idea of an unending existence after death, we deem it proper to devote a few pages to its special consideration.

The prevailing belief among Christians, is, that when Christ again appears he will raise all the dead—the just and the unjust—that they will all be summoned before his judgment-seat and judged; and that the wicked shall go away into everlasting punishment, while the righteous will inherit eternal life. But the new theory recently promulgated, asserts that the wicked, having been raised from the dead and judged, will then be stricken out of being, or utterly annihilated.* So far as we are aware, this

* Materialists are not exactly agreed upon this particular point. Mr. Ellis, in his "*Bible vs. Tradition*" contends that the wicked shall cease to exist, but dodges the question whether or not they shall be raised from the dead. See page 234, where he asks in capitals, "WILL THE WICKED DEAD BE RAISED TO LIFE AGAIN?" but leaves it unanswered.

doctrine is confined almost exclusively to the class of Second Adventists already alluded to; and as they profess to found their belief upon this point also upon the Scriptures, it may be well to notice some of the more prominent passages upon which they depend.

I. Those Scriptures that speak of the wicked as to be "*destroyed*," are claimed as teaching that they shall be annihilated. But destruction and annihilation are very different things. A thing is said to be destroyed when it is seriously injured. Thus St. Paul said, "*Destroy* not him with thy meat, for whom Christ died," Rom. xiv. 15; but surely he did not mean to warn the Romans against annihilating each other. So Christ came to *destroy* the Devil, Heb. ii. 14; but did he annihilate him? And do the wicked who "*destroy* the earth," Rev. xi. 18, annihilate the earth? Though the term is used in a great variety of senses it never means to annihilate; consequently the threatened destruction of the wicked is no proof of their approaching annihilation.

II. It is said the wicked are to "*perish*," and must, therefore, go out of existence. But if we attach this sense to the term *perish*, we can prove not only the annihilation of the wicked, but of the right-

So far as he has shown to the contrary, he believed that when a sinner dies, that is the end of him forever. Mr. Dobney and Mr. Hudson, on the contrary, are plainly committed to a general resurrection, and the subsequent annihilation of the wicked; while Mr. Storrs teaches the resurrection of all, and the subsequent annihilation of all wicked men and devils. He says, "the death which is the wages of sin is—an actual *extermination of being*;" and also that the wicked "are not punished till after the judgment of the great day." Sermons, pp. 16, 17. Of course, then, their annihilation does not take place till after they are raised from the dead.

eous also. "There is a just man that *perisheth* in his righteousness;" Eccl. vii. 15. "The righteous *perisheth* and no man layeth it to heart;" Isa. lvii. 1. St. Peter says, 2d Epistle, iii. 6, that "the world being overflowed with water, *perished*." But was the globe then annihilated? Of the "heavens" and the "earth," it is said, "they shall *perish;*" Heb. i. 11; and yet when this perishing is explained, it is said, "and they shall be *changed*." They perish, but are not annihilated. So of the wicked—they shall perish, that is, they shall be condemned and sent away into everlasting punishment, but their *existence*, like that of the old world which perished by water, shall continue on forever and ever.

III. Several passages that speak of the wicked as to be "*consumed*," are urged in proof of their annihilation. But this term, like *destroy* and *perish*, is never used in the sense of annihilated. "I shall one day be *consumed* by the hand of Saul," said David, 1 Sam. xxvii. 1; but surely he did not expect Saul to *annihilate* him. So the Psalmist said, "Mine eye is *consumed*," Psa. vi. 7; and "My bones are *consumed*," Psa. xxxi. 10; and yet neither his eye nor his bones were annihilated. Of man as a race it is said, "For we are *consumed* by thine anger," Psa. xc. 7, though the race yet lived; and God said of the children of Israel, "I have *consumed* them in mine anger;" though they were then living by hundreds of thousands. "Take heed," says the apostle, "that ye be not *consumed* one of another." Gal. v. 15. Does the word "*consumed*," then, mean *annihilated?*

IV. But it is said, "The wicked are to be *burned up*, which must mean, put out of existence." By no means. Literal burning annihilates nothing. The wood may be decomposed, and its elements scattered in the form of flame, and vapor, and smoke, and ashes, but nothing goes out of existence by the process of combustion. Hence, "burning up" never implies annihilation.

Besides; The passages that most strongly assert the burning up of the wicked, are found in the last chapter of Malachi:

"For, behold, the day cometh, that shall burn as an oven; and all the proud, yea, and all that do wickedly, shall be stubble: and the day that cometh shall burn them up, saith the LORD of hosts, that it shall leave them neither root nor branch."

* * * * * * *

"And ye shall tread down the wicked; for they shall be ashes under the soles of your feet, in the day that I shall do *this*, saith the LORD of hosts."

And yet, this predicted burning up was all accomplished at the destruction of Jerusalem by the Romans, when few, if any of the wicked were literally burned, and not one of them literally became as ashes under the feet of the Christians.

Of the latter it was said, "But unto you that fear my name shall the Sun of righteousness arise with healing in his wings; and ye shall go forth, and grow up as calves of the stall." Accordingly they all escaped unhurt. But the Jews were slaughtered in great numbers, and their city, Jerusalem, was laid waste. And this is described in the glowing language of prophecy as "burning them up;" and making them as "ashes under the soles of their feet."

That the above is the true meaning of the passages

cited, is evident from the last two verses of the chapter:—"Behold, I will send you Elijah the prophet before the coming of the great and dreadful day of the LORD: and he shall turn the heart of the father to the children, and the heart of the children to their fathers, lest I come and smite the earth with a curse."

Now this Elijah, or Elias, who came, was John the Baptist. Gabriel had said of him before his birth, "And he shall go before him [Christ] in the spirit and power of Elias, to turn the hearts of the fathers to the children, and the disobedient to the wisdom of the just; to make ready a people prepared for the Lord." Our Saviour said, "For all the prophets and the law prophesied until John. And if ye will receive *it*, this is Elias, which was for to come." Matt. xi. 13, 14.

"And they asked him, saying, Why say the scribes that Elias must first come? And he answered and told them, Elias verily cometh first, and restoreth all things; and how it is written of the Son of man, that he must suffer many things, and be set at nought. But I say unto you, That Elias is indeed come, and they have done unto him whatsoever they listed, as it is written of him." Mark ix. 11–13.

John was Elias metaphorically, because he had "the *spirit* and *power* of Elias." And he was sent "before the coming of the great and dreadful day of the Lord," when he visited his chosen people with sore judgments, and made Mount Zion a perpetual desolation. It is evident, therefore, that this "burning up" of the wicked, upon which modern Annihilationists depend so much, not only falls infinitely short of the annihilation of anything, but has no reference whatever to the day of judgment, or the final destruction of the wicked.

Several other terms employed in the Scriptures to represent the punishment of the wicked, such as that they shall be "*slain*," "*devoured*," "*blotted out*," "*hewn down*," "*cut off*," etc., are urged as teaching the doctrine of annihilation; but such a use of these terms is so evident a perversion of their meaning that it would be a waste of time to consider them in detail. They are all of the same general class and import, when applied to the punishment of the sinner, and can never, by any fair construction, be pressed into the service of annihilationism.

V. The notion that the wicked are first to be raised from the dead and then struck out of existence, as the punishment for their sins, is not only without warrant from the Holy Scriptures, but is liable to many other insuperable objections.

1. It is in direct conflict with Eccl. iii. 14; "I know that, whatsoever God doeth, it shall stand forever: nothing can be put to it, nor anything taken from it: and God doeth it, that men should fear before him." That this passage relates to the doings of Jehovah in the work of *creation*, is obvious from the fact that it is true of him in no other respect. "Whatsoever God doeth," in creating, "shall stand forever;"—shall never go out of existence. "Nothing can be put to it"—no being can add to the creation of God,—"nor anything taken from it"—nothing which God ushers into being can be uncreated, or put out of being. "And God doeth it that men should fear before him"—that is, that they may know that

they shall forever exist, and may fear the unending consequences of a life of sin. But the wicked have little to "fear" if the worst that awaits them after death is an eternity of non-existence! Such an object of fear is precisely like the vacuity of being which filled eternal ages before our existence began.

2. This theory makes no distinction between the state of the sinner *before* and *after* the day of judgment. It generally assumes that their souls go out of existence at death; are re-produced by the resurrection; and then sent back again into non-existence, precisely as they were before they were raised. To what, then, does their condemnation and punishment amount, if they were suffering precisely the same penalty before as after the resurrection? They are simply raised up from the fathomless abyss of non-existence, to be plunged back again into the same infinite depths, to remain there forever!

3. This theory consigns the righteous to the same punishment from death to the resurrection, (which in some cases must be many thousand years,) which is inflicted upon the wicked in the last day. The souls of the righteous are said to become extinct with the death of the body. Not only does all consciousness cease, but their very *being* ends. And this is all that the wicked are said to suffer after the day of judgment. They are simply sent back where the righteous were from death to the resurrection!

4. The doctrine of the annihilation of the wicked is contrary to the Scripture doctrine of *degrees of punishment* in a future state. Christ said, "Woe unto you, scribes and Pharisees, hypocrites! for ye devour widows' houses, and for a pretence make long

prayer: therefore ye shall receive the greater damnation," Matt. xxiii. 14; implying that there are degrees of "damnation," or punishment, in reserve for the wicked.

Again he said, "And that servant, which knew his lord's will, and prepared not *himself*, neither did according to his will, shall be beaten with many *stripes*. But he that knew not, and did commit things worthy of stripes, shall be beaten with few *stripes*. For unto whomsoever much is given, of him shall be much required; and to whom men have committed much, of him they will ask the more." Luke xii. 47, 48. The "stripes," or punishment, is to be proportioned to the knowledge and guilt of the individual sinner.

To the same effect is the statement, Rev. xx. 12, that men are to be judged "according to their works;" and Rev. xxii. 12, that they are to be rewarded upon the same principle; "And, behold, I come quickly; and my reward *is* with me, to give every man according as his work shall be." These passages plainly involve the doctrine of degrees of punishment, for sins committed in this life. The hypocritical Pharisee, who, for a pretence makes long prayers, and yet devours widows' houses, is to receive a "greater damnation" than the common sinner. Some are to be beaten with few stripes, and some with many, according to their guilt.

But how can this be true if the wicked are to be annihilated? Are there any degrees in annihilation? Certainly not. Consequently if that is the penalty of sin, the punishment of all would be precisely alike, in direct opposition to the word of God.

5. The apostle speaks, Heb. x. 28, 29, of a "much

sorer punishment" than death. "He that despised Moses' law died without mercy under two or three witnesses: of how much sorer punishment, suppose ye, shall he be thought worthy, who hath trodden under foot the Son of God, and hath counted the blood of the covenant, wherewith he was sanctified, an unholy thing, and hath done despite unto the Spirit of grace?"

But if death is the extinction of conscious being, and this is to be the penalty visited upon the wicked after they are raised and judged, there *is* no sorer punishment than death. And though those who trample under foot the Son of God are "*worthy*" of a "much sorer punishment" than those who rejected the law of Moses, still no difference can be made. They must all drink the same lethean draught of annihilation, and go out of being alike and forever.

6. The penalty of sin is never represented as annihilation, but always as *positive* and *conscious suffering.* Take the following passages as specimens:

Matt. xxv. 30:—"And cast ye the unprofitable servant into outer darkness: there shall be weeping and gnashing of teeth."

Luke xii. 28:—"There shall be weeping and gnashing of teeth, when ye shall see Abraham, and Isaac, and Jacob, and all the prophets, in the kingdom of God, and you *yourselves* thrust out."

Luke xvi. 23:—"And in hell he lifted up his eyes, being in torments."

Rom. ii. 8, 9:—"Indignation and wrath, tribulation and anguish, upon every soul of man that doeth evil; of the Jew first, and also of the Gentile."

Such passages are utterly irreconcilable with the

doctrine that the wicked are to be annihilated. Their punishment is to consist of "anguish" and "torment,"—manifesting itself in "weeping and gnashing of teeth."

7. This theory is directly opposed to the plain teaching of the Scriptures, that the punishment of the sinner shall be everlasting.*

Matt. xxv. 46:—"And these shall go away into everlasting punishment: but the righteous into life eternal." In this text the Greek word rendered "everlasting" is *aionion*—a word which in its proper grammatical sense means *unending.* It is the word almost invariably used in the New Testament to represent the unending joys of the righteous. Take the following instances as examples:

Matt. xix. 16:—"And behold, one came and said unto him, Good Master, what good thing shall I do that I may have *eternal life?*"

Mark x. 30:—"But he shall receive an hundred-fold now in this time, houses, and brethren, and sisters, and mothers, and children, and lands, with persecutions; and in the world to come, *eternal life.*"

Luke x. 25:—"And behold, a certain lawyer stood up, and tempted him, saying, Master, what shall I do to inherit *eternal life?*"

John iii. 16:—"For God so loved the world, that he gave his only begotten Son, that whosoever believeth in him, should not perish, but have *everlasting life.*"

Besides, it is the very word used for this purpose in the passage first cited:—"But the righteous into

*For an excellent summary of the Scripture testimony upon this point, see Lee's Theology, pp. 311–331, inclusive.

zoen ten aionion—life eternal." The punishment of the wicked must be coeval, therefore, with the eternal life of the righteous.

But this cannot be true, if the wicked cease to exist just when the joys of the righteous begin. Upon this hypothesis their punishment is but for a moment, during the process of annihilation, or at most from the time they are raised from the dead till they again go out of being.

The only reply that can be made to this objection is, that as their non-existence is endless, the punishment thus becomes eternal. We answer, that *punishment* is "pain or suffering inflicted on a person for a crime;"* and necessarily implies a *subject* of such punishment. Surely the sinner cannot be "punished," ages after he has ceased to exist. If, then, he is to go away into everlasting "*punishment*," his *existence* must be unending.

No punishment or damnation can possibly exist, in reference to a being that has no existence. And if the wicked are to go away into everlasting punishment, as the Scriptures affirm, they must exist forever; and the idea of their annihilation is erroneous.

8. The doctrine under consideration is in direct conflict with every description of the day of judgment and the punishment of the wicked. To them it is to be said, "Depart from me, ye cursed, into everlasting fire," Matt. xxv. 41, and they shall "go away" into this "everlasting punishment." How can a being that is annihilated "*depart*" from Christ, or "*go away*" into punishment at all? The unprofitable

* Webster.

servant, verse 30th, is to be "cast into outer darkness," but not annihilated. The wicked shall be "cast into a furnace of fire," Matt. xiii. 50, but instead of its being the end of their existence, they shall still live on; for "there shall be wailing and gnashing of teeth." The man who had not on a wedding garment, Matt. xxii. 13, was "taken away and cast into outer darkness." But here also, was "weeping and gnashing of teeth;" i. e., intense and conscious suffering. "Except a man be born again, he cannot see the kingdom of God;" and "he that believeth not shall be damned." But in neither case is it said that they shall be annihilated. The foolish virgins are shut out of heaven, but they still live to cry, "Lord, Lord, open to us;" Matt. xxv. 10, 11. And those who seek improperly, or too late, and are consequently not able to enter in at the strait gate, are to "stand without and knock, and say, Lord, Lord, open to us." But to all such Christ will say, "Depart from me, all ye that work iniquity." Luke xiii. 24–27. How very different all this from the sentence of utter annihilation!

9. This doctrine really destroys all personal identity in the day of judgment, and all personal responsibility, on the part of the souls that shall then exist, for the acts of the previous life. For if man has no soul, distinct from his body, then memory, and knowledge, and moral accountability must be perpetuated in the grave, and their seat must be in the mouldering ashes of the dead, or they can have no perpetuity whatever. But as this cannot be, and is denied even by Annihilationists themselves, it follows upon their own theory, that the accountable moral agent becomes

extinct at death. So, if this theory be true, all memory, and knowledge, and consciousness, and accountability are then at an end.

But when the body is raised again, the power that thinks, and reasons, and remembers, is re-produced; or rather *a* soul is evolved; for it is in fact a *new creation.* That which before did not exist is brought into being. Now we should like to know what connection this conscious spirit can have with the spirit or soul of the former body? Is the electricity generated by an electrical machine to-day, the same that was generated by the same instrument a hundred years ago?

So of the risen dead: will the souls evolved in the resurrection, according to this theory, be the same as those evolved by the mortal bodies before they died? Will they *know* what was known by spirits of the former bodies, and *remember* the events of the present life? And if not, wherein consists the identity? What chain connects the resurrection spirit, so to speak, with the mortal spirit, or spirit that knew, and thought, and remembered in the first body? How can the soul of the resurrection body remember what took place before *it* came into existence? And how can it be accountable for what was done by the former spirit, that has long before ceased to exist?

Take away, then, the continued and conscious existence of the soul between death and the resurrection, and we have no means of personal identity—no link connecting the moral and accountable agents of the resurrection morning, with those who lived and sinned or served God here in the present life. The alleged extinction of the soul at death, creates a parenthesis of being—a yawning chasm of non-existence, over which the spirit shall never wing its backward flight to call up the memories of the life it once lived in the body.

If the theory be true, the soul that is evolved in the resurrection, is a new-born soul. It can no more know or remember what took place in the body before death, than we can remember what took place a thousand ages before we existed. Neither can it be responsible for anything back of its own conscious doings, after it is brought into being by the resurrection of the body. Why, then, should it be annihilated? or punished in any manner whatever? As well might Adam have been annihilated an hour after he was created, for the rebellion of Satan before the world was made. Such are some of the absurdities of this attempt to sustain one of the worst features of Deism by the word of God.

We have thus shown, in the first place, that the philosophical distinction between matter and spirit is a legitimate and proper one, founded in the very nature of things, and necessarily resulting from a study of the phenomena of mind and matter, and the application to both of the principles of classification, which lie at the foundation of all science, and of all human knowledge. Turning then to the Holy Scriptures, we have shown by the most conclusive and abundant proofs that they everywhere recognise the distinction between matter and spirit, and the two-fold nature of man, as clearly as they recognise the being of a God. True, they nowhere formally assert, in so many words, that man has a spirit distinct from the body in which it dwells, and capable of a separate and independent existence when the body is dissolved; but they *assume* it as a truth not to be called in question, precisely as the being of a God is everywhere assumed throughout the Bible.

After a brief chapter on the supposed origin of souls, we have proved from the Scripture, that as life began with the infusion of "the living Spirit" into the body of Adam, so death is the *reverse* of this process—the *separation* of the soul from the body—a putting off of the fleshly tabernacle—the giving up of the ghost—the departure of the soul—a flying away, to be absent from the body and present with the Lord.

Next in order we have proved from the same "sure word of prophecy," that souls thus separated from the body by death, live on in conscious joy or sorrow, in the place of departed spirits, from death to the resurrection; and that the idea of the cessation of conscious being, or the "sleep" of souls from death to the resurrection, has no warrant in the word of God.

In the chapter on the "Intermediate State," it is shown that instead of implying that souls have *no* reward or punishment till the second coming of Christ and the resurrection, those Scriptures which speak of rewards and punishments as to be distributed at the resurrection and final judgment, relate solely to the *perfection* or *fulness* of both, which will be brought to all men at the revelation of Christ to judge the world. Thus, all such Scriptures are shown to be in perfect harmony with the idea of conscious being, and partial rewards and punishments during the intermediate period, or *before* the resurrection and final judgment.

In the ninth chapter we have proved that the penalty of sin is not *annihilation*, but conscious suffering, —that Christ did not die to redeem men from non-existence, but from the "wrath to come," or the endless consequences of sin in another life; and that consequently our immortality or continued existence after death is not dependent upon our faith in Christ. And finally, we have shown that the declarations of the Bible that the wicked are to "perish," "die," "be consumed," "destroyed," "burned up," "slain," "devoured," "blotted out," "hewn down," "cut off," &c., in no wise imply their non-existence; and that the idea of the annihilation of the wicked at the day of judgment is in conflict with the whole tenor of the Sacred Writings.

And here we might close the argument so far as many of our readers are concerned. By the mouth of these many inspired witnesses, every principle of the Christian theory of the soul's separate and conscious immortality is fully established.

But there is another class of reasoners, who, while they admit that the Bible plainly teaches the two-fold nature of man, and the immortality of the soul, claim that *Reason* and *Nature*, or in other words, the phenomena of mental and physical development, of life, decay, and death, and of the natural world in general, all point to oblivion as the end of man, and are therefore in conflict with the idea of another life after death.

However complete, therefore, the demonstration from the Scriptures, it is due to the advocate of "Natural Religion," to accompany him also to his favorite field of research, and see if both reason and nature do not respond to revelation, that the soul of man lives on forever.

PART SECOND.

RATIONAL EVIDENCES OF A FUTURE LIFE.

CHAPTER I.

CHARACTER AND VALUE OF THE RATIONAL ARGUMENT.

WE have thus far confined our inquiries to the teachings of the Holy Scriptures. Let us now turn our attention to what are called the *rational evidences* of man's immortality.

I. By the *rational evidences* of a future life, we mean such evidences as may be gathered outside of the pages of Divine Revelation, by reflection upon the facts and phenomena of the natural world; the relations of man to the material creation; the powers and susceptibilities of the soul; and the various phenomena of life and death.

"The evidences of a future state," says Dr. Dick, "which the light of reason affords, though not so clear and decisive as those which are derived from Divine Revelation, are worthy of the serious consideration of every one in whose mind the least doubt remains on this important subject. The conviction they are calculated to produce, when attentively weighed, is sufficient to leave every one without excuse who trifles with the concerns of his future destiny, and overlooks his relations to the eternal world."

"Though the realities of a future world are not presented directly to the eye of sense, yet the faculties with which man is endowed, when properly exercised on all the physical and moral scenes which the universe displays, are sufficient to evince the highest degree of probability, if not absolute certainty, that his duration and his sphere of action are not confined to the narrow limits of the present world, but have a relation to a future and immortal existence." *

"I am not sure," says Dr. Erskine Mason, "in these days of physiological research and philosophic pride, that it is a waste of time or labor, or an inappropriate work for the advocate of truth to ransack the analogies of things, to trace the correspondence between the natural and the spiritual, if for no other purpose than to show that a skepticism as to 'the life to come' has no warrant whatever in any of the things which are seen and known as yet."†

II. The Author of the Bible is the author of nature; hence all true science is in perfect harmony with revealed religion. And the fact that in all the researches and discoveries of modern times, nothing has been found in the realm of nature to contradict any portion of the sacred writings, while all other ancient writings are in perpetual conflict with modern science, is one of the strongest proofs that the Bible is from God, the infinite Creator of all things. So of each particular truth of revelation: if, upon its being announced every fact and phenomena of nature is in harmony with it, this circumstance of itself

* Philosophy of a Future State, Chapter I.

† Sermon on the Life to Come, Pastor's Legacy, p. 190.

affords a presumptive and collateral evidence of its truth.

A mysterious murder is committed, and the supposed criminal is arrested. A theory of the murder is set forth by the press, or by the states attorney. If that theory is in conflict with any known facts in regard to the supposed criminal or his victim, such conflict goes far to discredit the theory; but if, on the other hand, the theory is in harmony with and explains all the known facts of the case, there at once arises a strong presumption of the truth of the theory.

So of all revealed truth, and especially of the doctrine of a future state. If it is found to agree most wonderfully with all we know of ourselves or of the natural world, such agreement goes far to corroborate the doctrine, and to strengthen in our minds the conviction of its truth.

III. Two errors, we think, have been committed in regard to the nature and value of the rational evidences of man's immortality. *First*, we deem it a mistake to suppose that such evidence is *primary;* or in other words that it could be discovered or understood at all, without the light of the Bible first thrown upon the problem of our being, and afterward reflected from all the works of God. Until that "star of eternity" gilds the scene, all natural intimations of immortality are latent. They are like hieroglyphics upon the walls of some dark cavern, existing but undecyphered, till the darkness of ages is dispersed by the flambeau of the curious traveler. *Then only* can he see and read them.

But suppose a gorgeous chandelier, suspended from

the ceiling of the cavern, had been burning for ages; and suppose, as in some of the mines of the old world, one were born and grew up there, and had never seen darkness. How natural for him to imagine, as he stood with his back to the central luminary, that he was not dependent upon it for a knowledge of the characters before him.

So with the Deist. The world has never been without revelation of some sort. The lamp from heaven has been shining upon our dark world for ages. We have had no opportunity to ascertain what we could or could not have done, in the absence of its beams. And yet the Deist says, "Man shall live forever. We learn it from nature, independently of all aid from the Bible." Lord Herbert, the apostle of English Deism, who affirmed the sufficiency of reason and natural religion, and rejected the Bible as unnecessary and superfluous, inserted as one of the five principles of his natural creed the doctrine of a future state of rewards and punishments.

The celebrated Thomas Paine was orthodox so far as the *fact* of another state of existence is concerned. Hence he wrote, "I believe in one God, and no more, and hope for happiness beyond this life."* This class of Deists read the hieroglyphics aright, but ignored the light without which they could never have read the first character.

An aged and otherwise intelligent Deist once affirmed in the hearing of the writer, that he was in no degree indebted to the Bible for a knowledge of God, or of his attributes; that he had demonstrated

* This passage taken from his "Age of Reason," is inscribed upon his monument at New Rochelle, N. Y.

all originally for himself, without aid or suggestion from revelation. When asked how old he was when he made the discovery, he fixed the period at twelve years; but when asked where he had lived for twelve years without ever hearing of a God, he was confounded. Neither could he tell how it was that he, a boy of twelve summers, could infer the being of one God, infinite, just, and unchangeable, from his works, while the sages of antiquity, with all their vast mental resources and discipline, multiplied their divinities by thousands, and invested them with every hateful attribute and passion of the human heart.

This, then, is the first error, we should rather say *abuse* of the rational evidences of another life—viz. to magnify them unduly, and install them in place of that only "sure word of prophecy," the sacred Scriptures.*

But it may be asked, if immortality may be inferred from reason and nature, why is not the belief universal? Why were the sages of Greece and Rome in doubt, even with the light of a traditional revelation to aid their perceptions? "I hope," said Socrates, "I am now going to good men, though this I would not take upon me positively to affirm."† "Which of these is true," said Cicero, (referring to the two theories of life or no life after death) God only knows; and which is most probable a very great

* "The evidences of human reason in favor of the immortality of the soul have their use; but they are not adapted to the comprehension of all. Neither can they, considered separate from Divine revelation, impart a sure hope and confidence."—*Helffenstein's Theology*, p. 371.

† Helffenstein's Theology, p. 15.

question." "When I read I assent; but when I have laid down the book, all that assent vanishes." All this led Seneca to say, that "Immortality, however desirable, was rather promised than proved by those great men."

IV. A *second* error, in our opinion, and one into which not a few writers upon the subject have fallen, is to ignore or undervalue the testimony of reason and nature to the great and glorious doctrine of Immortality.* Because the Deist has made too much of them ought we to fly to the opposite extreme, and make too little of them? Will it disparage revealed religion for us to listen to the voice of nature, whose echoes have been first awakened by the voice of God from heaven? Shall we refuse to read or apply the inscription upon the wall, lest we disparage the lamp by which we read it? The Bible is the source of all true knowledge of God and of a future life. Without it there would be no startling traditions, no "Natural Theology."

But while we thus magnify the "lively oracles," we are not confined to them. The Deist may reject Revelation, but the Christian need not, therefore, reject Nature. We are as welcome to all her "testimonies," as is the most ardent disciple of "Natural Religion;" and we study them with a Divine interpretation; and amid a celestial radiance against which he has closed his eyes for ever.

V. The Rational Evidences of Immortality, to which attention is called in the following chapters, is not then regarded as *primary* and *independent*, but rather as evidences made available by Divine Revela-

* Even some Christian writers have fallen into this error.

tion. It is consequently only *collateral* to our chief source of knowledge, the Holy Scriptures; and instead of being a sufficient guide of itself, should only be regarded as *corroborative* of that Book which brings life and immortality to light, and alone is able to make wise unto salvation. Thus the Bible shines on, peerless in the moral heavens, while the Christian believer exults in its undimmed brightness, and rejoices amid scenes of beauty and grandeur illumined by its effulgence. But as the moon is made conspicuous and beautiful by the light of the sun, so all nature shines in the light of the Bible, and thus helps to light up the moral universe, by reflecting back upon the human heart and understanding its celestial beams. Such we conceive to be the nature of the argument drawn from reason and nature, and its true relation to the clearer light of Divine Revelation.

CHAPTER II.

INDICATIONS OF ANOTHER LIFE IN THE STRUCTURE AND PHENOMENA OF THE NATURAL WORLD.

Read Nature; Nature is the friend of truth;
Nature is Christian; preaches to mankind,
And bids dead matter aid us in our creed.

I. A SQUADRON of ships are about to proceed to sea, or to engage in battle. Upon almost every ship may be seen a man waving a small red and white flag in various directions. It may be *noticed* by a landsman, but of its *utility* and *design* he is utterly ignorant. Much less can he understand the import or *meaning* of these signal flags and their singular movements. But tell him that these men with flags belong to the signal-corps of the fleet; and place in his hands the manual which explains the import of every flag and motion; and these otherwise unmeaning signals become as intelligible as the plainest language; and are invested with equal power to inspire courage, enkindle hope or fill with terror.

So in regard to many of the facts and phenomena of material existence. In the absence of the Bible, which brings life and immortality to light, they may seem altogether unintelligible and unmeaning; when in the light of that all-perfect manual of creation, every important natural phenomenon has its significance, and the whole material universe responds to the glorious announcement that man shall live forever.

II. Suppose man placed upon our planet with the constitution and phenomena of nature as they now are. Suppose him subject to death as at present, but with no intimation from any source that his brief and sad life would ever be renewed or prolonged after death. He steps upon our planet amid the glory of a bright spring-day, with no instructer and no experience. He has never seen *night* or *darkness*, and knows nothing of them. The sun is on the meridian, and for ought that he knows to the contrary, will remain there forever. In a short time, however, he notices that the shadows of objects are traveling around to the eastward. But this scarcely awakens a thought, much less excites alarm.

A few hours elapse and the sun is fast sinking towards the western horizon; the light and heat are sensibly diminished; and a slight foreboding seizes the mind of the stranger. Downward still sinks the orb of day, till at length his western limb reaches the horizon and he begins to disappear. The light fades from hill and vale and sea and sky, till all nature is wrapped in the pall of darkness.

But as the sun goes down, and darkness takes the place of his beams, that very darkness becomes the revealer of a scene of glory in the heavens above, of which the stranger had before no conception, and which with perpetual daylight had never greeted mortal vision, or filled the human mind with wonder and amazement. True, the beholder is surrounded with darkness and gloom, but it seems only ordained because needful, to extend his range of vision, and introduce him early to a knowledge of other and brighter, though more distant worlds. Here, then, is the first lesson of the first half day of his earthly being. Darkness is needful to reveal the unnumbered and far-off glories of the celestial concave, and write it on the physical universe that the fading of an earthly glory is but the precursor of a celestial effulgence that shall not grow dim with passing ages, but is enduring as the pillars of heaven.

Mysterious Night! when our first parent knew
  Thee, from report divine, and heard thy name,
  Did he not tremble for this lovely frame,
This glorious canopy of light and blue?
Yet, 'neath a curtain of translucent dew,
  Bathed in the rays of the great setting flame,
  Hesperus with the host of heaven came;
And lo! creation widen'd in men's view.

Who could have thought such darkness lay conceal'd
  Within thy beams, O Sun! or who could find,
Whilst fly, and leaf, and insect stood revealed,
  That to such countless orbs thou mad'st us blind?
Why do we then shun death with anxious strife?
If light can thus deceive us, may not life?

The night rolls on, and man, the stranger just placed amid these scenes, is left to his own reflections and forebodings. He has no tutor to explain to him the nature of the change that has taken place since he stood a few hours before amid the glories of noontide; and no experience to intimate to him that the surrounding darkness shall ever again give place to the light of day. He has never seen a sun-rising, or heard of one. To him the going down of the sun was the death of nature, and he has no hope or ground of hope that he will ever rise again. All is darkness, sorrow and despair.

But lo! as he bemoans the sad phenomenon that has draped the world in mourning, a dim light is seen in the eastern sky. More and more brightly it shoots up from the horizon; the gaze of the stranger is fixed; his heart throbs with emotions of hope and fear; till at length he beholds the hills and valleys disrobed of their dark vestments; and clasps his hands in rapture as he sees an orb of fire emerge from the horizon, and commence its journey up the eastern sky. Moreover, he marks how fresh and beautiful the landscape appears; how fragrant the flowers; how sweet the songs sent up from every grove, as if to welcome the coming day.

Now here is the second lesson of his first natural day upon the earth—a kind of *death, burial and resurrection*—a lesson that may quell his fears amid all coming changes; that may apply to himself as well as to other objects; and should at least assure him that the disappearance of a bright object from view, and the reign of darkness and uncertainty, affords no proof or presumption, even, that the retiring object is lost, or will not still pursue its path of glory to unnumbered ages. Observation and experience have taught him that

—— The star that sets
Beyond the western wave is not extinct.
It brightens in another hemisphere,
And gilds another evening with its rays.

We do not affirm that Adam and Eve so interpreted these natural phenomena. Our theory is that they could not so understand them as "foregleams of immortality" without first having communicated to them the knowledge of another life. But whether understood or not, the phenomena remain the same; and as if ordained to throw light upon the subject of man's descent to the tomb, warn us not to infer extinction from retirement, obscurity and darkness; but rather to look upward for the stars of immortality when life's sun goes down; and to look, though the night of death may come, for a bright and a glorious morning.

III. Suppose further that when man was first placed upon the earth the moon was at her full—a mild and lovely object passing nightly through the heavens. As the sun goes down in the west, she arises in serene majesty in the east. But the next evening she is later in her appearing, and when at length visible is sensibly diminished in her magnitude. From night to night she lingers more and more behind the hour of her first appearing, and contracts more and more in her magnitude till finally she is lost amid the effulgence of the sun, and disappears entirely from view. For ought the beholder knows to the contrary she has gone to her fiery sepulchre, and will shine upon man and his abode no more forever.

But wait a fortnight and that now dishonored, faded, buried celestial object will have re-asserted all her former splendor, and may be seen rising in the east, as at the first, the glorious queen of night. Though she seemed to be dead and lost, she emerges from her obscurity to shine again with undimmed effulgence in the open void of heaven. Such are the lessons of the first month—a celestial orb fading and retiring from view, but anon restored again to its original life and grandeur.

IV. But our pupil arrived and took his place here amid all the sweetness and beauty of Spring. Bright flowers of every form and hue greeted his vision and filled the air with their fragrance. The forests and hills were clothed with their vestments of green, and not an object of sorrow or decay greeted his vision throughout all the realm of vegetable life. And so far as he knows to the contrary this state of things is as unchangeable as the throne of the Creator.

A few months pass and the flowers have faded; the forests are stripped of their foliage; the streams are bound in icy chains; the hills and valleys are covered with snow; and death reigns over the whole realm of nature. With no experience and no one to tell him that this is but a pause in life, to be succeeded by new vigor and beauty, what would be the natural feelings of such a stranger? How certainly would he mourn the loss of those days of song, and bloom, and brightness, now gone to return no more. He has never seen a spring open on the land, or heard of the change from winter to spring; and is therefore left a prey to all the fears and forebodings with which the death of every leaf and flower and blade of grass would necessarily fill his mind and his imagination.

But the winter rolls on—the brighter suns and warmer breezes of spring melt the snows from plain and mountain; the buds swell and expand into foliage; the tender grass shoots up from the pastures; and again all nature is clad in robes of beauty, and her seeming death and burial give place to the most joyful life and animation. This is the lesson of a year—nature fading, dying, buried, and nature reviving, rising, restored to her wonted animation and beauty.

V. A few weeks of observation will reveal another not altogether insignificant fact, viz., that in a certain sense life is to a large extent evolved from death throughout the whole realm of nature. Living animals are sustained in life by food, composed of dead animals and vegetables; and living vegetation in turn is fed and nourished by decayed vegetable and animal substances. Though death does not *originate* life, it *sustains* it, and life seems to spring more vigorously from the very triumphs of death.

Remote as this fact may seem from the subject under discussion, it shows at least the intimate relation between death and life in their lower types, and may therefore be cited as a natural intimation that the death of man here is made tributary, in the wise economy of the Creator, to a higher and more enduring life hereafter.

VI. A fiery meteor is seen throwing his long train over half the heavens. It is in view when the stranger first looks up at the celestial concave. But in a short time it begins to retire from view, and at length entirely disappears. Man lives on, like Methuselah, one hundred, two hundred, four hundred years, but sees nothing more of the strange light in the sky. At length, perhaps after centuries,

Lo! from the dread immensity of space,
Returning with accelerated force,
The flaming comet to the sun descends.

Though long given up for lost, and perhaps forgotten, he too stands forth again among the living, a bright celestial emblem of immortality.

Such are a few of the intimations of a future state drawn from the structure and phenomena of the natural world—witnesses naturally mute to us because we fail to understand their language, but yet intelligible and important when consulted in the light of the glorious revealed truth that the spirit of man never dies. Then each star that glows in the heavens when the sun sinks below the western hills; each opening day when the gloom of night is past; each waxing moon emerging from her obscuration; each opening spring bursting every wintry chain and tomb, and filling all nature with beauty and fragrance; each long-lost comet returning again to our heavens after an absence of ages; and each material atom that defies annihilation—all these illustrate and corroborate the glorious truth that man shall live on immortal, despite the shadows of death, and the hiding of his mortal light for a time amid the dark recesses of the grave. We know they are but the alphabet of what we need to know of death and the world to come; but they afford instruction clear and cogent to this one point, that we *be not deceived by appearances* to regard any thing as lost or extinct that becomes robed in darkness, or is hidden for a time from the eyes of mortals. The very mechanism of nature seems to have been arranged so as to teach and reiterate this great lesson. And what pupil has she but man? To whom shall the lesson apply if not to him; and to what portion of his allotment on earth if not to the solemn period when the light of his mortal life shall fade, and his sun go down to rise no more on earth or time?

Let, then, each glowing star, and rising sun, and full-orbed moon, and opening spring, and fiery comet, yea every material object that God has made echo and re-echo the glorious truth, that though life's brief day will soon close, and the darkness of the tomb cover us, there is a bright and glorious day beyond earth's deepest shadows; and the life we now live is but the vestibule of Immortality.

CHAPTER III.

ARGUMENT DRAWN FROM THE GENERAL BELIEF OF MANKIND.

THE extent to which the doctrine of the immortality of the soul has prevailed among men, in all ages of the world, has generally been regarded as furnishing a strong presumptive proof of the truth of that doctrine. "When we discourse of the eternity of souls," says Seneca, "the general consent of all men either fearing or worshipping the hellish powers, is of very great moment." "In every thing," says Cicero, "the consent of all nations is to be accounted the law of nature, and to resist it, is to resist the voice of God."

Though few Christian writers would fully endorse these views, especially those of the latter, the consent of all nations to the doctrine certainly deserves to be noticed among the rational evidences of a future state. Let us then consider the chief points in the argument.

I. That the idea is almost co-extensive with the race of mankind, will scarcely be doubted. No matter what other opinions may enter into the religion of any people, these three will be found associated in almost every system, viz., the existence of a

Supreme Being, the immortality of the soul, and future rewards and punishments. Whatever may have been the *origin* of these opinions, the *fact* is undeniable, that upon these points all nations are in the main agreed.

"That the thinking principle in man is of an immortal nature," says Dr. Dick, "was believed by the ancient Egyptians, the Persians, the Phenicians, the Scythians, the Celts, the Druids, the Assyrians—by the wisest and most celebrated characters among the Greeks and Romans, and by almost every other ancient nation and tribe whose records have reached our times. The notions, indeed, which many of them entertained of the scenes of futurity were very obscure and imperfect, but they all embraced the idea, that death is not the destruction of the rational soul, but only its introduction to a new and unknown state of existence."

"The ancient Scythians believed that death was only a change of habitation; and the Magian sect, which prevailed in Babylon, Media, Assyria, and Persia, admitted the doctrine of eternal rewards and punishments." *

II. "It is well known," says Dr. Dick, "that Plato, Socrates, and other Greek philosophers, held the doctrine of the soul's immortality." †

In his admirable dialogue, entitled "The Phædon," Plato represents Socrates, a little before his death, encompassed with a circle of philosophers, and dis-

* Philosophy of a Future State, Book 1.

† This is no doubt true in a general sense, though it must be admitted, as elsewhere shown, that they hold this doctrine with a measure of doubt and uncertainty.

coursing with them on the arguments which prove the eternal destiny of man. "When the dead," says he, "are arrived at the rendezvous of departed souls, whither their angel conducts them, they are all judged. Those who have passed their lives in a manner neither entirely criminal, nor absolutely innocent, are sent into a place where they suffer pains proportioned to their faults, till, being purged and cleansed of their guilt, and afterwards restored to liberty, they receive the reward of the good actions done in the body. Those who are judged to be incurable, on account of the greatness of their crimes, the fatal destiny that passes judgment upon them, hurls them into Tartarus, from whence they never depart.

"Those who are found guilty of crimes, great indeed, but worthy of pardon, who have committed violences, in the transports of rage against their father or mother, or have killed some one in a like emotion, and afterwards repented—suffer the same punishment with the lost, but for a time only, till, by prayers and supplications, they have obtained pardon from those they have injured. But those who have passed through life with peculiar sanctity of manners, are received on high, into a purer region, where they live without their bodies to all eternity, in a series of joys and delights which cannot be described."

III. From such considerations Socrates concludes:

"If the soul be immortal, it requires to be cultivated with attention, not only for what we call the time of life, but for that which is to follow, I mean eternity; and the least neglect in this point may be attended with endless consequences. If death were the final extinction of being, the wicked would be great gainers by it, by being delivered at once from their bodies, their souls, and their vices; but as the soul is immortal, it has no other means of being freed from its evils, nor any safety for it, but in becoming very good and very wise; for it carries nothing with it, but its good or bad deeds, its virtues and vices, which are commonly the consequences of the education it has received, and the causes of eternal happiness or misery."

The following additional extract from the same dialogue, is perhaps still more pertinent.

Socrates. "Answer me; what is that which, when in the body makes it alive?"

Kebes. "The soul."

S. "Will it always be so?"

K. "How can it be otherwise?"

S. "Will the soul, then, always bring life to whatever it occupies?"

K. "Certainly."

S. "Is there anything contrary to life, or nothing?"

K. "There is."

S. "What?"

K. "Death."

S. "Will the soul receive the contrary to what it introduces?"

K. "By no means."

S. "But what do we call that which does not receive death?"

K. "Immortal."

S. "The soul will not receive death, you say?"

K. "No."

S. "Is the soul, then, immortal?"

K. "It is immortal."

S. "When, therefore, death comes upon man, what is mortal in him perishes, as it is seen to do; but what is immortal withdraws itself from death, safe and uncorrupted?"

K. "This is clear."

S. "We may, then, be sure that, more than all things, O Kebes! the soul is immortal and incorruptible, and that our souls will still be in existence in Hades." *

"Having held such discourse with his friends, he kept silence for some time, and then drank off the whole of the poisonous draught, which had been put into his hand, with amazing tranquility, and an inexpressible serenity of aspect, as one who was about to exchange a short and wretched life, for a blessed and eternal existence."

When Cato found it in vain to attempt to animate his soldiers against Cæsar, he resolved to die by his own hand. After supping cheerfully as usual, he retired to his bed-chamber and read over this dialogue of Plato upon the soul's immortality two or three times, and then committed the crime of self-destruction by which he has blackened his character for all coming time. But the reading of the dialogue under such circumstances shows if not a belief in, at least a desire to be assured of an immortal existence after death.

In Cicero *De Senectute* he puts the following language into the mouth of Cato:

"Oh happy day when I shall quit this impure and corrupt multitude and join myself to that divine com-

* Turner's Sacred History, Vol. I. p. 102.

pany and council of souls who have quitted the earth before me. There I shall find not only those illustrious personages to whom I have spoken, but also my Cato, who I can say was one of the best men ever born and whom none ever excelled in virtue and piety. I have placed his body on this funeral pile whereon he ought to have laid mine. But his soul has not left me, and without losing sight of me he has only gone before, into a country where he saw I should rejoin him. This, my lot, I seem to bear courageously; not indeed that I do bear it with resignation; but I shall comfort myself with the persuasion that the interval between his departure and mine will not be long."*

IV. Plato tells us of an ancient law concerning men which was always and is still in force among the gods, that those who lived just and holy lives should after their death go into the isles of the blessed, where they should enjoy all manner of happiness without the least intermixture of misery; but that those who lived here unjustly and ungodly should be sent into that prison of just punishment which is called Hell."†

The apostrophe of the Roman Emperor, Adrian, to his soul, is also equally in point:—

"Poor, little, pretty, fluttering thing,
Must we no longer live together?
And dost thou prune thy trembling wing,
To take thy flight, thou know'st not whither?

"Thy pleasing vein, thy humorous folly,
Lies all neglected, all forgot!
And pensive, wavering melancholy,
Thou hop'st and fear'st thou know'st not what."

* Dr. Adam Clarke on 2 Samuel xiii. 33.
† Plat. Geor. p. 311.

The descriptions and allusions, contained in the writings of the ancient poets, are a convincing proof that the notion of the soul's immortality was a universal opinion in the times in which they wrote, and among the nations to whom their writings were addressed.

Homer, the oldest and greatest of the Greek poets, who lived and wrote about the time of Solomon—say a thousand years before Christ—embodies the doctrine of the soul's immortality both in the *Iliad* and the *Odyssey*. Indeed it is the first doctrine that arrests attention at the very commencement of the Iliad.

> Achilles' wrath, to Greece the direful spring,
> Of woes unnumbered, heavenly goddess sing;
> That wrath which hurled to Pluto's gloomy reign
> The *souls* of mighty chiefs untimely slain;
> Whose *limbs* unburied on the naked shore,
> Devouring dogs and hungry vultures tore.*

Nothing could be plainer than that this extract teaches the true nature of death—that it is a separation of the soul from the body—and that the soul is immaterial and immortal.

His account of the descent of Ulysses into hell, and his description of Minos in the shades below, distributing justice to the dead assembled in troops around his tribunal, and pronouncing irrevocable judgment, which decides their everlasting fate, demonstrate that they entertained the belief that virtues are rewarded and that crimes are punished in another state of existence.

"The poems of *Ovid* and *Virgil* contain a variety of descriptions, in which the same opinions are in-

* Pope's translation of the Iliad, Book 1, v. 1–6.

volved. Their notions of future punishment are set forth in the descriptions they give of *Ixion*, who was fastened to a wheel, and whirled about continually with a swift and rapid motion—of *Tantalus*, who for the loathsome banquet he made for the gods, was set in water up to the chin, with apples hanging to his very lips, yet had no power either to stoop to quench his raging thirst, or to reach to the other to satisfy his craving appetite—of the *Fifty Daughters of Danaus*, who for the barbarous massacre of their husbands in one night, were condemned in hell to fill a barrel full of holes with water, which ran out as fast as it was filled—of *Sisyphus*, who, for his robberies, was set to roll a great stone up a steep hill, which, when it was just at the top, suddenly fell down again, and so renewed his labor—and of *Tityus*, who was adjudged to have a vulture to feed upon his liver and entrails, which still grew and increased as they were devoured."

"Their notions of future happiness are embodied in the descriptions they have given of the Hesperian gardens, and the Elysian fields, where the souls of the virtuous rest secure from every danger, and enjoy perpetual and uninterrupted bliss."

Pindar, the prince of lyric poets, wrote about four hundred years before Christ. The following translation of his Second Ode, will illustrate the theology of the Greeks touching a future state, at the time it was written.

TRANSLATION OF PINDAR'S SECOND ODE.

The islands of the blest they say,
  The islands of the blest
Are peaceful and happy by night and day
  Far away in the glorious west.

They need not the moon in that land of delight,
  They need not the pale, pale star;
The sun he is bright by day and night,
  Where the souls of the blessed are.

They till not the ground, they plough not the wave,
  They labor not—never! oh, never!
Not a tear do they shed, not a sigh do they heave,
  They are happy forever and ever.

Soft is the breeze, like the evening one,
  When the sun hath gone to his rest;
And the sky is pure, and the clouds there are none,
  In the islands of the blest.

The deep, clear sea, in its mazy bed,
  Doth garlands of gems unfold;
Not a tree but it blazes with crowns for the dead,
  Even flowers of living gold.*

Such were the views held by the ancients in regard to a future life, and the conscious happiness or misery of souls in the world to come.

That the original idea of another life after death was matter of direct revelation from God, communicated to Adam and Eve, and confirmed to others after them, is no doubt true; but the idea being in the world, however obscured or distorted in its traditional progress from age to age, men were enabled to reason upon its probable truth or otherwise, and compare the supposition with the facts and phenomena of the mind and of the natural world around them. Hence the general impression among the ancients that the soul survives the dissolution of the body. "Right reason," said Osterwald, more than a century ago, "informs us that the soul is of a substance entirely different from the body, and not liable to corruption;

* Cambridge University Magazine

hence the very Heathen believe in the immortality of the soul."*

VI. And as the nations of antiquity recognized the doctrine of a future state of existence, so there is scarcely a nation or tribe of mankind, presently existing, however barbarous and untutored, in which the same opinion does not prevail.

"The natives of the *Society Isles* believe that after death there is not only a state of conscious existence, but degrees of eminence and felicity, according as men have been more or less pleasing to the *Eatova*, or Deity, while upon earth."

"The chiefs of the *Friendly Islands* believe in the immortality of their souls, which at death, they say, is immediately conveyed in a fast-sailing canoe, to a distant country called *Doobludha*, which they describe as resembling the Mahometan paradise,—that those who are conveyed thither are no more subject to death, but feast on all the favourite productions of their native soil, with which this blissful abode is plentifully furnished."

"The *New Zealanders* believe, that the third day after the interment of a man, the heart separates itself from the corpse, and that this separation is announced by a general breeze of wind, which gives warning of its approach, by an inferior divinity that hovers over the grave, and who carries it to the clouds. They believe that the soul of the man whose flesh is devoured by the enemy, is doomed to a perpetual fire, while the soul of the man whose body has been res-

* John Frederick Osterwald was a celebrated divine of Switzerland, who died in 1741. See Compendium of Christian Theology, translated from the Latin by Rev. John McMains, 1788.

cued from those that killed him, and the souls of all who die a natural death, ascend to the habitations of the gods."

"The inhabitants of the *Pelew Islands*, according to the account of Captain Wilson, although they have few religious rites and ceremonies, believe in one Supreme Being, and in a future state of rewards and punishments."

"In the religion of the *Kalmuc Tartars*, the doctrine of a future state holds a conspicuous place. They believe that hell is situated in the middle region, between heaven and earth, and their devils are represented with all sorts of frightful forms of a black and hideous aspect, with the heads of goats, lions, and unicorns. Their holy Lamas, who have obtained a victory over all their passions, are supposed to pass immediately into heaven, where they enjoy perfect rest, and exercise in divine service."

"The *Samoiedians* of northern Tartary believe, that there is one Supreme Being, that he is our all-merciful and common Parent, and that he will reward with a happy state hereafter, those who live virtuously in this world."

"The *Birmans* believe in the transmigration of souls, after which they maintain, that the radically bad will be sentenced to lasting punishment, while the good will enjoy eternal happiness on a mountain called *Meru*."

"The various tribes which inhabit the continent of Africa, in so far as we are acquainted with their religious opinions, appear to recognize the doctrine of a future state. * * * The inhabitants of the interior, according to the account of Mr. Park, believe in one Supreme Ruler, and expect hereafter to enter into a state of misery or felicity. The *Gallas* of Abyssinia, though they reject the doctrine of future punishment, admit the reality of a future state. The Mandingoes, the Jaloffs, the Feloops, the Foulahs, the Moors, and all other tribes who have embraced the Mahometan faith, recognize the doctrine of the immortality of the soul, and of future rewards in a celestial paradise."

"The natives of *Dahomey* entertain the same belief; and hence, it is a common practice with the sovereign of that country, to send an account to his forefathers of any remarkable event, by delivering a message to whoever may happen to be near him at the time, and then ordering his head to be chopped off immediately, that he may serve as a courier, to convey intelligence to the world of spirits."*

"The *Persians* are said to leave one part of their graves open, from a belief that the dead will be re-animated, and visited by angels, who will appoint them to their appropriate abode in a future state. From a similar belief, thousands of Hindoo widows annually sacrifice themselves on the funeral piles of their deceased husbands, in the hope of enjoying with them the felicities of eternal life."†

"The *Japanese* believe that the souls of men and beasts are alike immortal; that a just distribution of rewards and punishments takes place after death; that there are different degrees of happiness as well

* M'Leod's Voyage to Africa, 1820, p. 64.

† This was no doubt true in 1827, when Dr. Dick wrote, but the suttee has since been abolished over all that country. But this in no wise affects the argument.

as of punishment, and that the souls of the wicked transmigrate, after death, into the bodies of animals, and at last, in case of amendment, are translated back again into the human form."*

"From a conviction of the reality of a future world, the *Wahabbe Arabs* regard it as impious to mourn for the dead, who, they say, are enjoying felicity with Mahomet in paradise; and the *Javanese* make several feasts, on the decease of their friends and relations, to commemorate their entrance into a world of bliss."

"The ancient *Scandinavians* taught that the brave were to revel forever in the halls of Valhalla, and drink mead offered them by maidens, from the skulls of their enemies. Some of the Pagan Arabs said, that of the blood near the brain a bird was formed, which once in a century visited the sepulchre; and others believed in a resurrection.

"The *Patagonians* in mentioning the dead, call them those who are with God, and out of the world. The *Tongo* people suppose the souls of their dead chiefs to be in a delightful island of shadows. The *Yucatanese* represent the abode of the good as a pleasant land of plenty, under the shade of a mighty tree.

The first natives of this continent seen by the Spaniards, taught that the souls of good men went to a pleasant valley, where all kinds of fruit were abundant; and that the dead walked abroad in the night, and feasted with the living. Charlevoix says, that the Indians paid a great regard to dreams, as embracing an intercourse with spirits. They imagined

* Thunberg's Travels.

a paradise in the West, a land where nature glowed with an eternal sunset.

"The ancient *Mexicans* supposed three places for the departed: the house of sun, for such as fell in battle, or died captives, and women who perished in childhood; the place of the god of water for the drowned, for children, and for those who died of dropsy, tumors, and similar diseases, or of accidental wounds; and the place of darkness, in the centre of the earth."

To these very ample testimonies we may add that of our own native Indians, who uniformly believe in an immortal existence after death, in the celestial hunting grounds—the beautiful islands—where deer, and buffalo without number graze on the hills and through the valleys—where the good are always successful in the chase, and the wicked ever pursue in vain. To this "better country" they believe the Great Spirit will conduct them at the close of life. Hence their bow and arrows are often deposited with their bodies, that they may have them to use in the spirit world.

"The *Chickasaws* believed that the souls of red men walked up and down near the place where they died, or were laid; and said that they had often heard cries and noises where prisoners had been burned. The Indians of Cumana supposed echo to be the voice of the departed.

Lo the poor Indian whose untutored mind,
Sees God in clouds, or hears him in the wind,
Whose soul proud science never taught to stray,
Beyond the solar walk or milky way—
Yet simple nature to his hope has given,
Beyond the cloud-topped hill, an humble heaven;

Some safer world in depth of woods embraced,
Some happier island in the watery waste,
Where slaves once more their native land behold,
No fiends torment, no Christians thirst for gold,—
And thinks, admitted to yon equal sky,
His faithful dog shall bear him company.

"Thus it appears, that not only the philosophers of antiquity, and the most civilized nations presently existing on the globe, have recognized the doctrine of the immortality of man, but that even the most savage and untutored tribes fortify their minds in the prospect of death, with the hope of a happiness commensurate with their desires, in the regions beyond the grave. Among the numerous and diversified tribes that are scattered over the different regions of the earth, that agree in scarcely any other sentiment or article of religious belief, we here find the most perfect harmony in their recognition of a Supreme Intelligence, and in their belief that the soul survives the dissolution of its mortal frame. And, as Cicero long since observed, 'In everything the consent of all nations is to be accounted the law of nature, and to resist it, is to resist the voice of God.' For we can scarcely suppose, in consistency with the divine perfections, that an error, on a subject of so vast importance to mankind, should obtain the universal belief of all nations and ages, and that God himself would suffer a world of rational beings, throughout every generation, to be carried away by a delusion, and to be tantalized by a hope which has no foundation in nature, and which is contrary to the plan of his moral government."

VII. "To whatever cause this universal belief of a future existence is to be traced—whether to a universal tradition derived from the first parents of the human race; to an innate sentiment originally impressed on the soul of man; to a Divine revelation disseminated and handed down from one generation to another, or to the deductions of human reason—it forms a strong presumption, and a powerful argument, in favor of the position we are now endeavoring to support. If it is to be traced back to the original progenitors of mankind, it must be regarded as one of those truths which were recognized by man in a state of innocence, when his affections were pure, and his understanding fortified against delusion and error. If it be a sentiment which was originally impressed on the human soul by the hand of its Creator, we do violence to the law of our nature, when we disregard its intimations, or attempt to resist the force of its evidence. If it ought to be considered as originally derived from Revelation, then it is corroborative of the truth of the Sacred Records, in which 'life and immortality' are clearly exhibited. And, if it be regarded as likewise one of the deductions of natural reason, we are left without excuse, if we attempt to obscure its evidence, or to overlook the important consequences which it involves.

"As the consent of all nations has been generally considered as a powerful argument for the existence of a Deity, so the universal belief of mankind in the doctrine of a future state ought to be viewed as a strong presumption, that it is founded upon truth. The human mind is so constituted, that when left to its native unbiassed energies, it necessarily infers the existence of a Supreme Intelligence, from the existence of matter, and the economy of the material world; and, from the nature of the human faculties, and the moral attributes of God, it is almost as infallibly led to conclude, that a future existence is necessary, in order to gratify the boundless desires of the human soul, and to indicate the wisdom and rectitude of the moral Governor of the world.

"These two grand truths, which constitute the foundation of all religion, and of everything that is interesting to man as an intelligent agent, are interwoven with the theological creed of all nations; and in almost every instance, where the one is called in question, the other is undermined or denied: so that the doctrine of the immortality of man may be considered as resting on the same foundation as the existence of a Supreme Intelligence." *

We have quoted thus largely from Dr. Dick in the present chapter, not that the argument is original with him, or because the main statement with which this chapter commences, needed to be thus fortified in order to be credited by the well-informed and candid reader; but rather because of the amount of testimony condensed into a small compass, and as a tribute to the memory of one who while on earth treated with a master's hand the glorious theme of immortal existence after death.

* Philosophy of a Future State, Part I. Chap. I.

CHAPTER IV.

THE RELATION OF MAN TO THE LOWER ANIMALS.

Stupendous link in Nature's endless chain
Midway from nothing to the Deity.

THE relation of the different species of animals to each other, and of man to the whole, affords a strong presumption that though allied to them by his animal nature, he has also a higher and spiritual nature, by which he is also allied to superior beings in the great chain of intellectual existence.

I. If we look abroad over the vast field of animal creation, we shall find that no species stands alone, or isolated from its fellows of other species; but that all are related by resemblances more or less striking, and linked together in one grand chain, from the lowest forms of unorganized matter, up to the most perfect of all organization, the human body.

The *oyster*, with only the senses of taste and feeling at most, seems to link the animal world to the mineral. The *polypi*—half vegetable and half animal —link together these two kingdoms. The *bat* unites the birds and the quadrupeds; and the flying-fish the birds and the fish.

"The bat, the flying-squirrel, the flying-opossum, are instances of animals of the class mammalia, approximating to that of birds in the possession of wings, or organs resembling them, whilst the ornithorhynchus resembles them in the structure of its mouth, and its mode of producing its young by eggs.

On the other hand, the ostrich, the cassowary, and the dodo, which have wings so short as to be incapable of flying, and therefore always run or walk, are instances of birds approaching, in some degree, to the character of quadrupeds. So, too, the cetaceous tribe affords an example of the transition from mammalia to fishes; the flying-fish, of the transition from birds to fishes; the dragons of that from birds to reptiles." *

Thus through all the realm of nature, each inferior tribe is linked to the next above; and the link by which they are united shares the natures of both the superior and the inferior races. Indeed, nature is one grand chain, from the crudest forms of unorganized matter, through the whole vegetable and animal kingdoms, up to man at the head of all.

> "Of systems possible, if it's confessed
> That wisdom infinite must form the best,
> Where all must fall or not coherent be,
> And all that rises, rise in due degree;
> Then, in the scale of *reasoning life*, 'tis plain,
> There must be somewhere such a rank as man;
> And all the questions (wrangle e'er so long)
> Is only this, if God has placed him wrong."

"In the chain of animals," says Smellie, "man is unquestionably the chief or capital link. As a highly rational animal, improved with science and arts, he

* Smellie's Philosophy of Natural History, Boston Ed. p. 309.

is, in some measure, related to beings of superior order, wherever they exist."*

"Man," says President Hopkins, "has been called the microcosm, or little world, because, while he has a distinctive nature of his own, he is a partaker and representative of every thing in the inferior creation. In him are united the material and the spiritual, the animal and the rational. He has instincts, propensities, desires, passions, by which he is allied to the animals; he has also reason, conscience, free-will, by which he is allied to higher intelligences and to God."†

II. Now the manner in which the various kingdoms of nature—the animal, vegetable, and mineral—and also the different species in each kingdom are linked together requires, if the analogy is to hold good throughout creation, that man, who stands at the head of this lower world, should connect with the next link above in the chain of being, which would require a nature distinctly spiritual, and quite above that of the beast that perishes.

Look nature through, 'tis neat gradation all,
By what minute degrees her scale ascends!
Each middle nature joined at each extreme;
To that above it joined, to that beneath,
Parts into parts reciprocally shot,
Abhor divorce. What love of union reigns!
Here dormant matter waits a call to life;
Half-life, half-death, join there; here life and sense,
There sense from reason steals a glimmering ray;
Reason shines out in man. But how preserved
The chain unbroken upward to the realms
Of incorporeal life? Those realms of bliss,

* Smellie's Philosophy of Natural History, p. 307.

† Lectures on the Evidences of Christianity, p. 167.

Where death hath no dominion? Grant a make
Half-mortal, half-immortal; earthly part
And part ethereal: grant the soul of man
Eternal, or in man the series ends.
Wide yawns the gap; connection is no more;
Checked reason halts; her next step wants support;
Striving to climb, she tumbles from her scheme,
A scheme analogy pronounced so true;
Analogy! man's surest guide below.

The relation of man to this lower world is not only precisely that assigned him in the Scriptures, but just the relation to suggest his connection with superior beings, and a more exalted state of existence. "Thou hast made him a little lower than the angels, and hast crowned him with glory and honor. Thou madest him to have dominion over the works of thy hands; thou hast put all *things* under his feet: all sheep and oxen, yea, and the beasts of the field; the fowl of the air, and the fish of the sea, *and whatsoever* passeth through the paths of the seas." Ps. viii. 5–8.

Standing, there, where the Scriptures place him, at the head of all that lives and moves; on the land or in the air and sea, and tracing the wonderful gradating from the crudest form of animal life, upward to himself, man may truthfully exclaim,

"The chain of being is complete in me,
In me is matter's last gradation lost,
And the next step is spirit—Deity!
I can command the lightning, and am dust!
A monarch and a slave! a worm, a god!"

And being thus at the head of this lower world, and only "a little lower than the angels," he occupies the *place*, to say the least, of the connecting link between the terrestrial and the celestial. And when to this fact we add the obvious fact of his superior intellectuality, the conviction is strengthened that in his higher nature he is a SPIRIT, and thus allied to those invisible beings called angels, who throng the shores of immortality.

CHAPTER V.

THE IMMORTALITY OF THE SOUL INFERRED FROM THE STRUCTURE OF THE BODY IN WHICH IT DWELLS.

I. "I AM fearfully and wonderfully made," said the Psalmist three thousand years ago; and modern physiology fully justifies the exclamation. Of all living organisms the human body is the most perfect. Taken as a whole it is the grand climax of all animal existence, the embodiment of the grand ideal of organic perfection, toward which all other animals, tribe by tribe, seem to have been advanced by the Creator by regular and successive approaches. As it was the last created, so it was superior to all others, and worthy to be the palace of that celestial nature, who, under God, should rule this lower world.

"It is a wonderful fact developed by geology, combined with comparative anatomy, that all the forms of animal existence find the perfected completion of their type in man. Their whole system through ages, converges individually and collectively, like a vast pyramid in him, as its apex. Termination in man is the tendency in which they all advance. Hence man is the being of which all the past animal system was a prophecy."*

* Methodist Quarterly Review for April 1859.

"The recognition of an ideal exemplar for the vertebrated animals," says Professor Owen: "proves, that the knowledge of such a being as man, must have existed before man appeared. * * * * The archetypal idea was manifested in the flesh under divers modifications upon this planet long prior to the existence of those animal specie that actually exemplify it."

"It is evident," says Professor Agassiz: "that there is a manifest progress in the succession of being on the surface of the earth * * especially in their increasing resemblance to man.

Hugh Miller tells us in his "Testimony of the Rocks" that "man is pre-eminently what a theologian would term the antetypal existence—the being in whom the types meet and are fulfilled,"—and Oken calls him "the sum of all the animals."

Such is the testimony of these students of physical nature given entirely out of view of its bearing upon the question of the immortality of the soul. The *fact*, therefore, upon which we insist, namely, that the human body is the most perfect of all animal organizations, will scarcely be disputed. For beauty of figure, grace of motion, utility, strength and convenience all combined it has no equal in all the realm of animal life. The human hand alone with its bones and joints and muscles and tendons and nerves and arteries and veins—its exquisite form and adaptation to the wants of man—has been the wonder and admiration of the anatomist in every age. And so of other portions of the human organism.

"We cannot, with propriety, say that one complete animal is nobler than another, because of any prominence of particular organs as compared with its whole body ; nor is one creature to be called monstrous or ugly, in comparison with another, for each is exactly fitted to its place in the grand scale of existence, and therefore, all are alike beautiful, as exhibiting the wonderful wisdom and beneficence of God. But creation is graduated, and every creature has its proper place. The totality of an animal's framework, its position on the scale of being. If we measure man according to this standard his superiority is at once evident."*

II. "The organization of man," says Lavater, "peculiarly distinguishes him from all other earthly beings ; and his physiognomy, that is to say, the superfices and outlines of his organization, show him to be infinitely superior to all those visible beings by which he is surrounded."†

Of all the numberless animal organisms with which the beneficent Creator has peopled the globe, and with all their wonderful variety and beauty and exquisite workmanship, and adaptation to their various abodes and habits of life, *the body of man alone is adapted to the occupancy and demands of an intelligent spirit.*

"As the habits of certain animals have been correctly inferred from the examination of detached portions of their structure, so from almost any part of man's body we may at once discover that it was constructed for the accommodation and delight of an intellectual being. In fact, the excellency of man (as an animal) consists in the delicate adaptation of his structure, for without this the reasoning principle would

* Power of the Soul over the Body by George Moore, M. D. p. 18.

† Essay on Physiology.

be out of place. He is the most delicate creature on the earth."*

Nor is this all. He is not only the most delicate creature on the earth in his physical organization, but, as already stated, the human body is the *only* animal organization in existence, through which the soul of man could exercise all its functions, and fully manifest and develope all its capabilities.

Suppose, for illustration, the soul of some tailor or watch-maker should be transferred from the body in which it dwells to that of a dog or swan; what could he do in such a body? Could he handle a needle or use a forcep in either of those bodies? The horse is among the most beautiful and noble of animals. Look at him as described by Job: "Hast thou given the horse strength? hast thou clothed his neck with thunder? Canst thou make him afraid as a grasshopper? the glory of his nostrils *is* terrible. He paweth in the valley, and rejoiceth in *his* strength: he goeth on to meet the armed men. He mocketh at fear, and is not affrighted; neither turneth he back from the sword. The quiver rattleth against him, the glittering spear and the shield. He swalloweth the ground with fierceness and rage: neither believeth he that *it is* the sound of the trumpet. He saith among the trumpets, Ha, ha! and he smelleth the battle afar off, the thunder of the captains, and the shouting."

But suppose the spirit of Milton had been lodged in such a physical organization, perfect as it seems to be, could he ever have produced Paradise Lost? Could he have held a pen with his uncloven hoof, or dictated his poem to an amanuensis through the throat

* Moore on the Soul and Body, p. 21.

of such an animal? Most certainly not. And the same would be true of every quadruped, and bird and fish throughout nature. And why? Simply because there is not another animal body on earth adapted to become the abode of a rational spirit. The bodies of the lower animals are all adapted to their uses—to cleave the air or shoot through the waters, and seize their prey, or otherwise supply their physical wants; but not a body among them all is adapted to the demands of an intellectual life. What animal but man could play a flute, or a piano, even if endowed with the musical talent of a Mozart?

"How nice a structure must be called into play when a skillful pianist, by the aid of an additional instrument fitted to his convenience, executes an intricate piece of music, not only in a wonderfully rapid succession of mechanical movements, but also in a manner fully to express the very feelings of the soul?

"But how much more forcibly is the same power manifested in the human voice! By it the spirit speaks, not only in infinite variety of articulated sounds, but more marvellously still by the modulated language of tones, so as to excite into ecstacy or agony every sympathy within us."

But we must not forget that as the soul requires a peculiar body through which to manifest its wondrous powers, so the exquisitely wrought body of man, would be utterly useless to a less intelligent spiritual being than the soul which occupies it. Like the lamp in the distant light-house, it is the spirit in man after all that illuminates the body, and gives to it its chief importance and utility. Without it there would be no music or poetry or sculpture or painting or scientific or mechanical creations, however capable the *body* might be of doing its part towards their production.

"What is it that so skillfully touches the musical instrument? What is it that enjoys as well as actuates, receives as well as communicates, through this inscrutable organization? It is, as we have said, the soul or spirit, without which this body were more unmeaning than a statue, and only fit, as it would tend, to decay. It is the soul which animates the features and causes them to present a living picture of each passion, so that the inmost agitations of the heart become visible in a moment, and the wish that would seek concealment betrays its presence and its power, in the vivid eye, while the blood kindles into crimson with a thought that burns along the brow. It is this which diffuses a sweet serenity and rest upon the visage, when our feelings are tranquilized, and our thoughts abide with heaven, like the ocean in a calm, reflecting the peaceful glories of the cloudless skies. This indwelling spirit of power blends our features into unison and harmony, and awakes "the music breathing from the face," when in association with those we love, and heart answering to heart, we live in sympathy, while memory and hope repose alike in smiles upon the bosom of enjoyment. It is a flame from heaven purer than Promethean fire, that vivifies and energizes the breathing form. It is an immaterial essence, a being, that quickens matter and imparts life, sensation, motion, to the intricate framework of our bodies; which wills when we act, attends when we perceive, looks into the past when we reflect, and not content with the present, shoots with all its aims and all its hopes into the futurity that is forever dawning upon it."

So pertinent to the general subject is this extract, that we could not well withhold it from the reader, even though a portion of it has but a slight bearing upon the particular point to which this chapter is devoted. To return, then, to the topic in hand:

"If the body of man had been constituted on any inferior model, art and science could have had no outward existence, and reason must have been imprisoned in brute form. Supposing human knowledge then possible, man could only have been manifest as a subtle beast. 'It is mind that makes the body rich,' but the soul needs a corresponding body, and God has wedded them together, in perfect suitability to their present business and abode."

The body of man alone is adapted to the demands of an occupant possessed of intelligence, genius, science, art, and skill; and may therefore be regarded as indicating in itself the exalted nature of the soul of which it is the dwelling-place. We lack the speed of the antelope, the strength of the bison, the hearing of the elk, the sight of the panther, and the keen scent of the fox-hound, but all these qualities together, and every other in which the bodies of the lower animal excel that of man, are more than compensated for by the single apparatus by which these lines are written —the human hand. God made the human body to be the abode of an angelic nature. As it lay there fresh from the all-forming hand, before he breathed into it the immortal spirit, it was the fit abode for a seraphic nature, such as God placed within it.

Now as we may logically infer the character of the occupant of the house, from the character and appearance of the house itself, so we may logically infer the character, dignity and destiny of the soul of man, from the character of the earthly house in which the Creator has assigned it its present, and we may add, its everlasting abode. For we may not only contemplate the body as it now is, but also as it shall be beyond the resurrection, and when mortality is swallowed up of life.

The perfection of the human body, therefore, as compared with other animal bodies, betokens the exalted character of its occupant, and suggests for the soul of man a destiny unlike that of the beast that perishes.

> Look on that glorious face!
> There the quick play of varied passions see!
> Look on that brow of thought! must it not be
> A spirit's dwelling-place?
>
> Would God a palace rear
> For a frail being of no nobler life,
> Than that which closes with the dying strife,
> A life that endeth here?
>
> Ah, no! the tenant must,
> More glorious than its glorious mansion be;
> Whose dome and column soon alas! we see
> All crumbling back to dust.

CHAPTER VI.

DOMINION OF THE SOUL OVER THE BODY.

THE dominion of mind over matter in general, and especially of the soul over the body, proves the latter to be a mere instrument of the soul, and not the soul itself.

I. The general supremacy of mind over matter will scarcely be questioned. It is shown in all the mechanical arts, in sculpture and painting, and in all the improvements effected in the animal and vegetable kingdom. The original wild rose, from which man, "working together with God," has developed a score of exquisite varieties, was originally a simple four leaved flower, neither beautiful nor fragrant. And the same may be said in general of scores of our floral beauties and favorites—they are to a great extent human productions. Our fruits, whether berries or peaches, pears or apples, have become what they are by cultivation, from very unpromising beginnings. So of our grains and garden vegetables.

And is not the same true of our domestic animals—horses, oxen, sheep, swine, and fowls of all kinds? Were not their ancestors in their wild state feeble and worthless pigmies, compared with their domesticated posterity? By careful observation upon cause and effect, and the use of such means as were adapted to produce the desired end, these different animals have been improved to double the size and value of their progenitors, while in a wild state.

And what is all this but the triumph of spirit over matter?—of the soul of man, over the obstacles in the way of the complete development of portions of the vegetable and animal kingdoms? Indeed, it is more than this; it is carrying out a general plan, by laws established by the Deity, and with his continued co-operation, to an extent that seems scarcely to have been contemplated in the original creation.

II. The almost complete subserviency of material creation, in one form or another, to the wants and happiness of man, seems to justify the conclusion that the material universe was created after all the angelic hosts, and, in some way to minister to the development and happiness of intellectual life. The heavens declare the glory of God, not only to men but to angels. And who that believes in those bright celestial spirits can doubt the complete subjection of all material things to their convenience and happiness? If men in the body can do what we see done, in the creation of unnumbered forms of beauty and utility from the various elements of nature, what must be the power of an angel over material things?

Were the globe a solid mass of crystal, the beams of the sun would pass through it as swiftly as through vacant space. And could not a celestial do as much? If Gabriel were to meet a vast planet in his ethereal flights, would he be obliged to turn aside and go around it, as a ship at sea would sail around an island? Such is the superiority of spirit over matter, that angels and disembodied human souls can doubtless fly through solid marble and granite as easily and as swiftly as in the open void of heaven!

III. It is believed by many to be a matter of consciousness that they dwell in a body, from which they are as distinct as light is from the crystal through which it passes. We "feel" that we (the thinking power) are not the body, and the body is not ourselves. Nor is it a valid objection to this view to affirm that if it were a matter of consciousness, all men would arrive at the same conclusion, and there would be no dispute upon the subject. A metaphysician may be conscious of certain mental phenomena, of which others may have no knowledge, for the simple reason, that he has made the subject a study, and is accustomed to noting with care and accuracy his mental states and processes. So in regard to the occupancy of the body—the vast majority of mankind never think of the subject, and have therefore no distinct consciousness in regard to it. But let a person sit down and, turning his thoughts within, calmly contemplate the relation of that which thinks, and reasons, and remembers within him, to the physical frame with which it is connected; and if he does not realize a consciousness that *he* is *not the body*, but merely its occupant, we believe it will be either because such consciousness is at war with his creed, or because he is unaccustomed to distinguishing between his consciousness and his sensations. Who that reflects ever confounds the thinking principle within him, with his feet or hips, or arms, or even with the brain?* Are we not conscious that these are but instruments through which we communicate with the external world?

IV. But whatever may be thought of our consciousness of the *occupancy* of the body, as a distinct question, there is another point, equally pertinent to our argument, as we conceive, and, upon which there can be no dispute.

Every person is conscious of the control he exercises over his own body, as over a machine to be operated by him at will. At his bidding the hand rises or falls, or moves horizontally; or the feet convey the body to a different locality. With the exception of a few involuntary motions, like that of the heart, or of the lungs during sleep, the whole machine is obedient to the will. The mind sits enthroned like a mariner at the helm, or an engineer at his post, and the body obeys all its mandates.

And even when through fracture, or dislocation, or paralysis, an arm or a leg becomes immovable, how distinct the consciousness that the difficulty is in the *machine* which is out of order, and not in the operator, who retains all *his* powers and capabilities unimpaired. We are distinctly conscious that the mind controls the body, and not the body the mind. The material is consciously subject to the spiritual.

V. All these facts point unmistakably to the conclusion that the body is not the soul, or any part of it, but the mere *instrument* through which the mind

* We are conscious of an effort in connection with the brain, in thinking and hard study; but it is equally true that "the mind is sensibly in every limb, and acts wherever it pleases to act, provided the mechanism be fit for use." Moore's Power of the Soul over the Body, p. 70.

holds intercourse with the material world. No part of the body indicates that it is, in itself, the moving power. On the contrary the relation of some of the organs, at least, to artificial aids to sensation, show conclusively that like them they are mere instruments of a higher power, which uses them. Take for illustration the human eye and ear.

"We are accustomed to say the eye sees, the ear hears, the finger feels, and so forth; but such language is incorrect, and only admissible because we are accustomed to the error, and our expressions are necessarily accommodated to ignorance, or are not equal to our knowledge. The eye itself no more sees than the telescope which we hold before it to assist our vision. The ear hears not any more than the trumpet of tin, which the deaf man directs towards the speaker to convey the sound of his voice, and so with regard to all the organs of sense. They are but instruments which become the *media* of intelligence to the absolute mind, which uses them, whenever that mind is inclined or obliged to employ them. Or, perhaps, they might be more correctly represented as the seats or proper places of impressions, because of their exact adaptation to external influences."

"The slightest examination of the organs of sense will convince an observer that they are constructed merely as instruments. What is the eye but a most perfect optical contrivance? * * No mechanism invented by man was ever so well contrived or so well placed, or could move so precisely as required under the action of its pullies. No servant was ever so obedient; for without a conscious effort of the will, without a command, and as if instinct with the mind that employs it, this exquisite aparatus, which is both a camera obscura and a telescope, instantaneously takes the direction of a desire, and accommodates itself to the range of distance and the degree of light."

"And so of the *ear:* it is a complete acoustic instrument, with its exterior trumpet to collect sounds, and its vibrating tympanum, and its chamber and winding passages, and its dense fluids, so well calculated to propagate and modify vibrations, and its minute and sensitive muscles, to act as cords to brace the drum, just as required, and to move the jointed piston, which regulates the water in its channels, according to circumstances, and the whole built up within a stone-like structure, which prevents the sound from being wasted."*

And so of the organs of speech and song and that most wonderful of all contrivances, the human hand. They are all adapted to perform the will of an indwelling and controlling rational spirit—such duties as no other original organism is ever called upon or is competent to perform.

V. The same general idea is thus forcibly elaborated by Bishop Butler:

"If we consider our bodies somewhat more distinctly, as made up of organs and instruments of perception and of motion, it will bring us to the same conclusion. Thus, the common optical experiments show, and even the observation how sight is assisted by glasses, shows, that we see with our eyes, in the same sense as we see with glasses. Nor is there any

* Dr. Moore on the Power of the Soul over the Body, American Ed. pp. 25–27.

reason to believe, that we see with them in any other sense; any other, I mean, which would lead us to think the eye itself a percipient. The like is to be said of hearing: and our feeling distant solid matter by means of somewhat in our hand, seems an instance of the like kind, as to the subject we are considering. All these are instances of foreign matter, or such as is no part of our body, being instrumental in preparing objects for, and conveying them to the perceiving power, in a manner similar, or like to the manner in which our organs of sense prepare and convey them. Both are, in a like way, instruments of our receiving such ideas from external objects, as the Author of nature appointed those external objects to be the occasions of exciting in us. However, glasses are evidently instances of this; namely, of matter, which is no part of our body, preparing objects for, and conveying them towards the perceiving power, in like manner as our bodily organs do. And if we see with our eyes only in the same manner as we do with glasses, the like may justly be concluded from analogy, of all our other senses. It is not intended, by anything here said, to affirm, that the whole apparatus of vision, or of perception by any other of our senses, can be traced, through all its steps, quite up to the living power of seeing, or perceiving; but that, so far as it can be traced by experimental observations, so far it appears, that our organs of sense prepare and convey on objects, in order to their being perceived, in like manner as foreign matter does, without affording any shadow of appearance, that they themselves perceive. And that we have no reason to think our organs of sense percipients, is confirmed by instances of persons losing some of them, the living beings themselves, their former occupiers, remaining unimpaired. It is confirmed also by the experience of dreams; by which we find we are at present possessed of a latent, and what would otherwise be an unimagined unknown power of perceiving sensible objects, in as strong and lively a manner without our external organs of sense, as with them."*

VI. It is no sufficient reply to the above view to allege that the control of which we speak is simply the dominion of the *brain* over the muscles and bones, through the medium of the nervous system. For if we attribute this conscious supremacy and control to the brain alone, as a purely material substance, then we must attribute to it all the other functions and powers of the human soul, or rather declare the brain to be the soul itself, and not the mere instrument through which the mind operates upon other portions of the body. This brings us squarely on to the platform of materialism, and justifies a glance at the notion that the brain in itself considered, is the original source of thought and consciousness.

"The brain has been analyzed, and more than eight tenths of its substance has been found to be *water*. Indeed this, mixed up with a little albumen, a still less quantity of fat, osmazome, phosphorus, acids, salts and sulphur, constitute its material elements. In all cases water largely predominates. Take even the *pineal gland*—that interior and mysterious organ of the brain, supposed by Descartes, and by many philosophers after him, to be the peculiar seat of the soul—even this has been analyzed. Its prin-

* Butler's Analogy, Part I. Chapter i.

cipal elements are found to be phosphate of lime, together with a small proportion of carbonate of lime and phosphates of ammonia and magnesia."

"If the brain at large constitutes the soul, then the soul is only a peculiar combination of oxygen and hydrogen with albumen, acids, salts, sulphur, etc. Or, if the pineal gland constitutes the soul, then the principal element of soul is phosphate of lime!

"If this wonderful theory is true, it may be safely conceded that we gain *something* by it. We have at last found out *what the soul is.* And when the wise man again inquires, 'Who knoweth the spirit of man?' these sage philosophers may respond, 'We! it is phosphate of lime.' But what! has a peculiar combination of a few elemental substances; has *phosphate of lime* been the cause, the *fons et origo,* of all the glorious manifestations of intellect that have been made among men? Is it osmazome that has given origin to the creations of art? Is it oxygen that blazes out in the glowing fires of eloquence? Was it hydrogen that soared in the philosophy of Newton, and sought with all-comprehending grasp to encircle the universe of God? Was it phosphate of lime that wove the garlands of poetry, and thus touched the tender chords of human sympathy, taste and sentiment?"*

And what has materialism to respond to this point blank challenge? Is it prepared to attribute effects so ethereal and rapturous, to the gross and ponderable cause to which it belongs if its assumption be true? Will it thus elevate the stream above its source, or gather grapes of thorns and figs of thistles?

* Dr. Clark's "Man all Immortal," p. 58.

But we must pass to another topic. We have shown in the present chapter the dominion of mind over matter, in general, as shown in the arts, and in the development by man of portions of the vegetable and animal creation. We have also suggested the probable order of creation, and the relation of the material to the spiritual universe. Consulting our personal consciousness upon the question of our spiritual occupancy of the body, we have shown by the control which the spirit exercises over the physical organism, and the relation of some of our organs to certain artificial helps to sensation, that the body as a whole is the mere *instrument* of the mind, and no more the mind itself, than the locomotive is the engineer that runs it. And finally, that the idea that the *brain* is the living agent that controls the wondrous mechanism, and is the source of all our mental phenomena, is upon its face a palpable absurdity.

From all this we conclude that although the body may be laid aside at death, as one lays down a telescope or a musical instrument, the mind will still live on, unconscious of disability, and unaffected by the fate of the material organism with which it was for a time connected, and over which it once held dominion.

CHAPTER VII.

UNEQUAL DEVELOPMENT OF THE MIND AND BODY.

THAT the body and soul are distinct essences, and that the latter is not wholly dependent upon the former for its powers and capabilities, may be seen by a comparison of various physical and mental phenomena, in the relations which the body and spirit bear to each other in their present state of union.

I. The body reaches its acme of vigor and power at the age of thirty-five or forty.* From that period it is first stationary for a few years, and then, gradually declines. Not so the mind. When the body halts, as if to rest from its toilsome progress, the mind presses onward as if spurning all impediments and continues her progressive march for years after the body has begun to decline.

These facts go to corroborate the doctrine of man's two-fold nature, and of the capability of the soul to exist even independently of the body.

* Bishop D. W. Clark fixes the zenith of bodily vigor at twenty-five or thirty, and the period of the greatest intellectual vigor at from forty to fifty. See Man all Immortal, p. 127. We think he fixes both these points too early in life, though that by no means affects the general fact, or the force of the argument.

II. But to this it is replied that the decay of the mental faculties in extreme age, when the bodily powers give way, justifies the inference that when the body utterly fails, the mind will become extinct with it. But this by no means follows; because in the first place, the mind does not always decay with the body, as numerous and striking instances attest. Dryden translated the Iliad at the age of sixty-eight. Sir Isaac Newton solved the famous problem of the trajectories at the age of seventy-three. Hobbs translated the Odyssey at the age of eighty-seven and the Iliad at the age of eighty-eight. Dr. Adam Clarke died at the age of seventy-two and John Wesley at the age of eighty-eight, both as vigorous intellectually as at the age of forty.

Now if the body and mind were identical, they would not only fail together in most instances, but *always;* hence a single exception, like those above cited, (and many others still more striking,) proves the distinct spirituality of the mind, and its power to exercise its functions independently of the condition of the body in which it dwells. In the second place it is a law of the universe that few changes that take place in nature shall be abrupt and sudden. The refracting power of the atmosphere renders gradual the approach and departure of the king of day. But for this the gloom of midnight would suddenly give place at the sun-rising to the painful glare of his untempered beams; while at his going down the full blaze of day would be suddenly succeeded by deep and blinding darkness. Little by little the light fades from us, as the sun sinks down towards the western horizon, that the transition from day to night may be both expected and agreeable. So in regard to man's brief day; the rule of nature is that the transition from this life to another shall be gradual, and therefore the more welcome; and that failing powers of body and mind shall herald our departure out of time, and our entrance upon an eternal state of existence.*

Why then should the seeming mental decay of man as the body fails, even if that were the universal law, be regarded as furnishing even a presumption that the change of death is to terminate his existence? Does not nature herself furnish us with analogies upon which we may found a far more cheering expectation?

Let us not, then, misinterpret

> The gentle interlude,
> Of second childhood's sweet simplicity,
> A spring in autumn gentle and subdued,
> Telling of life to be.
>
> Flushing the weary heart
> With loving pictures of life's early bowers,
> Wreathing the spirit ere it doth depart,
> With sweet immortal flowers.

* Upon the subject of "Growing Old," Henry Ward Beecher has somewhere uttered the following characteristic remarks: "Who cares, then, whether the hair be white or black? Who cares whether the eye be far-sighted or near-sighted? Who cares whether the hearing be poor or good? Who cares what becomes of the senses? This is not my whole life. This body is not my only heritage. I go to that bright land where the immortal part shines up and on forever and ever. And this consideration takes away the sadness occasioned by the consciousness of the failure of the earthly faculties."

But what of the resurrection, and the "glorious body" in which the saints shall dwell after that event? Will the soul be disembodied "forever and ever?"

III. It is claimed by those who deny the immortality of the soul, that intelligence is a simple result of animal organization, as electricity is a result of the combination of certain elements in the galvanic battery; and that consequently when the body is dissolved or dies, all mind or intelligence will cease, as galvanic action ceases when the battery is destroyed. But if this were true, the development of intelligence should in all cases be in exact proportion to the development and perfection of the bodily organism. No one expects the same galvanic power from a small Leyden jar that he does from a large one. Neither does he expect the same result from a single jar, that he does from a combination of jars in a battery. And, upon the principle above assumed, the same should be true of human bodies in the development of intelligence—such development should be in exact proportion to the size and perfection of the physical organization. The man of the most healthful and stalwart body should invariably exhibit the most intelligence; while the effeminate, sickly, and diminutive should develope mental weakness and imbecility. But such is not the case.

For, while it is admitted that the mind and body sympathize with each other, and that a healthy body is favorable to mental development, while the opposite in some cases seriously affects the intellect; it nevertheless remains true that *there is no such correspondence between the development of the mind and the body*, as the doctrine of materialism demands. For,

1. Persons of the same age and of equal physical

development often have a very unequal mental development.

2. It often happens that persons of very small or delicate or feeble bodies possess wonderful intellectual powers.

Isaac Watts, Richard Watson, Henry Kirk White, and Robert Pollok may be cited as examples. And even "General Tom Thumb," as he is called, and Calvin Edson, "the living skeleton," seemed to possess their mental powers in full vigor, though their respective bodies were anomalies in human physiology.

The newspapers for October 1861, contained an account of an Indian dwarf in Central America, 30 years old, but 17 inches high, born without arms or legs, yet perfect in health, and speaking two languages.

Persons are not unfrequently to be met with whose souls seem to be so out of proportion to their bodies, as to remind one of a frail ferry boat propelled by a marine engine of a thousand horse power, causing it to tremble from keel to capstan at every revolution.

3. Thousands of persons of the most robust and perfect physical organizations, rise but little above the rank of idiots in point of intelligence. As animal organisms they are well nigh faultless, while in matters of thought and knowledge they are strikingly weak and deficient.

All these are facts so well known as to require no further proof or illustration. And yet they are diametrically opposed to the fundamental principles of materialism. They not only indicate a distinction between body and spirit, and that the latter is not dependent upon the former for its being and powers; but they also go to establish the idea that the mind may exist separate from the body, and when all the organs through which it held communion with the material world have crumbled back to dust.

CHAPTER VIII.

ENERGY OF THE SOUL, IN CASES WHERE PHYSICAL ORGANS ARE WANTING.

THE energy often displayed by the soul of man in extemporizing for herself new channels of communication with the external world, when any of her natural organs are destroyed, is another of the "signals" of her immortality. Are the *eye* and *ear* both wanting or useless, the smell and touch—the hands, and feet, and nose are made, to a great extent, to supply their place.

I. James Mitchell, who was deaf, blind, and dumb, could tell if a stranger were present, and in what direction, by the sense of smell alone. Dr. Moyse, a blind man, could distinguish a black dress on his friend by the same means. A blind man of Puiseaux, in France, could determine the quantity of fluid in a vessel, by the sound it produced by running from one vessel to another. Dr. Rush speaks of two blind brothers who once resided in Philadelphia, who knew when they approached a post in walking across a street, by the peculiar sound which the ground under their feet emitted in the neighborhood of the post; and could tell the names of a number of tame pigeons, with which they amused themselves in a little garden, by only hearing them fly over their heads. Dr. Saunderson, who lost his sight in very early youth, and remained blind through life, acquired such acuteness of touch that he could distinguish, by merely letting them pass through his fingers, spurious coins, which were so well executed as to deceive even skillful judges who could see. John Metcalf, of England, though perfectly blind, became an efficient surveyor.*

II. Mr. Fela, of Antwerp, was a successful painter. And yet he had no hands or arms. Insurmountable as this obstacle might seem it was overcome by his incontrollable genius. Holding the pencil between his toes instead of his fingers, he succeeded better than many others with arms and hands, but destitute of his artistic inspiration.†

* Upham's Mental Philosophy, pp. 60–65.

† A writer in the *New York Evening Post* for August 21, 1862, thus refers to this "armless painter of Antwerp.

"A little over a year ago I sauntered one day into the museum of that quaint and clean city, and from lingering here and there before prim Dutch pictures, my attention was attracted by the singular movements of a person in the distance seated before his easel. The thermometer was somewhere in the 'nineties,' and the seated artist was using his *foot*kerchief."

"Seat yourself on an ordinary chair; doff boots; so trim the inner covering of your feet, commonly called socks, that your toes will be free to do your bidding; take now your kerchief between the toe and 'index' finger of, say your right foot, and with the kerchief so held 'cool off' and dry your face, the back part of your head and your neck fore and aft. Transfer now the kerchief to the grasp of the left foot, and let a like *foot*ipulation be gone through with until the left side be made comfortable, and you will, in part, have done what, to my great astonishment, that armless artist Fela accomplished with apparent ease."

"Mr. Fela was copying a little figure from a group by an old master. His picture was far advanced; he worked on the eye, and the delicacy of the touch seemed the most marvellous feat of his feet that I saw accomplished."

III. Miss Mary Collins of New Jersey had been blind from infancy. At the age of forty she embraced Christ as her Saviour and hope, and conceived a strong desire to read the word of God. By the sale of ballads of her own composing in the streets of Philadelphia, she obtained money with which to procure a "spelling book," in raised characters, and two weeks' tuition in some school for the blind. She went on, studying and reading with her fingers, till she had mastered the alphabet, and could read easy words and sentences. A copy of the Psalms in raised letters was then procured for her, and when the writer saw her at a camp-meeting in 1841, she had read most of the Psalms several times over.

But what arrested attention more than anything else was that all her fingers were wrapped up, each in a white cloth, except one on each hand, then in use to read with; and on opening the book of Psalms, whole pages were found stained, line after line, with blood! The tops of the raised letters, though of paper, were hard and sharp, so that in a short time they wore through her finger ends; and before she was aware of it, the blood would be oozing from her fingers, as she was feeling out the letters, words and sentences, line after line, and drinking in divine knowledge therefrom, as from fountains of living waters. "Blessed be the Lord my strength," she exclaimed, "which teacheth my *hands* to war and my *fingers* to fight." Ps. cxliv. 1.

"Never," said she, "shall I forget my feelings when, trying to read a little in a raised New Testament, I came to a long and hard word which I had never found in the Psalms, and began to spell it out, r-e-s-u-r-r-e-c—and it flashed upon my mind that it was RESURRECTION! It was the first time I had ever read that startling word, and my soul was thrilled as by an electric shock."

She spent most of her time in reading, and when one set of fingers were worn through, and became painful, she would wrap them up to heal a little and undo the next best pair. Thus she kept four fingers on each hand, almost constantly worn through and bleeding, that they might serve as eyes to convey to the soul a knowledge of the form of the letters, and through the letters and words a knowledge of the mind of God.*

Now if the body of man is a kind of galvanic battery, and intelligence a mere result of certain material combinations, why this struggle of the soul to assert herself, when her natural channels of intercourse with the outside world are destroyed? Will electricity make its way through glass if a proper conductor be wanting? Will light penetrate sheet iron if it cannot enter or escape by a window? And if intelligence, after all, is but a phenomenon of matter under certain conditions, why does it spurn all material laws, and cut out new channels for itself where its natural media are destroyed?

All this fertility of resource—this energy of the

* Such cases strongly support the opinion of Diderot, that persons deprived of both sight and hearing, might so increase the sensibility of touch as to locate the soul in the tips of the fingers. See *Upham's Mental Philosophy*, p. 66.

soul amid physical adversity—is but an advertisement of her unlikeness to anything else on earth, and a token of the subordination of the body to the spirit, and the relation of the latter to an enduring and an immortal state of existence.

CHAPTER IX.

UNIMPAIRED MENTAL POWERS UNDER BODILY MUTILATIONS.

THE ability of the soul to retain all her faculties unimpaired while the body is subjected to great mutilation, is a striking proof of her independence, and of her immortal destination.

I. If the mind were material and mortal like the body, or rather, were it a mere phase of a bodily function, as materialism assumes, not only should intelligence be in all cases in exact proportion to the size and power of the body, and ebb and flow as health fades or returns; but every case of physical mutilation should be attended with a corresponding loss of intelligence. The loss of an arm or a leg should be just so much abstracted from the mind of the subject.

II. But such is not the case. A survivor of the wars of the first Napoleon lost an *eye*, an *arm*, a *leg*, and a *piece of his skull*, (which was substituted by a silver plate,) and yet not a thought was lost, neither was there the slightest diminution of intelligence. In the battles of the late rebellion of 1861, one man lost both arms, and both legs, but lost none of his grammar, or geography, or military tactics. He was conscious that his soul was still entire and unimpaired, though the body in which it dwelt was reduced to an inert and unseemly trunk of human flesh. How, then, are we deceived by our very consciousness, if the mind, by remaining intact amid such physical mutilation does not thereby indicate her independence of the body, and her destination for immortality.*

III. But it may be replied that the *brain* is the thinking power and the seat of knowledge, and consequently the loss of the legs and arms ought not to affect the intelligence. Let us see: the spinal marrow is but an elongation of the brain, and is of the same medullary substance. And so of all the nerves that branch off from it, from the head to the pelvis ;—they are all of the same general substance as the brain. While, therefore, the amount of cerebral matter in the limbs is much less than is left in the cavity of the skull, it is certainly an appreciable amount, as compared with the whole,—an amount the loss of which ought sensibly to affect the intellect, if materialism be true. For if brain is all the soul man possesses, and the nerves are in reality a part of the brain; then whoever loses part of his nervous system by the loss of a limb, inevitably loses part of his brain power, or

* A young officer in the British army had engaged himself in marriage to a young lady in England, before embarking for this country. While here, he was wounded and lost a leg. He accordingly wrote his affianced bride that he was maimed and disfigured, and so different from what he was when the engagement was formed, that he felt it his duty to release her from all obligation to become his wife. To this manly and honorable letter the lady returned the equally noble reply, that she was willing to marry him *if there was enough of his body left to hold his soul*,—a reply that indicated her appreciation of the two-fold nature of man, and the subordinate importance of the body to the immortal spirit.

soul, and should know less and have less mental capacity than before the amputation. But as this is not the case, it follows that though the mind may operate through the nervous system, it is nevertheless distinct from that system, and may survive, though that may perish.

IV. Even the brain itself may be extensively diseased, if not wholly removed, without affecting the reasoning faculties.

Bishop Clark refers to a case mentioned by Abercrombie in which one half of the entire brain of a lady had been reduced to a mass of suppuration by disease, and yet she had retained her faculties to the last, and had been enjoying herself at a convivial party only a few hours before her sudden death. He also cites a case mentioned by Dr. Ferrier in which a man who died suddenly, but who had retained all his faculties unimpaired till the moment of death, was found upon examination to have a brain the right hemisphere of which was destroyed by suppuration.*

"The celebrated Saussure was affected with extensive disorganization of the brain for the space of five years, without any sensible alteration of the intellectual powers. Mr. Howship relates a case where, in consequence of a slight blow on the head, the whole lobe of the brain was found in a state of *scirrhus* forty years afterward. But with the exception of occasional pain, the subject had no other symptoms till towards the decline of life, when she became gradually sleepy and stupid.

"A lad aged eleven years received a kick from a horse, which fractured the frontal bone. In two hours

* Man all Immortal, p. 64.

after, he recovered every faculty of his mind, and they continued vigorous for six weeks, and to an hour of his death, which took place on the forty-third day. He sat up every day, often walked to the window, frequently laughed at the gambols of the boys in the streets, &c. On dissection, the space of the skull previously occupied by *the right anterior and middle lobes* of the *cerebrum*, presented a perfect cavity, filled with sero-purulent matter, the lobe having been destroyed by suppuration. The *third lobe* was much disorganized. The *left hemisphere* was in a state of *ramollissement* (or softening) down to the corpus callosum."*

To the same effect is the celebrated case recorded by O'Halloran, where there was great destruction of the brain without any derangement of the intellect.

"The whole brain," says Dr. Payne, "may be sliced down to the medulla oblongata, or beginning of the spinal cord, without affecting, at the time, the organic functions."†

"Morgagni and Haller," says Bishop Clark, "claim to have ascertained by a wide induction of facts, that every part of the brain has been found to be destroyed or disorganized, in one instance or another, while yet the individuals have not been deprived of mind, or even affected in their intellectual powers."‡

"M. Flouren's experiments," says Dr. Moore, "are too numerous and extensive to quote; but they prove that the brain may be destroyed to a large extent, in

* *Medical and Physiological Commentaries*, Vol. 2, p. 139, *note; also Payne on the Soul and Instinct*, note, p. 90.

† Payne on the Soul, Instinct and Life, p. 36.

‡ Man all Immortal, pp. 63, 64.

any direction, without destroying any of its functions."*

Such instances not only disprove the fundamental assumptions of Phrenology, but they equally overthrow materialism in general, and foreshadow an immortal life for the spirit, by indicating her ability to live on undisturbed in her functions not only while the body is mutilated, or wasted by disease, but even while her most vital medium of connection with the material world is more or less removed, indurated or dissolved.

"The mutilations which the human body undergoes," says Chalmers, "and yet without the destruction of the living powers, warrant the conclusion, not that the soul *must*, but that the soul *may* survive the entire dissolution of that material frame-work wherewith it is now encompassed."†

* "Soul and Body," p. 54.

† Lectures on Butler's Analogy, Posthumous works, Vol. 2, p. 62.

CHAPTER X.

REVERY, SLEEP, DREAMING AND CATALEPSY.

In the previous chapter we have called attention to a variety of physical and mental phenomena, exhibited by the body and mind in their present state of union, and which go to prove the distinct spiritual nature of the latter, and its power to survive the decay of the body, and live on, with all its functions unimpaired, when the body is dissolved. In continuation of the same general topic—the relations of the soul to the body—let us now look at another class of phenomena, namely, those that occur in *revery, sleep, dreaming, catalepsy*, &c., and see if they also do not all converge to the same point, and furnish strong presumptive proof that the spirit of man is immortal.

I. "Revery," says Dr. Good, "is the dream of a man while awake. He is so intently bent upon a particular train of thought, that he is torpid to every thing else: he sees nothing, he hears nothing, he feels nothing; and the only difference between the two, (revery and dreaming) is, that in common dreaming, the sensitive and irritative power of the external senses is exhausted progressively and generally, while the will partakes of the exhaustion; and that in revery the whole is directed to a single outlet, the will, instead of being exhausted, being riveted upon this one point alone; and the external senses being alone rendered torpid from the drain that is thus made upon them to support the superabundant flow of a sensitive and irritative power expended upon the prevailing ecstacy."*

The celebrated Rittenhouse was so absorbed in witnessing the transit of Venus across the sun's disc in 1799 as to lose all control over his muscular system, and become helpless in the observatory. Another modern astronomer passed a whole night in his observatory, witnessing a celestial phenomenon, and on being accosted in the morning replied that he would go to bed before it was late. He had gazed the whole night and did not know it.

The mathematician Viote was sometimes so absorbed by his calculations that he has been known to pass three days and three nights without food. It is related of the Italian poet Marini, that while he was intensely engaged in revising his Adonis, he placed his leg on the fire, where it burned for some time without his being aware of it.†

Such cases seem almost incredible, and yet they can scarce be doubted. Budhist devotees so far abstract themselves as not only to endure what would cause extreme suffering to others without the least apparent pain, but also to become unconscious of all bodily existence.

II. Look also at the phenomenon of *sleep*. Suppose, instead of the present order of things, it had been ordained that man should sleep only once a year,

* Book of Nature, p. 253.

† Moore's Power of the Soul, &c., p. 105.

and then only for a few hours; and suppose men had lived a year without any experience or knowledge, upon the subject before the first instance of sleep occurred. At length one of their number begins to grow languid, ceases to talk, seeks a couch as if sick, his eyes close, and he becomes inactive. In vain is he called upon to explain the difficulty—he neither sees nor hears. All intelligence is as perfectly suppressed for the time being as if he were dead.

Now in the absence of experience what reason would his comrades have for supposing he would ever again awake to consciousness and intelligence? Would not the natural inference rather be that all thought and knowledge were at an end forever?

"What can possibly be more opposite to each other," says John Mason Good, "than the two states of wakefulness and sleep?—the senses in full vigor and activity, alive to every pursuit, and braced up to every exertion,—and a suspension of all sense whatever, a looseness and inertness of the voluntary powers, so nearly akin to death, that nothing but a daily experience of the fact itself could justify us in expecting that we should ever recover from it." *

And yet in a short time the sleeper awakes, and is more vigorous and active than before. A mysterious change has come over the body, but the mind still lives on—a natural intimation that it may survive still greater changes, and live even when we sleep our last sleep, and the body is dissolved.

III. But the activity and achievements of the mind, at times, in what are called *dreams*, is perhaps still more pertinent to the subject under consideration.

* Book of Nature, Sec. vii. p. 243.

A student retires to bed perplexed with a difficult problem, and perhaps despairing of its solution. He falls asleep and in a dream solves the problem, and on waking finds his solution correct. A mechanic or inventor is in trouble about some piece of machinery, and in that state of mind retires to rest. He falls asleep, but the mind goes on with its operations, and in a dream, he sees how the difficulty may be obviated, and that very idea, reached while the body was asleep, may be the most important item in a valuable invention and patent.

"A gentleman engaged in a banking establishment made an error in his account, and, after an interval of several months, spent days and nights in vain endeavors to discover where the mistake lay. At length, worn out by fatigue, he went to bed, and in a dream recollected all the circumstances that gave rise to the error. He remembered that on a certain day several persons were waiting in the bank, when one individual, who was a most amazing stammerer, became so excessively impatient and noisy that, to get rid of him, his money was paid before his turn, and the entrance of this sum was neglected, and thus arose the deficiency in the account." *

"Tartini, a celebrated violin player, composed his famous *Devil's Sonata* while he dreamed that the devil challenged him to a trial of skill, on his own violin. Cabanis often, during his dreams, saw clearly into the bearing of political events which baffled him when awake. Condorcet frequently left his deep and complicated calculations unfinished when obliged to

* Moore's Soul and Body, p. 117.

retire to rest, and found their results unfolded in his dreams."*

"I have formerly referred," says Abercrombie, "to some remarkable cases in which languages long forgotten were recovered during a state of delirium. Something very analogous seems to occur in dreaming, of which I have received the following example from an able and intelligent friend. In his youth he was very fond of the Greek language, and made considerable progress in it; but afterwards, being actively engaged in other pursuits, he so entirely forgot it that he could not even read the words. But he has often dreamed of reading Greek works which he had been accustomed to use at college, and with a most vivid impression of fully understanding them." †

Sir John Herschell, the famous astronomer, declared that the following stanza was composed by him while asleep and dreaming November 28, 1841, and written down immediately on waking:—

Throw thyself on thy God, nor mock him with feeble denial?
  Sure of his love, and oh! sure of his mercy at last;
Bitter and deep though the draught, yet shun not the cup of thy trial,
  But in its healing effect, smile at its bitterness past.

Coleridge, the poet, says that as he was once reading in the Pilgrimage of Purchas an account of the palace and garden of Khan Kubla, he fell into a sleep, and in that situation composed an entire poem of not less than two hundred lines, some of which he afterwards committed to writing. The poem is entitled Kubla Khan, and begins as follows:

* Moore's Soul and Body, p. 82.
† Intellectual Philosophy, p. 205.

In Hanadu did Kubla Khan
A stately pleasure dome decree;
Where Alph, the sacred river, ran
Through caverns measureless to man
Down to a sunless sea.*

And how often is it the case that the mind keeps up its exertions during our sleeping hours to such an extent that we feel oppressed with fatigue on waking, as if we had been toiling rather than sleeping.

Now upon the hypothesis that the body and mind are alike material, how are these things to be accounted for? The body is at rest, why is not the spirit? Why, when the body is prostrate and quiet does the soul seem often to seize the occasion, to roam abroad into unexplored regions, and hear, and see, and act, and suffer, or rejoice, without the intervention of material organs? Surely this is a strange phenomenon if the body and mind are identical, and the soul is destined now and hereafter to share the fate of its material tenement. Should not our very dreams by night instruct us that we have within these changing bodies of ours a living active principle —a spirit—which disdains implicit obedience to physical laws, refuses to share in the vicissitudes of the material body—to rest when it rests, and die when it dies,—and may, therefore, live on when the body shall crumble back to dust.

"Her ceaseless flight, though devious, speaks her nature
Of subtler essence than the trodden clod;
Active, ethereal, towering, unconfined,
Unfettered with her gross companion's fall;—
Even silent night proclaims my soul immortal:
Even silent night proclaims eternal day."

* Upham's Mental Philosophy, p. 108.

IV. The conscious activity of the soul while the body is in a state of *trance*, or *catalepsy*, is another indication of her independency of the body, and her probable immortality.

"We have all heard and read," says Dr. Good, "of such extraordinary occurrences of trances, or apparent absences of the soul from the body; we have heard and read of persons who, after having been apparently dead for many days, and on the point of being buried, have returned to a full possession of life and health; and although most of these histories are wrapped up in so much mystery and superstition, as to be altogether unworthy of notice, there are many too cautiously drawn up and authenticated to be dismissed in so cursory a manner."*

In the early history of "camp meetings" in this country instances of catalepsy induced by religious excitement were frequent. In those cases all the animal functions were suspended; the countenance was pale as a corpse; the body grew stiff and cold; and nearly every indication of death appeared. And yet during these periods the subject was usually intensely conscious, and upon recovery would describe the activity and the experiences of the mind during that strange parenthesis, in the most glowing language. But perhaps no one case will more fully illustrate this general subject, than that of REV. WM. TENNENT, a Presbyterian minister of Freehold, N. J.

"He was conversing one morning with his brother, in Latin, on the state of the soul, when he fainted

* Book of Nature, p. 252.

and died away. After the usual time he was laid out on a board, according to the common practice of the country, and the neighborhood were invited to attend the funeral on the next day. In the evening his physician and friend returned from a ride into the country, and was afflicted beyond measure at the news of his death. He could not be persuaded that it was certain; and, on being told that one of the persons who had assisted in laying out the body thought he had observed a little tremor of the flesh under the arm, although the body was cold and stiff, he endeavored to ascertain the fact. He first put his own hand into warm water, to make it as sensitive as possible, and then felt under the arm, and at the heart, and affirmed that he felt an unusual warmth, though no one else could.

"He had the body restored to a warm bed, and insisted that the people who had been invited to the funeral, should be requested not to attend. To this the brother objected as absurd, the eyes being sunk, the lips discolored, and the whole body cold and stiff. However, the doctor finally prevailed, and all probable means were used to discover symptoms of returning life. But the third day arrived, and no hopes were entertained of success but by the doctor, who never left him night or day. The people were again invited, and assembled to attend the funeral. The doctor still objected, and at last confined his request for delay to one hour, then to half an hour, and finally to a quarter of an hour.

"He had discovered that the tongue was much swollen, and threatened to crack. He was endeavoring to soften it by some emollient ointment, put upon it with a feather, when the brother came in, about the expiration of the last period, and mistaking what the doctor was doing for an attempt to feed him, manifested some resentment, and said, in a spirited tone, 'It is shameful to be feeding a lifeless corpse;' and insisted, with earnestness, that the funeral should immediately proceed.

"At this critical and important moment, the body, to the great alarm and astonishment of all present, opened its eyes, gave a dreadful groan, and sank again into apparent death. This put an end to all thought of burying him, and every effort was again employed, in hopes of bringing about a speedy resuscitation. In about an hour, the eyes again opened, a heavy groan proceeded from the body, and again all appearance of animation vanished. In another hour life seemed to return with more power, and a complete revival took place, to the great joy of the family and friends, and to the no small astonishment and conviction of the very many who had been ridiculing the idea of restoring to life a dead body."*

"The writer of these memoirs," says his biographer, "was greatly interested by these uncommon events; and on a favorable occasion, earnestly pressed Mr. Tennent for a minute account of what his views and apprehensions were, while he lay in this extraordinary state of suspended animation. He discovered great reluctance to enter into any explanation of his perceptions and feelings at that time; but being importunately urged to do it, he at length consented, and proceeded with a solemnity not to be described:

"While I was conversing with my brother," said

* Life of Rev. William Tennent, pp. 23, 24.

he, "on the state of my soul, and the fears I had entertained for my future welfare, I found myself, in an instant, in another state of existence, under the direction of a superior being, who ordered me to follow him. I was accordingly wafted along, I know not how, till I beheld at a distance an ineffable glory, the impression of which on my mind it is impossible to communicate to mortal man. I immediately reflected on my happy change, and thought—Well, blessed be God! I am safe at last, notwithstanding all my fears. I saw an innumerable host of happy beings, surrounding the inexpressible glory, in acts of adoration and joyous worship; but I did not see any bodily shape or representation in the glorious appearance. I heard things unutterable. I heard their songs and hallelujahs of thanksgiving and praise, with unspeakable rapture. I felt joy unutterable and full of glory. I then applied to my conductor, and requested leave to join the happy throng; on which he tapped me on the shoulder and said, 'You must return to the earth.' This seemed like a sword through my heart. In an instant I recollected to have seen my brother standing before me disputing with the doctor. The three days during which I had appeared lifeless, seemed to me to be not more than ten or twenty minutes. The idea of returning to this world of sorrow and trouble gave me such a shock that I fainted repeatedly.

"Such was the effect on my mind of what I had seen and heard, that if it be possible for a human being to live entirely above the world and the things of it, for sometime afterward, I was that person. The ravishing sounds of the songs and hallelujahs that I heard, and the very words that were uttered, were not out of my ears, when awake, for at least three years. All the kingdoms of the earth were in my sight as nothing and vanity; and so great were my ideas of heavenly glory, that nothing which did not in some measure relate to it, could command my serious attention."*

How strikingly does such a narrative remind one of the trance of Peter, Acts x. 10, and of the words of Paul, 2 Cor. xii. 2–4: "I knew a man in Christ about fourteen years ago, (whether in the body, I cannot tell; or whether out of the body, I cannot tell: God knoweth;) such an one caught up to the third heaven. And I knew such a man, (whether in the body, or out of the body, I cannot tell: God knoweth;) How that he was caught up into paradise, and heard unspeakable words, which it is not lawful for a man to utter."

What reason have we for doubting that the trance of Mr. Tennent was similar to that of St. Paul, and that in both instances the soul was temporarily separated from the body? We base no argument on this assumption, however, being content with the indisputable fact in all these cases, that the mind is *conscious and active* though the body is apparently dead.

V. Persons resuscitated from apparent drowning often relate similar experiences of the consciousness and activity of the mind, while every animal function of the body was suspended. Memory, will, consciousness, hope and fear were as active as if the body was in its normal state, and all its functions in active play.

VI. In other instances, though the heart and lungs,

* Life of Tennent, pp. 28–31.

which are among the most vital portions of the human frame, have ceased to perform their functions, and have continued inactive for a greater or less period of time, the mind has retained not only its consciousness, but the unimpaired use of all its faculties and powers. Take the following instance copied from the *Book of Nature* by Dr. John Mason Good, as an illustration in point:

"In the year 1769, Mr. John Hunter, being then forty-one years of age, of a sound constitution, and subject to no disease except a casual fit of the gout, was suddenly attacked with a pain in the stomach, which was shortly succeeded by a total suspension of the action of the heart and lungs. By the power of the will, or rather by violent striving, he occasionally inflated the lungs, but over the heart he had no control whatever; nor, though he was attended by four of the chief physicians in London from the first, could the action of either be restored by medicine. In about three-quarters of an hour, however, the vital actions began to return of their own accord, and in two hours he was perfectly recovered.

"In this attack," observed Mr. (now Sir Everard) Home, who has given an interesting memoir of his life, "there was a suspension of the most material involuntary actions; even involuntary breathing was stopped; while sensation, with its consequences, as thinking and acting, with the will, were perfect, and all the voluntary actions were as strong as before."

"In the whole history of man," continued Dr. Good, "I do not know of a more extraordinary case. The functions of the soul were perfect, while the most important functions of the body, those upon which life depends absolutely, in all ordinary cases, were dead for nearly an hour. Why did not the soul depart from the body? and why did not the body itself commence that change, that subjection to the laws of chemical affinity which it evinces in every ordinary case of the death or inaction of the vital organs? Because in the present instance, as in every instance of suspended animation from hanging or drowning, the vital principle, whatever it consists in, had not ceased, or deserted the corporeal frame. It continued visible in its effect, though invisible in its essence and mode of operation."*

Is there no significance in all these facts? How strikingly do they comport with and corroborate the revealed doctrine of the soul's immortality. And how completely do they refute the opposite idea that the mind is merely a function of the body, necessarily sharing its condition of quiescence or activity, and doomed to perish when the body dies. Ah, no!

Cold in the dust this perished heart may lie,
But that which warmed it once shall never die.

* Book of Nature, pp. 253, 254.

CHAPTER XI.

VIGOR AND ACTIVITY OF THE SOUL IN THE HOUR OF DEATH.

Life makes the soul dependent on the dust,
Death gives her wings to mount above the spheres.

THE vigor and activity of the soul in the hour of death, and amid bodily dissolution, is an evidence of its independency of the body, and its consequent immortality.

I. The history of the Christian martyrs furnishes many striking illustrations of the power of the soul to rise superior to the terrors of death, and the agony of bodily dissolution, and show herself essentially indestructible and immortal.

Polycarp sang hymns of praise to God while his body was being consumed by the fires of martyrdom. While *John Huss* was being burned he sang a hymn with so loud and cheerful a voice that it was heard above the crackling of the fagots, and the noise of the multitude. *Jerome* of Prague sang amid the flames of martyrdom till his voice was stifled by them.

"Thus we hear *Lambert* while consuming by a slow fire, exclaiming, 'None but Christ! none but Christ!' Thus also died Cranmer—the soul triumphing over all that was terrible in bodily suffering—steadily hold his hand in the flame, and exclaim, while it is being consumed, 'This hand! this wicked hand.'

"So also *Mrs. Cecily Ormes*, who was added to the noble host of martyrs at the early age of twenty-two. Approaching the stake, already charred by the fires that had consumed two martyrs before her, she clasped it with her hands, exclaiming, 'Welcome! welcome, Cross of Christ!'

"But a still more striking instance of the triumph of the soul over the body is the case of *James Bainham.* When his legs and his arms were half consumed, and his body scorched and seething in the flame, he cried out to the bystanders, 'Ye look for miracles! Here, now, ye may see one. *This fire is to me a bed of roses.*'

"Before being led to the stake, *Mr. Hawkes* agreed with his friends upon a signal by which to express his feelings when he should be no longer capable of speech. When he was so nearly consumed that all thought him dead, and when his whole body was crisped with the fire, the skin of his arms drawn up, and his fingers literally consumed, suddenly seeming to recollect the appointed signal, he raised his fingerless hands above his head and clapped them three times in token of triumph." *

Thus triumphed many of the martyrs, while their bodies were being devoured by wild beasts, or consumed by fire.

II. Numerous instances of unimpaired and even unusual intellectual vigor in the hour of death, by

* Man all Immortal, pp. 60, 61.

disease, and when the body was already a ruin, fully demonstrate that the body and spirit are distinct; and that the latter may remain uninjured and vigorous, though the former has crumbled back to dust.

"The *Rev. Alanson Reed*, only half an hour before his last breath, said, 'I know full well that I am at the point of death, but the idea of a spirit being extinguished in death, is utterly inconceivable. The soul is going forth, but it has no consciousness of dying; rather the consciousness of living on rises above every other feeling, and it is impossible for me to doubt.'

"The celebrated *Boerhaave* contemplated the perceptible difference between his mind and his body, in his last illness, as being like a philosophical experiment to him, that his intellectual self would not perish with his bodily dissolution.

"*Haller*, as death advanced to the mastery over his bodily system, could only measure its progress by keeping his fingers upon his own pulse. 'The artery, my friend,' said he at length, 'ceases to beat;' and almost instantly expired.

"The *Rev. Mr. Halyburton*, when dying, said to a brother minister, 'I think my case is a pretty fair demonstration of the immortality of the soul. My bones are rising through my skin. This body is going away to corruption, and yet my intellectuals are so lively, that I cannot perceive the least alteration or decay in them.'"*

"It seems," said *Dr. Payson* amid his dying agonies, "as if the soul disdained such a narrow

*Man all Immortal, p. 68.

prison, and was determined to break through with an angel's energy—until it mounts on high. It seems as if my soul had found a pair of new wings, and was so eager to try them that, in her fluttering, she would rend the fine net-work of the body to pieces."

"I now feel," said *Dr. Fisk*, when near his end, "a strength of soul, and an energy of mind which this body, though afflicted and pained, cannot impair. *The soul has an energy of its own.* And so far from my body pressing my soul down to the dust, I feel as if my soul had almost power to raise my body upward, and bear it away." In view of such a death, well might the poet exclaim,

> **Oh may I triumph so,**
> **When all my warfare's past;**
> **And, dying, find my latest foe,**
> **Under my feet at last!**

III. It will not be denied that the hope of eternal life which inspires the bosom of the dying Christian, has a tendency to invigorate the soul, and impart in the hour of death a supernatural strength and courage. And yet it cannot be said that the above recited mental phenomena are *wholly* due to this cause. The soul has exhibited the same intellectual vigor, and superiority to the body, even when the unhappy subject was dying in despair. To give but a single illustration, take the case of the young man of high position, and of superior talents and education, whose last hours are so touchingly described by Dr. Young. To spare the feelings of his relatives and friends, he speaks of him under a fictitious name.

"This body," says the wretched Altamont, "is all weakness and pain; but my soul, as if stung up by torment to greater strength and spirit, is full powerful to reason, full mighty to suffer. And that which thus triumphs within the jaws of mortality, is, doubtless, immortal."

IV. The bearing of such instances upon the subject of the soul's immortality is obvious. They clearly show that the mind is not the body; that it does not waste with it, and does not die with it.

"To make the argument plain," says Dr. Lee, "we say that a single instance in which the mind kindles up at the moment of death, and blazes out with unwonted intellectual fires, while the body is wan and cold and helpless, cannot be reconciled with the idea that the mind is any part of the material body, and that it wastes and dies with it. On the other hand those cases in which the mind appears to waste with the body and go out like the sun, passing gradually behind a cloud, deeper and darker, until its last ray is lost, can be explained in perfect harmony with the theory of the immateriality of the mind, and even its immortality. Does the mind fail, as in second childhood—or does it grow gradually dim as the body wastes under the influence of disease? The explanation is this: the bodily organs through which the mind communicates with the material world, in these particular cases, are impaired by age or disease. In many cases of death from sickness, the mind appears to waste away, or gradually sink into a state of sleep, merely because the will does not determine it in a direction to develope itself to the world without. But that the mind is there, distinct from the wasting, dying body, is clear from the many cases already referred to, in which the mind, being roused by the prospect of heaven, or seized with the terror of impending perdition, flashes with the fires of immortality, and sheds a living glare as it quits its house of clay, and enters upon the destinies of the spirit world.

"This has often been witnessed in the dying moments of both the Christian and the sinner. There are but few Christian pastors who have been long devoted to their work, that have not in their visits among the sick and dying, more than once stood by the bedside of those whose last moments left upon their minds a vivid impression of the undying nature of the soul."*

O change! O wondrous change!
Burst are the prison bars;
This moment there so low,
So agonized, and now
Beyond the stars!

O change! Stupendous change!
There lies the soulless clod;
The sun eternal breaks,
The new immortal wakes,
Wakes with his God!

* Lee's Theology, p. 267.

CHAPTER XII.

THE DISSOLUTION OF THE BODY AFFORDS NO PRESUMPTION THAT THE MIND PERISHES WITH IT.

I live, move, am conscious; what shall bar my being?
Where is the rude hand to rend this tissue of existence?
Not thine, shadowy Death, what art thou but a phantom?
Not thine, foul Corruption, what art thou but a fear?
For death is merely absent life, as darkness absent light;
Not even a suspension, for the life hath sailed away.

HOWEVER clearly the Bible may teach the doctrine of a future state, and however loudly Nature may respond to this revelation, we have no *practical* acquaintance with disembodied spirits. All that we have known of the human soul has been in its connection with the body. All our experiences and habits of thought and utterance, associate the mind of man with the body, in relations so intimate, that it is but a natural, though an erroneous induction, that when one perishes the other must perish also. And yet a moment's attention to the subject, in the light of other physical phenomena with which we are acquainted, might convince us that the dissolution of the body does not afford even a presumption that the soul perishes with it.

I. It is a general fact in nature that the dissolution

of a compound substance, does not involve the elements of which it is composed, in the same common destiny. If we burn a piece of hard coal, a portion "goeth downward," returning to the earth as it was, in the form of ashes; while other and more volatile elements ascend, and are either consumed by combustion, or mingle with the atmosphere. And so of almost every element in nature; let it be submitted to any great and radical change, and certain portions of it are almost sure to elude our grasp and escape.

Let a man be placed upon an insulating stool, and charged with electricity till every hair of his head stands erect. Could he be reduced to ashes, or got into a coffin without the escape of the electricity? We might handle him with the greatest care, and with gloves made of non-conducting substances, and yet it would escape; if in no other way the very atmosphere would gradually remove it.

Have we not, then, in these facts, an analogy in the natural world—one that might at least guard us against the conclusion that the dissolution of the human body, necessarily involved the entire man in a common destiny and ruin?

If there is an element in nature with which the human body may be charged, which will inevitably escape unimpaired, though the body be destroyed, may there not also be an ethereal principle in man, which thinks and reasons and hopes and fears, and which will escape uninjured though the body be dissolved?

II. Every person is conscious of his personal and intellectual identity, from childhood to old age, no matter what changes may have taken place in the body.

1. How great the change in the size and form and appearance of every human body, from childhood to maturity. A few years, even, will often so change and disguise a person that their most intimate friends can scarcely recognize them.

2. A man may lose both arms, and both legs, and yet he is conscious of being the same thinking spiritual being that he was before.

3. It is said to be a well-established fact in human physiology, that the body is completely changed, so that every person has an entirely new body, so far as the matter of which it is composed is concerned, every seven years. Take, then, for example, a person eighty years of age; upon the supposition just stated; the substance of his body has been changed no less than ten times since he was ten years old. And, yet though he has had ten new bodies during the previous seventy years, he is conscious that so far as the *mind* is concerned, he is *the same identical person* who saw and heard and laughed and wept seventy years before.

"The identity of the organization is preserved only as the identity of a watch is preserved, which when seventy years old, has had every wheel and part supplied with new ones ten times. All the wheels have been used up and supplied ten times, but it is the same watch."

"This may be seen by the unlettered reader who has never studied physiology. He knows that he must take food every day to supply the perpetual waste of his system—that what he eats forms blood, and flesh, and bones. This could not be necessary, were there not a perpetual waste. This is further proved from the fact that the moment we cease to receive a sufficient degree of nutriment, the body begins to waste and become thinner, as the saying is, it grows poor. A person may be nearly starved to death, or emaciated with sickness, until reduced to one quarter his usual weight, and then in a few weeks recover, and be as full and heavy as before. Does the body consist of the same particles of matter now that it did before? Certainly not; the waste has been supplied with new matter, and yet the person is conscious of having preserved his identity through all these changes; he is certain that he that thinks and feels now, is he that thought and felt before these changes took place."*

4. But we have no such consciousness that the *body* in which we find ourselves at three-score years, is in its substance the same body in which we played in childhood. If consciousness gives any testimony upon this point, her verdict will be that the outer man has been changing from year to year, during all our pilgrimage, not only in its *form and magnitude*, but also in the very elements of its being.

How different with the mind. Instead of feeling that *that* has changed while these great changes have taken place with the body, we retain amid all these changes, a distinct consciousness of our own spiritual identity—that we are the same identical conscious intelligence that hoped and feared in our childhood bodies sixty years before.†

Now what is the legitimate inference from a fact

* Lee on the Soul, new edition, pp. 33, 34.

† See Moore's Power of the Soul over the Body, p. 15. Also, Butler's essay on personal Identity.

like this, if it be not that the mind is not the body, but is distinct from it; and that however the body may be changed, either gradually or imperceptibly, or suddenly or palpably, that the mind will live on, retaining its personal identity, and its powers undestroyed, through all subsequent bodily mutations.

III. Bishop Butler has thus forcibly stated the same general argument:

"We have already, several times over, lost a great part, or perhaps the whole of our body, according to certain common established laws of nature; yet we remain the same living agents; when we shall lose as great a part, or the whole, by another common established law of nature, death, why may we not also remain the same? That the alienation has been gradual in one case, and in the other will be more at once, does not prove anything to the contrary. We have passed undestroyed through those many and great revolutions of matter, so peculiarly appropriate to ourselves; why should we imagine death to be so fatal to us?

"Nor can it be objected, that what is thus alienated or lost, is no part of our original solid body, but only adventitious matter; because we may lose entire limbs which must have contained many solid parts and vessels of the original body; or if this be not admitted, we have no proof that any of these solid parts are dissolved or alienated by death; though, by the way, we are very nearly related to that extraneous or adventitious matter, whilst it continues united to and distending the several parts of our solid body. But, after all, the relation a person bears to those parts of his body to which he is the most nearly related, what does it appear to amount to but this, that the living agent and those parts of the body mutually affect each other? And the same thing, in kind, though not in degree, may be said of *all foreign* matter, which gives us ideas, and which we have any power over. From these observations, the whole ground of the imagination is removed, that the dissolution of any matter is the destruction of a living agent, from the interest he once had in such matter."*

IV. But an objection to the argument based upon the conscious identity of the mind, amid bodily changes, has been founded upon the acknowledged *sympathy* of the mind with the body, and especially upon the well-known fact that in many cases an injury to the brain destroys consciousness. This would be somewhat forcible, perhaps, were it true that in *every* case where the brain was diseased or partially removed, the *mind* was impaired to the same extent. But if cases occur where even the brain may be seriously injured or disorganized, while the mind remains with all her faculties unimpaired, the objection falls to the ground. The instances of mental derangement in such cases, no more prove that the mind will perish when the entire brain is dissolved, than the unconsciousness of one man during sleep, proves that all who sleep are meanwhile unconscious.

But it is not only true that the soul indicates her immortality by retaining her powers and faculties unimpaired, amid extensive bodily mutilations; but even the *brain*—the especial organ of the mind—may suffer largely, as we have shown in a previous chapter,†

* Analogy, Part I.

† See chapter ix. page 215.

without deranging a thought of the indwelling and undying spirit. And so of the entire body. It is not the soul or any part of it, and may waste and be dissolved without the extinction of that other and higher nature, which is spiritual, indestructible and immortal. As the swift-winged arrow may be speeding on its way, though the bow from which it is sent may be snapped and ruined, and as the light of the fixed stars might continue to shoot on through space for ages, though the stars themselves were suddenly annihilated, so the life of the soul will go on in the future forever, though the body from which it springs at death has crumbled back to dust.

CHAPTER XIII.

ARGUMENT DRAWN FROM THE INDESTRUCTIBILITY OF MATTER.

It has generally been assumed by those who deny the immortality of the soul, that annihilation is even more natural than creation. How that may be we care not to inquire. Neither are we disposed to deny that so far as power to effect the result is concerned, God *could* annihilate the entire universe in a moment of time. But so far as we have any light upon the subject, instead of its being even an occasional event, it seems to be established as a law of nature, that nothing that is once launched into being shall ever go out of existence.

I. Natural philosophy teaches us that of all this vast creation no substance has yet been found, however subtle or refined, which man has power to annihilate, or put utterly out of being. It may be a hailstone or a drop of water, and we may freeze it, or heat it to steam, or decompose it into its elementary gases, and explode it; or evaporate it; but *it still exists*, every atom of it; and disperse or change its elements as we may, they will forever defy all efforts at their annihilation. And so of every substance, solid or fluid, animal, mineral, or vegetable, through the whole realm of nature. *Annihilation* is a name for what never yet occurred to matter, and never can.

"A mass of atoms may be separated and changed from one form to another by chemical and mechanical forces, but not one of them can ever be lost; for in all cases where a body is apparently destroyed, it can be shown experimentally that the parts are only separated, and can be collected again. Thus, when wood is burned in the fire, it appears to be annihilated; but if we collect the products—the smoke and ashes, we shall find the same quantity in weight that existed in the wood. In fact, we shall find a larger amount of matter than was originally contained in the wood, owing to the oxygen of the air which has combined with the wood in the process of combustion.

"When gunpowder is exploded, the products may all be collected again. The same is found true in every case where matter changes its *form* or *composition*. We know that the material atoms of our own bodies are constantly changing, but not one of them is ever annihilated. That atom of matter which was struck from its kindred particles ages since, may have passed through many forms, solid, liquid, and gaseous, perhaps through animal and vegetable bodies, before it entered the kernel of grain, and became a portion of our own system; and there are many changes which it will undergo there before it shall be cast out into the air as pure as at first, to enter other forms and nourish other systems. Matter is thus ever changing, but never destroyed." *

* Gray's Elements of Natural Philosophy, pp. 22, 23.

Here, then, is a distinct intimation of a great law in nature herself, that *change* is not extinction of being; and therefore that *death* may not be the last of man.

II. The Holy Scriptures teach the same philosophy, "Whatsoever God doeth, it shall be forever: nothing can be put to it, nor anything taken from it: and God doeth *it*, that *men* should fear before him."

"*It shall be forever*"—shall always exist. "*Nothing can be put to it.*" A congress of archangels could not add a pebble to the universe. "*Nor anything taken from it.*" All the intelligent universe, God excepted, could not annihilate a grain of sand. "*And God doeth it that men should fear before him.*" This fixedness of the material creation is ordained that we, knowing that whatever God launches into being by his creative fiat, must exist forever, may understand our own immortal destination, and may fear to provoke the unending displeasure of the Almighty.

III. Such being the fact in the material world, namely, that so far as we have knowledge nothing can be annihilated, the advocate of the non-existence of souls after the change of death, reasons against the undeniable and stubborn fact, that all philosophy is against him. Every analogy of nature is a protest against his cold and cheerless creed. In talking of "annihilation," he talks of that which has never yet occurred even to a grain of sand; and employs a name which represents nothing but an imaginary nonentity.*

* Some writer, perhaps Samuel Drew the metaphysician, coined the word *zamiff* to represent an imaginary something as yet unknown, which should be neither matter nor spirit. The term *annihilation* has an analogous import; as it is used to represent an imaginary event that never did occur and never can.

IV. In contemplating this characteristic of the material world, we should not forget that it applies as well to the elements of which our bodies are composed, as to any other.

> Corruption, closely noted, is but a dissolving of the parts.
> The parts remain, and nothing lost, to build a better whole.

The oxygen, and iron, and lime, and phosphorus that enter into the composition of our bodies, are to exist forever. Why, then, should the spirit cease to be?

But it may be replied that the body no longer exists *as a body.* We grant it; but it exists *as matter*, and still retains all its original attributes and capabilities as such, and may live again in other forms and under other auspices from age to age. And if the same be conceded in regard to the essence of the soul, notwithstanding failing powers and perhaps a seeming parenthesis of unconscious being just before death, we shall still have an immortality with all our powers *as spirits* unimpaired and vigorous forever.

We have thus shown that so far as we can learn from all observation and experience, matter is indestructible; and that it is a law of the universe that whatever is once launched into being shall, in one form or another, exist forever.

Now if this be true of *matter* much more of *mind*, unless it can be shown that mind is inferior to and more perishable than matter. If it were granted, even, that the soul is a material substance, its endless existence would be a legitimate inference from the indestructibility of matter. And in proportion as the soul is found *superior* to matter, is the inference strengthened that she might survive, though matter should cease to exist.

Would not the idea of the extinction of the spirit by any means be contrary to all the analogies of nature?

> "Can it be so?
> Matter immortal, and shall spirit die?
> Above the nobler shall less noble rise?
> Shall man alone for whom all else survives,
> No resurrection know? Shall man alone,
> Imperial man be sown in barren ground?
> Less privileged than the grain on which he feeds?"

No! The idea is not only repulsive to every instinct of our natures, but is both irrational and absurd. Shall the pyramids of Egypt resist the corroding power of time, and stand undecayed for ages, when the mind that designed them has long since ceased to exist? Even the body, though doomed to dissolution, will still exist, with all its capabilities of reconstruction and immortal vitality. Why, then, should its occupant and ruler cease to be? The superior utterly perish, while the inferior survives?

> Why should this gross integument endure
> If its undying guest be lost forever?
> Oh! let us keep the soul embalmed and pure,
> In living virtues, that when both must sever,
> Although corruption may our frame consume,
> The immortal spirit in the skies may bloom.

CHAPTER XIV.

THE SOUL IMMATERIAL AND THEREFORE IMMORTAL.

In the preceding chapters our inquiries have been exclusively confined either to the materia. world, or to the relations which the soul sustains to matter, and its phenomena under various material changes. With a few slight exceptions no allusion has been made to the abstract mental and moral powers of man, as furnishing in themselves considered, a strong presumptive argument that the soul is immortal. Let us now pass to this branch of the general argument, namely, to the evidences of immortality which may be drawn *from the powers and susceptibilities of the soul herself.*

I. We think it may safely be assumed at the outset that, if he who made the soul at the first designed her to exist forever, every power and attribute of her being would correspond with this design. Not only her relations to the body, and the various phenomena of life and death would harmonize with the idea of continued existence, as shown in the previous chapters, but the *effects* of all influences brought to bear upon our spiritual natures, while in connection with the body, would be such only as are compatible with the idea of immortal existence after death.

II. If the question of durability related to some

ponderous and solid substance, such as materials for a building, and we had no experience to guide us in its solution; we should most probably proceed *analytically*, to ascertain its composition; its power of resisting heat and cold and moisture; its relation to other durable substances; and how it is affected by the ordinary causes of dissolution. May not a similar process be employed in considering the question of the soul's immortality? True, the soul is not susceptible of physical analysis like a block of granite; and yet so numerous and various are her powers, and so distinct from each other, that their separate contemplation is not wholly unlike the chemical analysis of a compound substance, and the determining of its general character by the study of its component elements. Let us inquire then, whether or not there is anything in the nature or attributes of the soul herself, that foreshadow her continued and conscious existence when the body is dissolved.

III. In the preceding chapter we have shown that continued being is a law of the material universe; and that consequently the soul of man will survive the event of death, unless it can be shown to be more liable to perish than the material world with which it is here connected. Let us now inquire whether the nature of the soul, as a spiritual and indissoluble essence, does not render her future non-existence even less probable than if she were a bar of gold, or a block of marble.

If the soul is really an immaterial essence—a pure spirit—wholly different from the body, in which it dwells, does not that fact *in itself* greatly strengthen the probability that it will continue to exist after the body is dissolved; or, indeed, that it is *in its very nature* incapable of annihilation. But here arises the great question, *Is the soul immaterial?*

IV. Different writers have varied greatly in the prominence which they have given to this question in their productions. *Flavel*, in his "*Treatise on the Soul of Man*," scarcely alludes to it, in a volume extending to nearly five hundred octavo pages.* *Samuel Drew*, the celebrated English metaphysician, makes it more prominent, and treats it more thoroughly and conclusively, in our opinion than any other writer.† But his style is metaphysical, and it requires the closest attention for an ordinary reader to understand and appreciate his arguments. On this account his book, though small in size, and eminently able, has never been a popular one, and his arguments are comparatively unknown. *Dr. Dick*, in his Philosophy of a Future State, barely mentions the subject of the soul's immateriality, but dismisses it, on the ground of the difficulty of so stating the proofs of the fact, as to have them understood and appreciated by ordinary readers. In *Bishop Clark's* recent work, we have little or nothing upon the subject, as a distinct topic.

It is not unlikely that the omission of this argument by modern writers, is to some extent a sort of reaction, caused by the excessive prominence given to it by Mr. Drew, and to the fact alluded to by Dr. Dick, that it is not easy to adapt it to popular apprehension.

Nevertheless, in our view it is an important element in this discussion; and one upon the settlement of which to a great extent the whole question of the

* London edition, 1739.

† Essay on the Immateriality and Immortality of the Human Soul.

soul's immortality depends. In our opinion, therefore, the true course lies between the extremes of an extended metaphysical discussion on the one hand, like that of Mr. Drew, and passing by the question in comparative silence.*

In the first and second chapters of part first we have touched briefly upon the subject, but recur to it again not only on account of its intrinsic importance, but because it is a question belonging as well to the department of rational investigation, as to that of Scriptural proof.

V. The superiority of mind over matter as shown elsewhere is witnessed on every hand. The control of the mind over the body; all the products of art, mechanical ingenuity and skill; and all the wonderful achievements of the human soul in the realm of nature, proclaim her what the Scriptures declare her to be, master of the material creation. Is it likely, then, that mind which exercises this wonderful control is of the same nature as the forms of being over which it reigns? Is it one mere animal having "dominion" over all other animals? Is it one part of the body ruling the other parts?

This very supremacy of man over the lower world, as read in the Scriptures, and seen everywhere in fact, betokens superior power and a superior nature; and as he reigns by his mental and not by his physical superiority,† his rule in this lower world implies a

* Dr. Luther Lee has hit this medium very happily in his work on the Immortality of the Soul, in which he treats this point very clearly and ably, and yet with admirable brevity.

† As a mere animal, and aside from its adaptation to the uses of a rational spirit, the human body is in some respects inferior to many other animals. The horse, and owl, lions, cats, &c., can see where man cannot. In strength, and speed, and hearing, and smelling, and endurance

spiritual nature, by virtue of which he sways his scepter.

VI. That either matter or spirit are indestructible in such a sense that God could not annihilate them, is absurd. He who created can with equal ease destroy the universe. But that he has so constituted both as that they will continue on despite all created powers, we fully believe. The soul is therefore *naturally* immortal; that is, God has *endowed* it with immortality as *a part of its very nature.** It seems to have been the opinion of Mr. Tupper, however, that but for redemption Adam and Eve would have been annihilated.

> "If then, as annihilated by sin, the soul was ever forfeit,
> Godhead paid the mighty price, the pledge hath been redeemed:
> He, from the waters of Oblivion raised the drowning race,
> Lifting them even to himself, the baseless Rock of Ages." †

But we regard this as an erroneous view of the grounds of our immortality. Christ did not die to save us from annihilation, but that the immortal ex-

and instinct, they are inconceivably his superiors. Take from man the single endowment of *reason;* or in other words, dispossess the human body of its indwelling immaterial spirit, and man is of all animals perhaps the most helpless and dependent.

* "Immortality," says Dr. Good, "is in every instance a special gift of the Creator; and so wide is the gulf that exists between the intelligence of man and that of the brute tribes, that there can be no difficulty in conceiving where the line is drawn, and the special endowment terminates. It is an attribute natural to the being of man, merely because his indulgent Maker has made it so; but there is nothing either in natural or revealed religion that can lead us to the same conclusion in respect of brutes; and hence to speak of their *natural immortality* is altogether visionary and unphilosophical.[1]

† Proverbial Philosophy, p. 95.

[1] Book of Nature, p. 331.

istence before us might be one of joy and gladness, and not one of endless remorse and sorrow.

But to return to the point in hand: if the soul is indestructible and immortal, it is so because God wills it, and not because of anything in the nature of either matter or mind, which renders annihilation impossible by the infinite Creator.

The true form of the argument drawn from the spiritual nature of the soul, is, therefore, as we conceive, to infer immortality from the *adaptation* of the soul, as a spirit, to exist forever; and not from any alleged impossibility of annihilation.

The Divine Being *will not* annihilate the souls of men, (a legitimate inference from his doings in the natural world,) and has made them incapable of annihilation by material agencies. We can form no conception of any method by which a pure spirit can be injuriously affected by material contact, or by physical power.

"Material bodies can never act but when they bring their surfaces in contact with each other. As an immaterial substance has no surface, it is a contradiction to suppose that matter can ever be brought into contact with it: to suppose such a contact possible, is to suppose a surface in an immaterial being, which at the same time is excluded by its natural immateriality. Whatever has an exterior must have an interior; and what has both must be extended: and what is thus extended, cannot be immaterial. An immaterial substance, therefore, can have no surface, and that which has no surface can never be brought into contact with that which has; it therefore follows that the soul must be inaccessible to all violence from matter, and that it cannot perish through its instrumentality." *

The soul of man is not a thing to be dissolved, or melted, or frozen, or pulverized. As well attempt to weigh a pain, or solidify a fear; so that if the soul has no power to dread beyond the realm of material creation, her passport to endless existence is clear, and immortality certain.

VII. Even some of the elements around us may aid our conceptions of the powers and capabilities of the immortal spirit. Who can trace the footsteps of the *magnetic currents*, either on our planet or through the celestial spaces? Could not *light* pass through a globe of crystal thousands of miles in diameter without obstruction? or *electricity* through a globe of iron in an instant of time, and experience no hindrance? How, then, with a spirit, which no chains can bind, or material prison detain. Can any one suppose that the angels on one side of our planet, who desire to visit an heir of salvation upon the other side, are obliged to fly around a hemisphere, soaring over continents and seas to reach their destination? If light can pass through the diamond, and electricity through the hardest steel, cannot a celestial being take the shorter route of the earth's diameter, and fly through rocks, and floods, and internal fires, as in the open void of heaven? Must they turn aside whenever they meet a material orb in the celestial spaces? Do they not rather dart through them, as a sunbeam through a window pane, and as if matter had no existence?

And so of the human soul: as a *spirit*, can material

* Drew on the Immortality of the Soul.

bonds confine her, or retard her movements? What retort can hold her, or alchymy dissolve her? What cords can bind her, or enginery crush her? What floods can drown or flames consume her? What men or angels will become her executioners, and undertake the task of her annihilation? Much better attempt to solidify a sunbeam, or convert the lightning's flash into a tangible thunderbolt.

Spirit may control matter, but matter has no dominion over *spirit.* No axe of steel can ever behead her, no polished blade can ever pierce her.

> The soul secure in her existence, smiles,
> At the drawn dagger and defies its point.
> The stars may fade away. The sun himself,
> Grow dim with age, and nature sink in years,
> But she shall flourish in immortal youth,
> Unhurt amid the war of elements,
> The wreck of matter and the crush of worlds.

CHAPTER XV.

POWERS OF THE SOUL—MEMORY.

Who reads his bosom reads immortal life;
Or Nature there, imposing on her sons,
Has written fables: man was made a lie.

In the preceding chapter an argument for the soul's immortality was based upon her nature as a spiritual essence. Let us now proceed to an analysis of her *powers* and *capabilities*, and see if they do not afford evidence in themselves that she is destined to an endless state of existence.

Among the most wonderful of all our faculties is that of MEMORY. It may be defined as the power of the soul to treasure up ideas, and to recall them at will, or have them recalled by association, contrast, &c. Of this power or faculty of the mind, the following may be affirmed:

I. Under favorable circumstances memory may be cultivated to an almost unlimited extent. It is related by Seneca of the Roman orator Hortensius, that, after sitting a whole day at a public sale, he gave an account, from memory, in the evening, of all things sold, with the prices and names of the purchasers; and this account, when compared with what had been taken in writing by a notary, was found to be exact in every particular.

An Englishman, at a certain time, came to Frederic the Great of Prussia, for the express purpose of giving him an exhibition of his power of recollection. Frederic sent for Voltaire, who read to the king a pretty long poem which he had just finished. The Englishman was present, and was in such a position that he could hear every word of the poem; but was concealed from Voltaire's notice. After the reading of the poem was finished, Frederic observed to the author that the production could not be an original one, as there was a foreign gentleman present who could recite every word of it. Voltaire listened with amazement to the stranger, as he repeated, word for word, the poem which he had been at so much pains in composing; and, giving way to a momentary freak of passion, he tore the manuscript in pieces. A statement was then made to him of the circumstances under which the Englishman became acquainted with his poem, which had the effect to mitigate his anger, and he was very willing to do penance for the suddenness of his passion by copying down the work from a second repetition of it by the stranger, who was able to go through with it as before.*

"An instance of remarkable power of memory in an Indian orator, is given in Smith's History of the Colony of New York. In 1689 commissioners from Boston, Plymouth, and Connecticut, had a conference with the five Indian Nations, at Albany; when a Mohawk sachem, in a speech of great length, answered the message of the commissioners,

* Upham's Mental Philosophy, pp. 168, 169.

and repeated all that had been said the preceding day."

"Cyrus knew the names of all the soldiers in his army. Lucius Scipio knew the names of the Roman people. Mithridates, who ruled over twenty-two kingdoms, delivered laws to them in as many languages, and publicly addressed the natives of each kingdom in their own tongue, without an interpreter. Charmidas, or rather Charmeades, could name all the books in a great library as they stood in order. Bonaparte is said to have had, in many respects, a wonderfully-retentive memory. It is related of Moderata Fonte, an Italian lady and an authoress of note, that she could repeat *verbatim*, a sermon or discourse which she had heard but once. The same is related of Thomas Fuller, author of the 'Worthies of England.'"

"Sir Walter Scott possessed a remarkable memory, Hogg, the Ettrick Shepherd, records a striking evidence of this. On a fishing excursion in the Tweed, the party sat down upon the bank. 'Scott,' says the Ettrick Shepherd, 'desired me to sing them my ballad of Gilman's cleuch. Now, be it remembered that this ballad had never been printed; I had merely composed it by rote, and, on finishing it three years before, had sung it once over to Sir Walter. I began it at his request, but at the eighth or ninth stanza I stuck in it, and could not get on with another verse; on which he began it again, and recited it every word from beginning to end. It being a very long ballad, consisting of eighty-eight stanzas, I testified my astonishment, knowing that he had never heard it but once, and even then did not appear to be paying particular attention."

"Sydney Smith had an extraordinary memory always ready. He could repeat pages of poetry, English, Latin, and French—when, where, or how he learned them no one of his family pretended to know; but they were always ready and appropriate in company, when conversation turned that way. The memory of Grotius was so retentive that he remembered almost everything he read."

"Professor Porson possessed a prodigious memory. When a boy at Eton school, he discovered the most astonishing powers of memory. In going up to a lesson one day, he was accosted by a boy in the same form—'Porson, what have you got there?' 'Horace.' 'Let me look at it.' Porson handed the book to the boy, who, pretending to return it, dexterously substituted another in its place, with which Porson proceeded. Being called on by the master, he read and construed Carm. I. x., very regularly. Observing the class to laugh, the master said, 'Porson, you seem to me to be reading on one side of the page, while I am looking at the other; pray whose edition have you?' Porson hesitated. 'Let me see it,' rejoined the master; who, to his great surprise found it to be an English Ovid. Porson was ordered to go on; which he did easily, correctly, and promptly, to the end of the ode."

"It is said that Dr. Leyden had so strong a memory that he could repeat correctly a long act of Parliament, or any similar document, after a single perusal. Woodfall's extraordinary power of reporting the debates in the House of Commons without aid of written memoranda, is well known. During a debate he used to close his eyes and lean with both hands upon his stick, resolutely excluding all extraneous associations. The accuracy and precision of his reports brought his newspaper into great repute. He would retain a full recollection of a particular debate a fortnight after it had occurred, and during the intervention of other debates. He used to say that it was put by in a corner of his mind for future reference." *

Pascal forgot nothing that he ever read or thought. Ben Jonson could recall every line which he had ever written. A blind Scotchman in Glasgow, who died a few years ago, could repeat the entire Scriptures, Old Testament and New.

The Roman emperor Adrian had a memory so tenacious that he recollected every incident of his life, and knew the name of every soldier in his vast army.

Dumas informs us that, when the emperor Napoleon decided to abandon the invasion of England, and attack the emperor of Austria, it was necessary to confide to the chief of his staff not only the idea of the plan of the campaign which he meditated, but, likewise, to develope all the details. He dictated to M. Daru, off-hand, and without once stopping, those memorable instructions, that admirable plan of the campaign, which was executed precisely as he had fixed it, doubtless after profound meditation. In these instructions, the march of every day, the places at which the army should arrive at successive periods, and the place and almost the day on which

* Man all Immortal, pp. 381–383.

the great battle should be fought, were minutely specified. With these previous instructions the actual result corresponded." *

"The power of a strong memory, even in its ordinary, unquickened state, is astonishing. So few people cultivate the memory that they are oftentimes incredulous of well authenticated instances of remarkable retentiveness."

II. It is matter of common experience, that events which we had not thought of for long years, and that we had apparently forgotten, are often brought distinctly to our knowledge again by some accidental remark or incident; so that of all that we have "forgotten" as we call it, or that we are now unable to remember, no man can tell how soon he may be able to remember more or less of which his mind is now wholly oblivious.

III. Distance of time, of itself, seems to have no unfavorable effect upon the memory. The aged remember the events of their youth even more distinctly than recent occurrences. This is no doubt due to the fact that the attention is more easily arrested and fixed in early life than in after years; but even if this be the case, it shows that the lapse of sixty or seventy years has little or no power to obliterate the records of memory.

IV. Under extraordinary excitements it often happens that memory seems to bring forth all her treasures, and to call up in review and in rapid succession, all the events of our past lives. Of the manifestations of this remarkable power of the soul, a few instances may be cited.

* Wayland's Intellectual Philosophy, p. 258.

1. "Mr. R. of Bowland, a gentleman of landed property in the vale of Gala, was prosecuted for a very considerable sum, the accumulated arrears of teind, (or tithe,) for which he was said to be indebted to a noble family, the titulars, (lay impropriators of the tithes.) Mr. R. was strongly impressed with the belief that his father had, by a form of process peculiar to the law of Scotland, purchased these lands from the titular, and therefore that the present prosecution was groundless. But after an industrious search among his father's papers, an investigation of the public records, and a careful inquiry among all persons who had transacted law-business for his father, no evidence could be recovered to support his defence. The period was now near at hand when he conceived the loss of his lawsuit to be inevitable, and he had formed his determination to ride to Edinburgh next day, and make the best bargain he could in the way of compromise. He went to bed with this resolution, and with all the circumstances of the case floating upon his mind, had a dream to the following purpose: His father, who had been many years dead, appeared to him, he thought, and asked him why he was disturbed in his mind. In dreams men are not surprised at such apparitions. Mr. R. thought that he informed his father of the cause of his distress, adding that the payment of a considerable sum of money was the more unpleasant to him, because he had a strong consciousness that it was not due, though he was unable to recover any evidence in support of his belief. 'You are right, my son,' replied the paternal shade; 'I did acquire right to those teinds, for payment of which you are now prosecuted. The papers relating

to the transaction are in the hands of Mr. ——, a writer (or attorney) who is now retired from professional business, and resides at Inveresk, near Edinburgh. He was a person whom I employed on that occasion for a particular reason, but who never, on any other occasion, transacted business on my account. It is very possible,' pursued the vision, 'that Mr. —— may have forgotten a matter which is now of a very old date; but you may call it to his recollection by this token, that when I came to pay his account, there was difficulty in getting change for a Portugal piece of gold, and that we were forced to drink out the balance at a tavern.'

"Mr. R. awoke in the morning, with all the words of his vision imprinted on his mind, and thought it worth while to ride across the country to Inveresk, instead of going straight to Edinburgh. When he came there he waited on the gentleman mentioned in the dream, a very old man; without saying anything of the vision, he inquired whether he remembered having conducted such a matter for his deceased father. The old gentleman could not at first bring the circumstance to his recollection; but, on mention of the Portugal piece of gold, the whole returned upon his memory; he made an immediate search for the papers and recovered them,—so that Mr. R. carried to Edinburgh the documents necessary to gain the cause which he was on the verge of losing."

"There is every reason to believe that this very interesting case is referable to the principle lately mentioned; that the gentleman had heard the circumstances from his father, but had entirely forgotten them, until the frequent and intense application of his mind to the subject with which they were connected at length gave rise to a train of association which recalled them in the dream. So the same principles are referable to the two following anecdotes, which we have received as entirely authentic.

2. "A gentleman of the law in Edinburgh had mislaid an important paper, relating to some affairs on which a public meeting was soon to be held. He had been making most anxious search for it for many days; but the evening of the day preceding that on which the meeting was to be held had arrived, without his being able to discover it. He went to bed under great anxiety and disappointment, and dreamed that the paper was in a box appropriated to the papers of a particular family, with which it was in no way connected; it was accordingly found there in the morning.

3. "Another individual, connected with a public office, had mislaid a paper of such importance, that he was threatened with the loss of his situation if he did not produce it. After a long but unsuccessful search, under intense anxiety, he also dreamed of dis covering the paper in a particular place, and found it there accordingly.*

4. "The following," says Dr. Abercrombie, "occurred to a particular friend of mine, and may be relied upon in its most minute particulars:—

"The gentleman was at the time connected with one of the principal banks in Glasgow, and was at his place at the teller's table, where money is paid, when a person entered demanding payment of a sum of six pounds. There were several people waiting, who were, in turn,

* Abercrombie's Intellectual Philosophy, pp. 203–7.

entitled to be attended before him; but he was extremely impatient, and rather noisy; and, being besides a remarkable stammerer, he became so annoying, that another gentleman requested my friend to pay him his money and get rid of him. He did so, accordingly, but with an expression of impatience at being obliged to attend to him before his turn, and thought no more of the transaction. At the end of the year, which was eight or nine months after, the books of the bank could not be made to balance, the deficiency being exactly six pounds. Several days and nights had been spent in endeavoring to discover the error, but without success; when, at last, my friend returned home, much fatigued, and went to bed. He dreamed of being at his place in the bank, and the whole transaction with the stammerer, as now detailed, passed before him in all its particulars. He awoke under a full impression that the dream was to lead him to a discovery of what he was so anxiously in search of; and, on examination, soon discovered that the sum paid to this person in the manner now mentioned, had been neglected to be inserted in the book of interests, and that it exactly accounted for the error in the balance."*

The following similar instance, is also to the same effect:

5. "A gentleman who was appointed to an office in one of the principal banks in Edinburgh, found on balancing his first day's transactions, that the money under his charge was deficient by ten pounds. After many fruitless attempts to discover the cause of the error, he went home, not a little annoyed by the re-

* Intellectual Philosophy, pp. 203–4.

sult of his first experience in banking. In the night he dreamed that he was at his place in the bank, and that a gentleman who was personally known to him presented a draft for ten pounds. On awaking, he recollected the dream, and also recollected that the gentleman who appeared in it had actually received ten pounds. On going to the bank, he found that he had neglected to enter the payment, and that the gentleman's order had by accident fallen among some pieces of paper, which had been thrown on the floor to be swept away."*

6. It is a well-known fact, that to men brought into sudden peril,—there comes flashing in upon their minds all the scenes of their past life.

"A friend of mine," says Theodore Tilton, "told me, a few days ago, of an accident which occurred to a relative of his while riding through one of the recently broken roads in West Philadelphia. His horse became frightened, and ran away; the rider feared that he would be dashed to pieces upon a pile of stones that lay by the side of the road; but, escaping without harm, he afterwards said that in that one solitary instance of imminent peril, there flashed through his mind a recollection of all past life, —his childhood, his youth, his early manhood, his business affairs, his family." †

7. Numerous instances are on record in which persons who have been recovered from drowning have declared that at a certain period in the process of suffocation, after the lungs had become filled with water, the mind became indescribably clear and

* Intellectual Philosophy, p. 204.

† Lecture in Music Hall, Boston, June, 1860.

active; and that the minutest events of their past lives arose distinctly to view, and passed rapidly before the mind.

"An individual of my acquaintance," says Bishop Clark, "was nearly drowned some years since. He stated that when first precipitated into the foaming deep, he fully realized the hopelessness of his condition; but almost at the very moment the recollection of former events and of former years came rushing upon the memory. Its action was intense and rapid. Everything was remembered with all the distinctness of present life. Incidents, events, acts, words—all started up in rapid succession, till his whole past life seemed to be reflected as from a mirror. His memory seemed to have grasped every event from very childhood to middle life, and hung them up, as though painted on canvas, before the broad glance of the drowning man. Almost by a miracle he was plucked from the very jaws of death; but ever after was he accustomed to dwell with astonishment and wonder upon the singular developments of his memory while the floods—compassed him about, and to declare that he believed it possible for the mind to recollect everything that had ever come within the range of thought and feeling." *

Admiral Beaufort of the British navy had a similar experience under similar circumstances. "Every incident of my life," said he, "seemed to glance across my recollection—not in mere outline, but the whole picture filled up with every minute and collateral feature. The whole period of my existence seemed to be placed before me in a kind of panoramic re-

* Treatise, p. 390.

view, and each act of it seemed to be accompanied by a consciousness of right and wrong."

Such instances might be multiplied, but it is not necessary.

8. In other cases the most astonishing powers of memory have been exhibited under the excitement of disease.

In a Catholic town in Germany, a young woman of four or five-and-twenty, who could neither read nor write, was seized with a nervous fever, during which she was incessantly talking Greek, Latin, and Hebrew, with much pomp and distinctness of enunciation. The case attracted much attention, and many sentences which she uttered, being taken down by some learned person present, were found to be coherent and intelligible, each for itself, but with little or no connection with each other. Of the Hebrew only a small portion could be traced to the Bible; the remainder was that form of Hebrew which is usually called Rabbinic. Ignorant, and simple, and harmless, as this young woman was known to be, no one suspected any deception; and no explanation could for a long time be given, although inquiries were made for that purpose in different families where she had resided as a servant.

Through the zeal, however, and philosophical spirit of a young physician, all the necessary information was in the end obtained. The woman was of poor parents, and at nine years of age had been kindly taken to be brought up by an old Protestant minister, who lived at some distance. He was a very learned man; being not only a great Hebraist, but acquainted also with Rabbinical writings, the Greek and Latin fathers, &c. The passages which had been taken down in the delirious ravings of the young woman, were found by the physician precisely to agree with passages in some books in those languages which had formerly belonged to him. But these facts were not a full explanation of the case. It appeared, on further inquiry, that the patriarchal Protestant had been in the habit for many years of walking up and down a passage of his house, into which the kitchen door opened, and to read to himself with a loud voice out of his favorite books. This attracted the notice of the poor and ignorant domestic whom he had taken into his family; the passages made an impression on her memory; and although probably for a long time beyond the reach of her recollection when in health, they were at last vividly restored, and were uttered in the way above mentioned, in consequence of the feverish state of the physical system, particularly of the brain.*

9. Abercrombie mentions the case of a poor woman, sick in a hospital, who, during a fever, talked in her sleep. The physician drew near to hear what she was saying, and to ascertain whether there was any coherency in her speech. She began to talk of the condition of other patients, describing with singular minuteness the aspects of their disease. The physician queried whether these remarks could apply to any of the patients in the hospital; but, on looking round at the various sick beds, he could see no proper application whatever. Calling some other physicians to examine the case, they all approached the bedside and listened attentively. One of the

* Upham's Mental Philosophy, pp. 185 186.

number remembered the face of the woman as that of a patient who had been in the hospital some two years before, sick with the same fever; and when the attendants were called, they also recognized her, and, as she murmured in her sleep, discovered that her remarks applied with wonderful precision to the sick persons in the hospital two years before. So that those impressions which, during her two years of comparative restoration to health had remained entirely dormant, now again the moment the hand of disease was laid upon her, were quickened into this strange life.

From cases like these, philosophers have concluded that no impression made upon the mind is ever utterly lost. Such was the conclusion of Lord Bacon, and of others after him.

As one has well said, "The resurrection of memory is a physical fact which science has proved and no man can gainsay. Every impression made upon the mind is abiding. What is written on this tablet endures as if it were written on tables of stone. There is no oblivion! The old mythological Water of Lethe, into which a sad thought once dropped, was fabled to be drowned forever, never flowed except in the myth." *

Though we may think we have utterly forgotten and lost a name, or an event, yet such is the constitution of the soul, that some word or incident may call up the long forgotten name or event, the very next moment of our life.

> Lulled in the countless chambers of the brain,
> Our thoughts are linked by many a hidden chain,

* Theodore Tilton, in the Lecture previously referred to.

Awake but one, and lo, what myriads rise !
Each stamps its image as the other flies.

V. Now what is the bearing of all these facts, illustrating the nature and power of the memory, upon the question of the soul's continued existence after death? Perhaps we may better understand their import and force in the light of an illustration or two drawn from the physical world.

1. A naturalist who has never seen a honey bee is called upon to observe its habits, and ascertain whether it has power to survive a northern winter, and live on through the summer, or must perish like the butterfly, by the first frosts of autumn. Watching its habits he observes, first, that it feeds and lives on the nectar and pollen gathered from flowers. In the second place, he observes that it is *storing up* both these elements of life in a secure and warm place, carefully sealing up every vessel, and eating nothing therefrom, till the frosts have killed the flowers, when it opens cell after cell of its stores to supply its daily wants.

Now without waiting for the issue of the coming spring, or even for the effect of intense cold upon the subject of his observations, would not a thoughtful mind inevitably come to the conclusion that whatever might be the result in this particular instance, the Creator *designed* this species of insect to survive confinement, cold and storm, and go forth amid the sunshine of other springs, to taste the sweetness, behold the beauty and breathe the fragrance of newborn flowers, when the rigors of winter have passed away.

2. Take another illustration: A naturalist who

has no knowledge of such an animal, is called upon to dissect the body of a *camel*, in order to ascertain its habits, abode, &c. Coming to the stomach, he finds it to consist of a central sack into which the food descends, and from which it is raised for further mastication, as is the case with the ox, goat, &c. But around this central stomach he finds several other subordinate cavities, so constructed that when filled their mouths are closed tightly by muscular action, or opened at pleasure. Moreover, he finds that some of these side cavities are filled with fresh water, while others are empty; and that although the camel has taken no water for several days, there is a quantity of fresh water in the stomach, as if he had just been drinking.*

From these facts he would infer that the fresh water in the main stomach was from the empty side stomachs—that the animal had power to unseal one of those reservoirs and empty its contents into the stomach proper whenever he was thirsty, or his food needed moistening—that he could drink a large supply of water at a time,—and go a long time without drinking; and was therefore adapted to and designed for *long journeys* over a desert country where water could seldom be obtained. Such would be the testimony of "Reason and Nature" as to the destiny of the species, and its capability of living amid burning sands, where the antelope and the bison would die

* Travelers in the deserts of Arabia are sometimes obliged to slaughter a camel out of their caravans in order to save their own lives by the water found in those wonderful reservoirs. "If worst comes to the worst," said an old Arab, "we can sacrifice one of our camels for the sake of the water which Allah has provided him with a reservoir in his stomach." *Life in the Desert, by L. Du Couret, pp.* 251–283.

of thirst. It would in no wise invalidate the argument to show that in this case the animal was born in a menagerie, and had never had occasion to store up water for long journeys over burning deserts. The use or disuse of his peculiar physical organism is an indifferent incident. His Creator has constructed the species so that they are adapted to and capable of such journeys, as no other animal is; they are therefore made for them; and, as a species destined to such journeys.

3. Let the same process of reasoning be applied to the problem of immortality. As the bee stores up the food on which she feeds in summer in quantities sufficient for the ensuing winter, so the mind treasures up in the store-house of memory the elements of her manifested life, and indicates unmistakably her power to retain and under favorable circumstances to reproduce every idea ever committed to her charge.

But of what avail would be this wonderful instinct of the bee, if she were destined to die in autumn, and leave all her treasures of food untasted? Not to speak irreverently would not such an anomaly be characterized as a mistake in the economy of Nature? Is not that frugal instinct in itself a prophecy of continued being in other years? So of the faculty of memory—is it not also a prophecy of the continued being of the soul when the vicissitudes of this mortal life are forever past?

And if the physical economy of "the ship of the desert," in itself indicates both her capabilities and her destination, does not the faculty of memory indicate with equal clearness that the soul of man is adapted to the long journey of immortality, and will open up all her treasures of thought and of knowledge in the world beyond the grave.

> Then shall the soul around her call,
> The treasures that she gathered here;
> And painted on the eternal wall,
> The past shall re-appear.

VI. The ability of the soul to re-produce, under favorable circumstances, all the events, words and thoughts of its past experience, has led some to regard the memory of man as one of the "books" to be opened in the day of judgment, and from which all men are to be judged. Rev. xx. 12. However that may be, of one thing we may be assured, that in the life to come all the scenes of the present life will rise again to view on the enduring tablet of memory, to become a source of joy or of sorrow through all the years of eternity.

> Each fainter trace that memory holds,
> So darkly of departed years,
> At one broad glance the soul beholds,
> And all that was at once appears!

If we add to a memory that will reproduce all the past; even "every vain and idle word," a conscience so quickened as not only to discriminate the nicest shades of right and wrong, of guilt and innocency, but also to tear the soul with keenest sense of guilt and of agonizing remorse, may we not have the embodiment of "the worm that dieth not, and the fire that shall never be quenched?" Mark ix. 45.

But as this question leads us beyond the range of our appropriate inquiry, we dismiss it to continue the argument for immortality based upon the powers of the soul herself.

CHAPTER XVI.

POWERS OF THE SOUL CONTINUED—RAPIDITY OF OUR MENTAL PROCESSES.

In man the more we dive, the more we see
Heaven's signet stamping an immortal make.

I. INTUITION is defined as "the act by which the mind perceives the agreement or disagreement of two ideas, or the truth of things, immediately, or the moment they are presented, without the intervention of other ideas, or without reasoning or deduction."* This may be sufficiently correct for a popular definition, and yet we think it needs qualifying. If it had said "without *conscious* reasoning or deduction," we believe it would have been more strictly correct. Is not what we call intuition a conclusion reached by a process of reasoning so rapid, that we are simply unconscious of it? Is not an intuition, so called, a *conclusion* or *judgment*, even though reached in an instant? and if so—is it not based upon some *data* or *premises*, which are the basis of the intuition?

We may not be able to point out the grounds of our intuition, in any given case, or to detect a process of reasoning, and yet such grounds exist, beyond all question, and govern our intuitions; and whether

* Webster.

conscious of it or not, every intuition is a process of reasoning instantaneously consummated. All intuitions, therefore, are specimens of the rapidity of our mental processes.

II. The rapidity with which an experienced accountant will add up long columns of figures, without error, affords another illustration of the same power. How inconceivably rapid must be the mental action in such cases. Beginning on the right the form of the first figure is first noted, from which the number of units it represents is ascertained. This noted, the operator passes to the next, carrying with him a distinct idea of the amount of the first figure. He passes to the second, notes its form, ascertains its value, adds it to the first, ascertains the amount, and with this new amount passes to the third figure, and so on to the end of the first column, and from column to column. A great variety of distinct acts take place in the mind, in regard to each figure; and yet thousands of persons will add a column of figures the height of an ordinary ledger page, and extending to five or six figures in width, in half the time it will take to read this paragraph.

III. The case of Truman Henry Safford, furnishes an illustration in point.

"After a very superficial attendance at a country school in Vermont, with an attenuated frame and feeble health, this boy, at the age of nine years and six months, produced the "Youth's Almanac for 1846," having made all the calculations of eclipses, the rising and setting of the sun, &c., &c., without any assistance whatever; and that recently, in the thirteenth year of his age, and in the same unassisted manner, he calculated the orbit of the telescopic comet of November, 1848, and with an accuracy, as I am informed, which is corroborated by the best astronomers. The interrogatories were of a very difficult nature, resolved mentally and according to the rules of science, and generally with great instantaneousness. For the purpose of testing the reach of his mind in computation, he was finally asked to "multiply *in his head* 365,365,365,365,365,365, by 365,365,365,365,365,365. He flew round the room like a top, and pulled his pantaloons over the top of his boots, bit his hand, rolled his eyes in their sockets, until, in not more than one minute, said he, 133,491, 850,208,566,925,016,658,299,941,583,225. What was still more wonderful, he began to multiply at the left hand, and to bring out the answer from left to right, giving first, 133,491, &c. Here, confounded above measure, I gave up the examination." *

Here we have the most satisfactory proof that a mere boy multiplied 365,365,365,365,365,365, by 365,365,365,365,365,365, in "not more than one minute," and gave the correct product!

Now whether it were performed in a day or a minute, one thing is certain; and that is, that the numerical value of each figure must have been distinctly comprehended, and also its increased value, as affected by its distance from the first figure on the right. Then each of the separate figures of the first line, must be multiplied by each of those in the second; and finally the result of each distinct multiplication must be added up, as one grand total.

But there are eighteen distinct figures in each

* Paine on the Soul, Instinct and Life, pp. 51, 52.

line. To multiply the eighteen figures in the first line, by the first figure of the second line, will require eighteen distinct multiplications, the product of which will be unlike in each distinct instance; and as there are eighteen distinct figures by which the first line is to be multiplied, there must be three hundred and twenty-four distinct multiplications, to say nothing of the effort of remembering each figure of the products, and their places, and of adding up the whole, mentally, without slate or blackboard. And all this in one minute! It seems incredible, and yet it cannot reasonably be doubted.

IV. Another illustration of this wonderful power of the soul, is found in the phenomena of dreaming. Events which would take whole days or weeks are sometimes gone through with in our dreams in a few minutes. The jarring of a door, which awakens us by its opening, may cause us to dream of robbers, or other calamities, in the very instant of awaking.

"A friend of mine," says Abercrombie, "dreamed that he crossed the Atlantic, and spent a fortnight in America. In embarking on his return, he fell into the sea; and, having awoke with the fright, discovered that he had not been asleep above ten minutes."

Count Lavallette, who some years since was condemned to death in France, relates a dream which occurred during his imprisonment as follows: "One night while I was asleep, the clock of the Palais de Justice struck twelve and awoke me. I heard the gate open to relieve the sentry; but fell asleep again immediately. In this sleep I dreamed that I was standing in the Rue St. Honoré, at the corner of the Rue de l'Echelle. A melancholy darkness spread around me; all was still; nevertheless, a low and uncertain sound arose. All of a sudden, I perceived at the bottom of the street, and advancing towards me, a troop of cavalry, the men and horses, however, all flayed. This horrible troop continued passing in a rapid gallop, and casting frightful looks on me. Their march, I thought, continued for five hours; and they were followed by an immense number of artillery-wagons, full of bleeding corpses, whose limbs still quivered; a disgusting smell of blood and bitumen almost choked me. At length the iron gate of the prison shutting with great force, awoke me again. I made my repeater strike; it was no more than midnight; so that the horrible phantasmagoria had lasted no more than two or three minutes; that is to say, the time necessary for relieving the sentry and shutting the gate. The cold was severe and watchword short. The next day the turnkey confirmed my calculations."

"Our dreams not unfrequently go through all the particulars of some long journey, or of some military expedition, or of a circumnavigation of the globe, or of other long and perilous undertakings, in a less number of hours than it would take weeks or months, or even years, actually to perform them. We go from land to land, and from city to city, and into desert places; we experience transitions from joy to sorrow, and from poverty to wealth; we are occupied in the scenes and transactions of many long months; and then our slumbers are scattered, and behold they are the doings of a fleeting watch of the night."*

V. The power of the soul to conduct her processes with inconceivable celerity is seen again in those instances of fright and of apparent drowning, recorded in a previous chapter.† Not only is memory true to reproduce the past, without a trace obliterated, but it is done in an instant. So far as reviewing every event of our past experience is concerned, so rapid is our mental action, under circumstances adapted to call into play the power of the soul, that it is but the work of a moment. From such developments we are warranted in the conclusion that under favorable circumstances the soul of man may be capable of minutely reviewing the history of our globe from the dawn of time to its close, in a single hour! We must not judge of the future even by our sublimest achievements in this mortal life. It doth not yet appear what we shall be. Oh what glory and bliss may await the righteous, even in the exercise of his mental powers alone! With the universe for his text book, a world taken at a lesson, and eternity for his school-days, who can anticipate the lofty goal to which he may at length ascend? Though now a little lower than the angels, may not the period arrive in the glorious future, when the present attainments of seraphim and cherubim shall appear to God's ransomed people but as the rudest elements of knowledge, the mere alphabet of man's intellectual endowments.

VI. Still another illustration of the rapidity of our

* Upham's Mental Philosophy, pp. 113, 114.

† See especially, page 268, of chapter xv.

mental processes, may be found in the flights of the imagination. Let this power be excited, and how marvelous the speed of thought!

> How swift is a glance of the mind,
>   Compared with the speed of its flight,
> The tempest itself lags behind,
>   And the swift-winged arrows of light.

Or as another has more strikingly depicted the same power of the soul,

> How swift thought travels. Lo the cannon's flash,
> The swift-winged lightnings, and the whirlwind's dash,
> Much slower move. Hoarse thunder's leaping sound,
> Hurled orbs careering through the void profound,
> And Time, swift charrioteer, all fly behind
> The speed of thought! Sunlight, our servant kind,
> Along the extended void each minute flies,
> Twelve million miles to greet our waiting eyes;
> Yet swifter thought. Yes, this winged power of soul,
> Can travel round the globe, call at each pole,
> Visit the Moon, the portals of the Sun,
> Thence step from world to world, through systems run,
> O'er fields of stars where blazing comets stray,
> To Nature's verge; trace back time's traveled way,
> Six thousand years to where creation rose,
> Thence back and onward to creation's close;
> To Heaven's metropolis where seraphs burn,
> And, but one minute gone, to earth return,
> Without the least fatigue; but ready quite,
> To stretch her wings, and take another flight.*

Such is the celerity with which the soul is capable of carrying on her various processes of remembering and reasoning and imagination. How wonderful, then, how subtle and ethereal must be that mysterious nature which is capable of such feats of activity. She has no inertia to be overcome by mechanical force; no liability to burst asunder like a Sheffield grind-stone,

* Triumph of Truth, by Rev. Charles Giles.

from her too rapid revolutions; and no tendency to spontaneous combustion from excessive friction.

Though she act with the speed of lightning, there is no material manifestation, no friction, no noise. Though she outstrips the sunbeams in the race, her form shall cast no shadow as she passes, nor jostle a dew-drop from the morning flowers. All this she can do because she is *a spirit*. Were she of earth, she must needs move like earthly things, and like them, might perish at last; but spurning the dull tediousness of inert matter, she acts like a celestial being, and thus proclaims, both her title to and her fitness for an immortal state of existence.

CHAPTER XVII.

POWERS OF THE SOUL CONTINUED—CAPABILITIES OF IMPROVEMENT, AND VAST ACHIEVEMENTS.

CONTINUING our analysis of the powers and susceptibilities of the soul, let us now look at her capacity for improvement, as compared with the lower animals, and as in some measure attested by her achievements even during this brief and inauspicious life.

I. That reason and instinct are not identical, we shall not pause to argue at length. When we see the lower tribes endowed with instinct to select their food; swim if thrown into the water; hide upon the approach of danger, &c., from the day of birth,—to migrate with unerrring precision, both as to the time and the direction, and a thousand other things for which man has no corresponding instinct, it is obvious that the Creator gave instinct to be the guide of the lower animals, leaving man to be governed by the higher endowment of *reason*. Hence man has but a single instinct, and that is to draw his food from his mother's breast; and even that is supplanted by reason before six months have elapsed. On the other hand the birds of the air, the quadrupeds, the insect tribes, and even the fish of the sea, are all richly endowed with various instincts, which continue through life, but have scarce a semblance of reason.

II. But though the endowment of instinct usually remains during the life of its possessor, there is no improvement. The beaver builds his dam and his house during the last year of his life, precisely as he did the first; and those of this generation precisely like those of a thousand generations past. So of the bee; she builds her honey-comb to-day, precisely as in the days of Samson or of David, three thousand years ago. And so on through all the animal tribes. There is no progress; no invention, no improvement upon the past, no building upon the acquisitions of preceding generations. Though some of them may live for a century, they reach their zenith of knowledge in a few short years, at longest, and can go no further.

A horse becomes accustomed to his stable;—it takes fire, but it is impossible to remove him except by deception or force; and even when fairly out, if left free to follow his instincts he will rush back into the flames and perish. And yet he is one of the most sagacious of animals. But capable as he may be of improvement in minor things, probably a century of training would fail to give him reason enough not to rush into the jaws of certain death, merely because he has been in the habit of being fed and of resting in a building now wrapped in flames. Such is the *quality* of the "reason" which materialism insists upon according to the brute creation.

III. From these undeniable facts, look now at the progressive character of reason. Step by step and link by link, the soul moves onward and upward from one principle to another, and from premises to remote conclusions, till she plants herself above the stars. So far as we know, there is no limit to her capacity for storing up knowledge. Failing bodily powers may arrest her progress and obscure her light for a time, but this argues nothing against continued vigor in the intermediate state nor when the soul shall come to dwell in her resurrection body. Even in this life, both the field of investigation and the capacity of improvement may be regarded as unlimited.

> Were man to live coeval with the sun,
> The patriarch pupil would be learning still,
> Yet, dying, leave his lesson half unlearned.

With all the disabilities under which the mind of man exists in our present fallen state, the capability of endless progress in knowledge is as apparent as the ability to acquire knowledge at all. In this we discover the broad line of demarkation which distinguishes man from the beast that perishes.

IV. In further illustration of the capacity of man for acquiring knowledge, look at his actual achievements in the various fields of human research. Take the sciences, for example. Here is one man, who like Solomon, knew every plant, and shrub, and flower, and tree, from the cedar of Lebanon, to the hyssop upon the wall. 1 Kings iv. 33. He can tell you of the structure, and habits, and abode of each, whether in the valleys or on the hills, on the land or in the depths of the sea. Another makes geology his study, and can tell you the origin, and age, and peculiarities of every rock, and gem, and mineral, and fossil in all the earth. It is his delight to dwell amid "the chief things of the ancient mountains, and the precious things of the lasting hills." Deut. xxxiii. 13. Another is equally familiar with the geography of every part of the globe, its continents and oceans, rivers and mountains, climate and productions. And so of optics and magnetism, pneumatics and chemistry, natural history and astronomy, mathematics and languages, mental philosophy and logic, rhetoric and history, physiology and medicine, law and theology, architecture, navigation, mechanics, invention, poetry, sculpture, and painting; and a thousand other minor departments of knowledge and skill which we cannot enumerate.

And how wonderful the elevation to which man has attained in each of these departments.

> Earth's disembowel'd! measured are the skies!
> Stars are detected in their deep recess!
> Creation widens! Vanquish'd Nature yields!
> Her secrets are extorted! Art prevails!
> What monuments of genius, spirit, power!

The astronomer will predict a transit or an eclipse to a minute a thousand years to come, and tell you precisely where it will or will not be visible on the earth's surface, and its precise extent and duration. So familiar is he with the mechanism of the heavens, and with "the geometry of God." The chemist will separate the gold from the silver, though thoroughly fused and blended together; or detect the smallest quantity of arsenic, though scattered through the whole human body. The physiologist knows every bone, and muscle, and artery, and vein, and nerve, and gland, and organ, from the crown of the head to the sole of the foot, with their proper offices, and functions, and perhaps the symptoms of every disease, and the effect of every remedy. And thus on through every department of human research.

No matter what speciality we single out, the amount that is already known by man in that single department is almost overwhelming to our contemplations. Think of all that is known of language, of history, of mathematics, of architecture, and of the mechanical arts. Look at the immense libraries, embracing scores of volumes in each branch of study. Look at the collections of minerals, and shells, and birds, and quadrupeds, and reptiles, and fishes, and insects gathered by man, to aid him in his investigations. There are enough objects of scientific interest in the Smithsonian Institute in Washington, or in the Academy of Natural Science in Philadelphia, to bewilder and almost overwhelm an ordinary observer. Go to the Patent Office in Washington and look at the fifty thousand models, more or less, deposited there by inventors. Think of the research and mental power of which each model is an embodiment.

In a word the height of knowledge to which man has attained in each department of skill and of knowledge is almost overwhelming to the common understanding. And yet, judging from the achievements of the last half century, our progress even in this world is but just begun. Look at the advance in the use of steam since Robert Fulton launched his first steam boat. So of the daguerreotype, of telegraphing, of printing, and stereotyping, and a thousand other branches of human industry.

> Whose footsteps these ?—Immortals have been here,
> Could less than souls immortal this have done ?
> Earth's covered o'er with proofs of souls immortal,
> And proofs of Immortality forget.

But we must forbear. The mind grows weary under the contemplation of even the briefest outline of the accomplished attainments of the human soul.

V. But it is not necessary to embrace all this in order to secure a foundation for the inference that the soul of man is immortal. The capability of unlimited progress is seen in the development of the mind in each particular case, without this overwhelming survey of the already hoarded treasures of the immortal spirit. The locomotive that comes thundering along the valleys, and burrowing through the hills with its thousands of passengers, or its hundreds of tons of merchandise, ascending the steep grade like a Titan, and scorning fatigue, and yet manageable as an infant, proclaims by every shout that it sends out on the air, reverberating along the hills, "*my builder is immortal!*" And such is the voice of every cotton factory, every cathedral, every steamer, every suspension bridge, every iron-clad war ship, every steam printing-press, every sewing or knitting-machine, every chronometer, or mariner's compass, diving-bell, or balloon.

The *works* of man are the witnesses of his capacity for improvement, the living monument attesting his adaptation to another state of existence.

VI. Should it be replied that although the amount of knowledge acquired by man is almost inconceivably vast, no one mind has comprehended it all—that it has been gathered by different persons, in different lands and ages, by each pursuing a speciality; we admit the fact, but deny that it vitiates the argument. Why does the linguist, for instance, devote his life to the study of language? Is it because he is *incapable* of learning history, or science, or law, or medicine? By no means; but because this life is too short to allow him to explore the whole field. Like a poor student, who can afford but a single term at an academy, and who, wishing to turn his opportunities to the best account, selects writing and book-keeping as his studies, and devotes all his time and energies to them; so with man here. His student life is too short for him to pursue the entire course which the Creator has placed before him. He must choose his speciality and pursue it, turn his attainments to the best account during this short life, and await the developments of the world to come.

It is not, then, a want of *capacity* that restricts him, but a want of *time*. How often have individuals been found who were equally at home in several vast fields of learning. And suppose vigor, and life, and opportunities were extended for centuries, who can say that the soul of one man is not fully competent to acquire all the knowledge within the reach of mankind? That the human soul is capable of this there can be no doubt. With the universe for our text-book, and eternity for our school-days, well may the apostle say, "it doth not yet appear what we shall be."

VII. Let us now apply these facts, illustrative of the powers of the soul, to the question of her continued existence after death. Have they such scope in this brief life, as to justify their bestowment by an all-wise Creator? Would a kind parent send his son to toil over Greek, and Latin, and mathematics, who knew that he must die before he could graduate? And is not the Deity equally economical in the bestowment of powers and opportunities? If so, the very *capacity* of the human soul for endless improvement, is both a token and a pledge that her way shall be onward, and that she is destined to another and an endless state of existence.

> Say, can a soul possessed
> Of such extensive, deep, tremendous powers,
> Enlarging still, be but a finer breath,
> Of spirits dancing through their tubes,
> And then forever lost in vacant air?

"When I consider," says Cicero, "the wonderful activity of the mind, so great a memory of what is past, and such a capacity of penetrating into the future; when I behold such a number of arts and sciences, and such a multitude of discoveries thence arising; I believe, and am firmly persuaded, that a nature which contains so many things within itself cannot be mortal." *

The progressive character of reason, and the capability of the soul for unlimited improvement, constitute a natnral argument for immortality that might well impress the mind of a heathen philosopher. And if it was of weight then, when science and the arts were but in their infancy, how is it now, when the achievements of the human mind are augmented an hundred fold? And yet our education is but just begun. We see but through a glass darkly, and know but in part. We have capacity for limitless improvement, but lack time and opportunity for full development. Shall, then these latent powers slumber unimproved forever? Are not the tiny unspread wings of the chrysalis a sure omen and pledge of its destination to flit from field to field and from flower

* De Senectute, Cap. 21.

to flower, as the gorgeous butterfly?* So of the powers of the soul, as yet undeveloped in this life.

> Nor are our powers to perish immature;
> But after feeble effort here, beneath
> A brighter sun, and in a nobler soil,
> Transplanted from this sublunary bed,
> Shall flourish fair, and put forth all their bloom.

* "The worm that crawls upon the ground and prepares its own grave in which to wait for its coming transformation, yet bears on its unsightly form those very prominences which mark the places of gold and silver spangles on the wings of the released and soaring insect."

CHAPTER XVIII.

IMMORTALITY INFERABLE FROM THE NATURE OF OUR DESIRES.

Our heads, our hearts, our passions, and our powers,
Speak the same language, call us to the skies.

In the last three chapters we have spoken somewhat at length of the powers of the soul, as furnishing a natural argument for immortality. Let us now turn from this survey of our intellectual energies, to the contemplation of our *desires.*

1. The *thirst for knowledge* which is so common to man, and which is exhibited in the natural curiosity of all men, as well as in the toils and achievements of the student, is incapable of satisfactory explanation, except upon the hypothesis of a future state of existence.

How true is it, that "the eye is not satisfied with seeing, nor the ear filled with hearing." Prov. i. 8. No matter how much knowledge one has acquired, he still thirsts and toils for more, till failing bodily powers arrest his upward progress, and terminate his earthly being in the midst of the race, his soul more conscious of its powers and capabilities than ever before, and more eager to reach a higher goal than at the beginning of its journey.

"I know not," said Sir Isaac Newton, "what I may appear to the world; but to myself I seem to have been only like a boy playing on the sea-shore, and diverting myself in now and then finding a smoother pebble or a prettier shell than ordinary, whilst the great ocean of truth lay all undiscovered before me. And yet, these 'smoother pebbles," which he had found, were the laws of gravitation which hold the stars in their serene courses, standing as pillars of adamant underneath them; these "prettier shells," were the method of Fluxions and the Binomial Theorem, a theory of colors established upon thousands of costly experiments, and laws of light so subtle and beautiful that their imprint upon science seemed to give it a new and celestial illumination."

"When William Herschell, dissatisfied with the musical profession to which he had been bred, determined to devote himself to the study of the stars, and to the minute investigation of their motions and laws, he found no telescope that could answer the demands of his exquisite and searching mind. He therefore determined to construct one for himself; and after what seemed to others a marvelous labor, he completed a refractor five feet in length. But this was not sufficient; and speedily transcending it he turned from the heavens, and commenced the construction of another more adequate to his enlarged wants, not ceasing from the effort till it was rewarded by the completion of an instrument seven feet in length, perhaps the most remarkable 'optic glass' at that time possessed by any similar observer.

"But still this could not give him all the answers which he sought to his nightly inquiries; so that the labors which had been for a little suspended were again renewed to construct another, now of ten feet; and yet a little while later, another still, of twenty feet in focal length. And it was not till at last he had planned and built that magnificent instrument erected at Slough, with its tube of forty feet in length, slung up amid pillars, braces, and beams, like a very mortar of observations bombarding the skies,—with its speculum of almost fifty inches in superficial diameter, and with its magnifying power of 6,500—that he was measurably satisfied with his apparatus for study.

"And even then, it is on record that this equipment did not fully meet his desires; and that nothing but what seemed the insuperable difficulties of the work at his age, prevented the erection of a still more stupendous instrument, before which the new nebula which he had discovered should be resolved into suns, or be shown the misty seed-plots of worlds, and by whose continued micometrical measurements of the relations of the fixed stars, the elements of the parallax should at last be ascertained.

"So always the scientific judgment of man is instinctively running forward to new attainments, and a more complete mastery. It treats all instruments, the most elaborate and complete, as the traveler upon the mountain treats the staff which he has cut in a hedge by the way-side; only using it as a helper, and throwing it away when the end has been gained, or retaining it as a memento of the course it has assisted. It will never pause satisfied, this faculty of the judgment, with any result accessible in time; but conscious of capacities unexhausted by use, and superior to any defined acquirement, it will press still upward till the universe shall be scrutinized, and then only will rest when clearly and fully it has reproduced by its analysis the thought of the Almighty.

"It is very instructive and impressive to observe, too, how age, in the absence of physical disease, and of protracting pain, does not oppose or retard this spontaneous movement. The principle of curiosity, as an intellectual principle, the desire for true and satisfying knowledge,—and the power of the judgment to satisfy this desire, exploring and explaining what attracts its attention,—both grow as they are used, while that use is legitimate and fills God's plan; and they are never so strong, unless sickness exhausts and shatters the frame, as when the studies already prosecuted have been largest and most profound. To the end of his life, the student whose frame remains unshaken, writes on morals and history, on science and on fine art, and his inquiries in all the departments of nature are marked by as keen and strenuous an enthusiasm as when in his youth he traversed the hills and the valleys on foot. As the skiff, which the boy builds, grows at last to the steamship, and the hut of the pioneer, to the palace which the citizen rears and adorns,—while yet neither of these is felt to be final with him, or adequate to the highest conception he can form,—so the thought of the child expands and accumulates to the science of manhood, and still is admitted insufficient.

"In this, then, we see, unmistakably declared, the

capacity of the soul for still higher attainments, through the use of its constructive and analytic power examinining truth, when it passes from the present to a future state of being. The fact that it goes on still triumphing and enlarging as long as it here is properly used,—unexhausted by its endeavors, yet still unsatisfied with any result, so far as we can follow or trace it,—seems a promise and the prophecy, if not the proof of the fact, that if its existence outlasts that of the body, a yet higher mission, on a more noble sphere, may be hereafter given it to accomplish. Having looked at the stars from beneath, and from afar, it may, with superior and immediate vision look upon them from above, when treading on the pavement, whose dust they are." *

"Were a man sure," says Dr. Moore, "that he could not possibly possess a better than this earthly life, to look off from this dull cold spot would only be to aggravate his doom. The glory of distant worlds would fall like a blight upon his being, for it would suggest possibilities of intelligence and delight forever beyond his reach." †

'Tis Immortality, 'tis that alone
Amid life's pains, abasements, emptiness,
The soul can comfort, elevate, and fill.

II. The *desire to be remembered on earth after we are dead*, may also be reckoned among the indices of our coming immortality.

How few are willing to be forgotten when the grave shall cover them.

* Graham Lectures, by Rev. Richard S. Storrs, Jr., D.D. pp. 290–294.

† Power of the Soul, &c., Harper's ed., p. 9.

For who, tc dumb forgetfulness a prey.
This pleasing anxious being e'er resign'd,
Left the warm precincts of the cheerful day,
Nor cast one longing, lingering look behind?

Men have even been known to commit deeds of infamy, that their names might be perpetuated on the records of time. Now upon what principle is this fact to be accounted for, if man is not destined to survive the stroke of death? Is it not in reality an outgrowth of the innate conviction, which despite all theories to the contrary, pervades the soul, that our being is not to end with the dissolution of the mortal body, and that in some way we may still have an interest in the living and conscious universe, and may wish to be remembered beyond the change of death?

"Why otherwise," says Dr. Dick, "should men be anxious about their reputation, and solicitous to secure their names from oblivion, and to perpetuate their fame, after they have descended into the grave? To accomplish such objects, and to gratify such desires, poets, orators, and historians, have been flattered and rewarded; to celebrate their actions monuments of marble and of brass have been erected to represent their persons, and inscriptions engraved in the solid rock, to convey to future generations a record of the exploits they had achieved. Lofty columns, triumphal arches, towering pyramids, magnificent temples, palaces, and mausoleums, have been reared, to eternise their fame, and to make them live as it were, in the eyes of their successors, through all the future ages of time. But, if the soul be destined to destruction at the hour of death, why should man be anxious about what shall happen, or what shall not happen hereafter, when he is reduced to a mere non-entity, and banished forever from the universe of God? He can have no interest in any events that may befall the living world when he is cancelled from the face of creation, and when the spark of intelligence he possessed is quenched in everlasting night." *

III. The *almost universal discontent* of man in this world is a prophecy of another state of existence.

Not only is it true of an Alexander that when the civilized world had been brought under his sceptre, he sighed and wept that he had not another world to conquer; † but the same principle is indigenous in every heart. Where do we find the person who is satisfied and quite contented? No matter what wealth, or fame, or knowledge, or power, or earthly pleasures; man still sighs for more. The patient ox, that has satisfied his appetite from the green and fresh pastures, seeks a couch upon the same soft carpet, and as he lies there ruminating, he is the living embodiment of satisfaction and contentment. Not a thought of future want disturbs his perfect tranquility. Not a desire of his nature remains unsatisfied, or is still reaching out for further gratification. Not so with man. From the king upon his throne, to the beggar upon the dunghill, all sigh for something beyond their present possessions and enjoyments.

* Philosophy of a Future State, Part I., Chap. i., Sec. 2.

† Augustus said even of the infamous Herod the Great, that his soul was too great for his kingdom. Watson's Theological Dictionary, Article Herod.

Man, ill at ease,
In this, not his own place, this foreign field,
Where Nature fodders him with other food
Than was ordained his cravings to suffice,
Poor in abundance, famish'd at a feast,
Sighs on for something more when most enjoyed.

Of the fact here asserted there will be no dispute. What, then, is its explanation? Has the Creator made "the beast that perishes," to find his every desire gratified, while man is created with immortal longings that shall have no satisfactory response either in time or in eternity?

Is Heaven then kinder to thy flocks than thee?
Not so; thy pasture richer, but remote;
In part remote; for that remoter part
Man bleats from instinct, though, perhaps, debauch'd
By sense, his reason sleeps, nor dreams the cause.
The cause how obvious, when his reason wakes!
His grief is but his grandeur in disguise,
And discontent is immortality!

The leopard or tiger that paces his cave hour after hour, the very genius of discontent, shows, by his very restlessness, that he was not created for the menagerie, but for the far reaching jungle. So of the human soul in the present life.

Man's misery declares him born for bliss;
His anxious heart asserts the truth I sing,
And gives the sceptic in his head—the lie.

IV. The *nature*, *influence*, and *universal prevalence* of *hope*, point unmistakably to another state of being beyond the grave.

We speak not here of the hope of the Christian, which entereth to that within the veil, and apprehends as its object a blissful immortality; but of those hopes that relate to future earthly objects, and are ever pointing to brighter scenes and happier years to come.

> Hope springs eternal in the human breast;
> *Man* never *is*, but always *to be* bless'd.

Though the promised objects are seldom reached, and, when attained, never satisfy the promises and expectations of the past, yet the soul is ever ready to receive each new promise with implicit confidence, so that life is made up of a succession of eager races from goal to goal, till the race of probation is run, and the goal eternal is reached.

Now why is this if man has but one life? Why this stretching out of her arms into the coming future at all, if the soul expires at death? Or, if she be constituted thus to gaze upon ideal bliss in years whose arrival she may never greet, why has not her Maker provided that at least in all such cases, the reality of what *is* enjoyed shall fully equal the brightest visions of hope?

But not so. We still hope and sigh for coming happiness, and are incapable of throwing off faith in the enchanting future, or becoming wise by our repeated disappointments. How strange if there is no future for man beyond the grave!

> The darkest of enigmas human hope;
> Of all the darkest, if at death we die.

Upon that dark hypothesis nature, reason, mental philosophy, all fail to furnish us with a key to the strange anomaly. But grant a Future Life and all is clear. The race we run under the stimulus of this wonderful power, is but a phase of a celestial attraction ordained of Heaven to draw us to the skies. The momentum generated under its impulses, bearing us onward through life, from stage to stage, was designed not so much to speed each minor and earthly race, as to bear the soul onward toward the heavenly goal, and finally across the river of death to her native country above. And the successive disappointments of this life, that are so soon and so easily retrieved by a new promise and hope cast into the distant future, are obviously intended to teach us that our rest and happiness are not to be found below —a lesson appropriate only to beings destined to immortality.

Thus, while on the one hand the soul is lured on by hope to her endless abode, she is weaned from earth by repeated disappointments, and taught to look for realization and satisfaction, not in this world, but rather in that beyond the tomb. Oh how salutary these divine lessons! Well may an immortal being, after such an experience here for a time, and when the light of a better world has dawned upon his delighted vision, lift his soul to heaven and sing,

Let me go, why should I tarry?
  What has earth to bind me here?
What, but cares, and toils, and sorrows?
  What, but death, and pain, and fear?
Let me go, for hopes most cherished,
  Blasted round me often lie,
Oh! I've gathered brightest flowers,
  But to see them fade and die.

Thus hope tells us of another life, not only by

the inspiration and solace which it draws from the mysterious, enchanting future, but also by the successive demise or failure of its brightest earthly creations. A wise and beneficent Creator could never tantalize us with the hope of future being, had we not been predestinated to immortality.

> Shall I be left forgotten in the dust,
> When Fate, relenting, lets the flower revive?
> Shall Nature's voice, to man alone unjust,
> Bid him, though doomed to perish, hope to live?
> Is it for this fair Virtue oft must strive
> With disappointment, penury, and pain?
> No! Heaven's immortal springs shall yet arrive,
> And man's majestic beauty bloom again,
> Bright through th' eternal year of Love's triumphant reign.

V. The *desire* of *immortality itself*, in the soul of man, is both an omen and a pledge of another life after death.

Look through all nature and show me if you can a single instance in which God has given to one of his sentient creatures,—quadruped, bird, fish, reptile, or insect—a desire for the gratification of which he has made full provision. Whether it relates to abode, or appetite, or pastime, or instincts, the law is universal—the means for its gratification is the counterpart of each desire, and answers to it as light answers to the eye, or water to the fins of the inhabitants of the deep.

Whenever the idea is once lodged in the human soul that there may be an immortal life after death, it immediately enkindles a *desire* to live forever. Henceforth we shudder at the thought of annihilation.

> "Could you, so rich in rapture fear an end,
> That ghastly thought would drink up all your joy."

Henceforth, though he may not be a Christian, he desires to exist forever. Even though clouds of doubt and uncertainty may shade his prospects of bliss in the life to come, the soul cries out "*let me still exist!*" Even the prospect of misery beyond the grave, is often more welcome to the mind and heart of man than the thought of non-existence; and that for the reason that while future misery to the unforgiven is in harmony as well with the nature of man as with the government of God, the future non-existence of the soul is opposed to both; and we might therefore expect to find every instinct and intuition and power of the soul arrayed against it.

And how is this desire strengthened by a virtuous life.

> Guilt only makes annihilation gain.

There is no one thought that can so effectually chill and petrify the devout heart, as that of non-existence after death. If, then, the alliances of virtue are with truth, and those of sin are with error, the doctrine of immortality must be true, and that of annihilation false.

According, then, to all the analogies of the natural world, the *existence* of a strong desire in the soul herself to live on forever, is a proof and pledge that her Creator formed her for such destiny, and has provided infallibly against all failure and disappointment.

It must be so; Plato, thou reasonest well;
Else whence this pleasing hope, this fond desire,
This longing after immortality?
Or whence this secret dread and inward horror,
Of falling into naught? Why shrinks the soul
Back on herself, and startles at destruction?
'Tis the divinity that stirs within us;
'Tis Heaven itself that points out an hereafter,
And intimates eternity to man.

CHAPTER XIX.

THE MORAL NATURE OF MAN, CONSCIENCE, REMORSE.

In considering the powers of the soul thus far, we have dwelt mainly upon her intellectual capabilities. Let us turn now for a moment to the contemplation of her *moral* powers, and see if they do not with equal clearness indicate another state of existence after death.

I. That mysterious principle or faculty of the soul called *conscience*, implies another life in which the soul may be held accountable for her doings in the present world.

Conscience has been defined as "the faculty, power, or principle within us, which decides on the lawfulness or unlawfulness of our own actions and affections, and instantly approves or condemns them."* Others call it the *moral sense*, merely. It seems to include a perception of the agreement or disagreement of our conduct and affections with some acknowledged standard of right and wrong, and a capability of feeling unhappy under the perception of our guilt.

One of the poets has said,

> Conscience is the mirror of our souls,
> Which represents the errors of our lives,
> In their full shape.

* Webster.

Another has described it as,

> The worm that never dies! the "thorn within"
> That pricks and pains! The whip and scourge of sin!
> The voice of God in man! which without rest,
> Does softly cry within a troubled breast.

II. Of the power of conscience alone to make its guilty possessor wretched, history furnishes a great variety of examples.

"While *Belshazzar* was carousing at an impious banquet with his wives and concubines and a thousand of his nobles, the appearance of the fingers of a man's hand, and of the writing on an opposite wall, threw him into such consternation, that his thoughts terrified him, the girdles of his loins were loosed, and his knees smote one against another. His terror, in such circumstances, cannot be supposed to have proceeded from a fear of man; for he was surrounded by his guards and his princes, and all the delights of music, and of a splendid entertainment. Nor did it arise from the sentence of condemnation written on the wall; for he was then ignorant both of the writing and of its meaning. But he was conscious of the wickedness of which he had been guilty, and of the sacrilegious impiety in which he was then indulging, and, therefore, the extraordinary appearance on the wall, was considered as an awful foreboding of punishment from that Almighty and invisible Being whom he had offended.

Tiberius, one of the Roman emperors, was a gloomy, treacherous, and cruel tyrant. The lives of his people became the sport of his savage disposition. Barely to take them away was not sufficient, if their death was not tormenting and atrocious. He ordered, on one occasion, a general massacre of all who were detained in prison, on account of the conspiracy of Sejanus his minister, and heaps of carcases were piled up in the public places. His private vices and debaucheries were also incessant, and revolting to every principle of decency and virtue. Yet this tyrant, while acting in the plenitude of his power, and imagining himself beyond the control of every law, had his mind tortured with dreadful apprehensions. We are informed by *Tacitus*, that in a letter to the Senate, he opened the inward wounds of his breast, with such words of despair as might have moved pity in those who were under the continual fear of his tyranny.* Neither the splendour of his situation as an emperor, nor the solitary retreats to which he retired, could shield him from the accusations of his conscience, but he himself was forced to confess the mental agonies he endured as a punishment for his crimes.

Antiochus Epiphanes was another tyrant remarkable for his cruelty and impiety. He laid siege to the city of Jerusalem, exercised the most horrid cruelties upon its inhabitants, slaughtered forty thousand of them in three days, and polluted, in the most impious manner, the temple, and the worship of the God of Israel. Some time afterwards, when he was breathing out curses against the Jews for having restored their ancient worship, and threatening to destroy the whole nation, and to make Jerusalem the common place of sepulture to all the Jews, he was seized with a grievous torment in his inward parts, and excessive pangs of the colic, accompanied with

* Tiberium non fortuna, non solitudines protegebant, quin tormenta pectoris suasque pœnas ipse fateretur, &c.—*Tacitus.*

such terrors as no remedies could assuage. "Worms crawled from every part of him; his flesh fell away piece-meal, and the stench was so great that it became intolerable to the whole army; and he thus finished an impious life, by a miserable death."* During this disorder, says Polybius, he was troubled with a perpetual delirium, imagining that spectres stood continually before him, reproaching him with his crimes.

Similar relations are given by historians, of *Herod* who slaughtered the infants at Bethlehem, of Galerius Maximianus the author of the tenth persecution against the Christians, of the infamous Philip II. of Spain, and of many others whose names stand conspicuous on the rolls of impiety and crime.

It is related of Charles IX. of France, who ordered the horrible Bartholomew massacre, and assisted in this bloody tragedy, that, ever after, he had a fierceness in his looks, and a colour in his cheeks, which he never had before;—that he slept little and never sound; and waked frequently in great agonies, requiring soft music to compose him to rest; and at length died of a lingering disorder, after having undergone the most exquisite torments both of body and mind.

D'Aubigne informs us that Henry IV. frequently told, among his most intimate friends, that eight days after the massacre of St. Bartholomew, he saw a vast number of ravens perch and croak on the pavilion of the Louvre; that the same night Charles IX. after he had been two hours in bed, started up, roused his grooms of the chamber, and sent them out to listen to a great noise of groans in the air, and among others,

* Rollin's An. His.

some furious and threatening voices, the whole resembling what was heard on the night of the massacre; that all these various cries were so striking, so remarkable, and so articulate, that Charles, believing that the enemies of the Montmorencies and of their partisans had surprised and attacked them, sent a detachment of his guards to prevent this new massacre. —It is scarcely necessary to add, that the intelligence brought from Paris proved these apprehensions to be groundless, and that the noises heard, must have been the fanciful creations of the guilty conscience of the king, countenanced by the vivid remembrance of those around him of the horrors of St. Bartholomew's day.

King Richard the III. after he had murdered his innocent royal nephews, was so tormented in conscience, as Sir Thomas More reports from the gentlemen of his bed chamber, that he had no peace or quiet in himself, but always carried it as if some imminent danger was near him. His eyes were always whirling about on this side, and on that side; he wore a shirt of mail, and was always laying his hand upon his dagger, looking as furiously as if he was ready to strike. He had no quiet in his mind by day, nor could take any rest by night, but, molested with terrifying dreams, would start out of his bed, and run like a distracted man about the chamber.*

This state of mind, in reference to another case, is admirably described, in the following lines of Dryden.

"Amidst your train this unseen judge will wait,
Examine how you came by all your state;

* Stow's Annals, p. 460.

Upbraid your impious pomp, and in your ear
Will hollow, rebel! traitor! murderer!
Your ill-got power, wan looks, and care shall bring,
Known but by discontent to be a king.
Of crowds afraid, yet anxious when alone,
You'll sit and brood your sorrows on a throne."

Bessus the Pæonian being reproached with ill-nature for pulling down a nest of young sparrows and killing them, answered, that he had reason so to do, "Because these little birds never ceased falsely to accuse him of the murder of his father." This parricide had been till then concealed and unknown; but the revenging fury of conscience caused it to be discovered by himself, who was justly to suffer for it.

That notorious skeptic and semi-atheist, Mr. Hobbes, author of the "Leviathan," had been the means of poisoning many young gentlemen and others with his wicked principles, as the Earl of Rochester confessed, with extreme compunction, on his death-bed. It was remarked, by those who narrowly observed his conduct, that "though in a humor of bravado he would speak strange and unbecoming things of God; yet in his study, in the dark, and in his retired thoughts, he trembled before him." He could not endure to be left alone in an empty house. He could not, even in his old age, bear any discourse of death, and seemed to cast off all thoughts of it. He could not bear to sleep in the dark; and if his candle happened to go out in the night he would awake in terror and amazement, a plain indication, that he was unable to bear the dismal reflections of his dark and desolate mind, and knew not how to extinguish, nor how to bear the light of "the candle of the Lord" within him. He is said to have left the world, with great reluctance, under terrible apprehensions of a dark and unknown futurity.

> "Conscience, the torturer of the soul, unseen,
> Does fiercely brandish a sharp scourge within.
> Severe decrees may keep our tongues in awe,
> But to our thoughts what edict can give law?
> Even you yourself to your own breast shall tell
> Your crimes, and your own Conscience be your Hell."*

How conscience spoke in the souls of Joseph's brethren, when they found themselves in trouble in the land of Pharaoh.

"And they said one to another, We *are* verily guilty concerning our brother, in that we saw the anguish of his soul, when he besought us, and we would not hear; therefore is this distress come upon us. And Reuben answered them, saying, Spake I not unto you, saying, Do not sin against the child; and ye would not hear! therefore, behold, also his blood is required." Gen. xlii. 21, 22.

How easily Herod could believe in the resurrection of the dead, after murdering John the Baptist. When he heard of the miracles of Christ, he was sure that John had risen again from the dead, and might soon appear and hold him to account for his bloody deeds.

"And king Herod heard *of him*, (for his name was spread abroad,) and he said, That John the Baptist was risen from the dead, and therefore mighty works do shew forth themselves in him." Mark vi. 14.

Other instances nearer home, and of more recent date are equally striking. Take the following which have appeared from time to time in the public prints during the last few years.

* Future State, pp. 72–75.

Rev. Daniel Lindly, after an absence of forty years—more than half of the time passed as a missionary in Africa—returned to this country, and recently revisited Athens, Ohio—the home of his childhood, the theatre of his youthful days. He trod again upon the old Campus, walked through the old college halls, stood upon the cliff—the rocky rostrum of college boys. He examined the old paths, and inquired for the companions of his youth. Changes had passed upon every scene, and few, indeed, were the associates of early life he could recognize there. But his name and presence were known, and he was asked to preach at night, and to give some account of his life in Africa. At the close of the services, a very respectable and aged gentleman approached, and desired him to take a walk.

They passed on, and when they had reached a somewhat retired place, the gentleman turned and said: "Brother Lindly! if a man has ever done a wrong, has committed a sin, don't you think he should confess it?"

"Why, yes," said Mr. Lindly, "if thereby he may glorify God; if it will make amends to the party wronged, or do good to the party who sinned."

"Well, that is just what I think. I am just in that predicament. I have long desired and prayed for an opportunity to make a confession and amendment to you. * * When we were boys together, fifty years ago, we were playing together.

"You dropped a quarter of a dollar, I snatched it up, and put it in my pocket: I claimed it as my own and kept it.

"It was, perhaps, a little mean, dirty trick, and it has worried and troubled me ever since."

"Oh! it was a small matter, and I have no recollection of it," said Mr. Lindly.

"Ah, you may call it a small matter, but it has been a mighty burden for me to bear.

"I have carried it now for fifty years. I would not carry it for fifty more for all the gold of California. And suppose I had to carry it for fifty thousand years, or for all eternity! No, sir; it is no small matter: it has been growing bigger, and heavier and heavier, and I want to get rid of it.

"I have no doubt you have forgotten it, but I could never forget it. I have not, for the last fifty years, heard your name mentioned, or the name of your father, or any of the family, but that *quarter* has come in connection. Why, the very buttons on your coat—every thing that is round, represents a quarter. Sun, moon, and stars, are magnified and illuminated quarters. You need not call it a little sin; if it was, it has grown mightily to plague me; and deservedly, too."

With this, the gentleman took from his pocket-book a five franc piece, worn bright and smooth, and said: "I wish you to take this; it belongs to you; it is rightfully yours, and will be no burden to you. And if this is not enough, I will give more." Mr. Lindly accepted it, and the gentleman raised himself erect and drew a long breath, as a man would who has thrown off a heavy load. He was at last relieved.

In February 1863, the following anonymous note, with its enclosure, was received at the Metropolitan Bank, New York.

NEW YORK, Feb. 14, 1863.

"MR. J. F. WILLIAMS: Enclosed please find $309, the property of the Metropolitan Bank."

Soon afterward a similar event occurred in another direction, as the following, cut from the *New York Tribune* of March 7, 1863, will show.

"On Wednesday, the President received, by Adams & Co's. Express, a package of 'greenbacks, amounting to $868, which sum the writer of an accompanying letter says he obtained from the Government dishonestly, and which he therefore returns. The letter is dated Brooklyn, March 2, 1863, and signed '*Candido Securo.*'"

On the second of February, 1864, the following also appeared in the columns of the same paper.

"The sum of $70 was received at the Treasury Department to-day, in a letter dated Boston, which said it was for duty on an article, not designed for sale, imported some years ago. The writer says the compound interest and premium on gold have been added to the amount originally due."

Such cases remind us of the unhappy Judas, who, after having betrayed his Lord and Master, was smitten with remorse of conscience, brought back the bribe for which he had committed the deed of infamy, threw down the money in the temple, and went out and put an end to his own life. Matt. xxvii. 3–5. Oh how terrible the power of conscience to agonize and ruin the guilty and unforgiven soul!

Now it is by no means probable that, in either of the above recent cases the parties had the least fear of detection or exposure in this world. In this respect they were no doubt perfectly safe; and if not there is no proof that restitution rendered their detection any less probable, or, in that respect, relieved them from any measure of anxiety. Evidently such was not the object of any one of these restitutions, but rather to relieve the soul of her sense of guilt and remorse,—to allay the forebodings of detection and exposure in a future and eternal state.

III. The following instances relate to still higher offences.

"One or two years since, a citizen of Alabama was tried for murder, but through some technicality was acquitted. He went forth, however, with the brand upon him, and wherever he wandered, people made room for the murderer to pass. He was shunned as one with the leprosy. Some weeks since, the man shut himself in a room with no companion but a barrel of whisky, and plunged into the deepest intoxication, drinking, it is said, a quart of the liquor at a draught. In this condition he lingered through two or three months in the most intense mental agony, and finally died."

So gnaws the grief of conscience evermore,
And in the heart it is so deeply grave,
That they may never sleep nor rest therefor,
Nor think one thought but on the dread they have.

Albert W. Hicks, the murderer, who was executed at Bedloe's Island, near New York, July 13, 1860, made the following statement to the reporters, as published in the New York daily papers at the time.

"For years conscience has slumbered; I have not

heard her voice at all. No deed of desperation has seemed to me too desperate; no crime has seemed too dark or bloody. My soul seemed dead to all remorse or dread, and fear has been a feeling which, until now, I have never known.

"But in this lonely cell, away from all the excitements which have always been the support of my restless nature—within these solemn walls, where I see none but those who guard me, or those come to look at me, as upon some wild beast; here, where no sounds fall upon my ear but the footsteps of the keeper, as he paces with measured tread the long corridor outside, or harsh, discordant clank of heavy doors slamming, or the grating of bolts and the creaking of hinges—conscience, so long dead, has at last awakened, and now stings me with anguish, and fills my soul with dread and horror.

"I look back upon my way of life, and see the path marked with blood and crime, and in the still midnight, if I sleep, I act the dreadful scenes anew. Again I imbue my hand in the red blood of my victims; again I rob the unsuspecting traveler, or violate the most sacred sanctities of life, to satisfy my greed of gold, or headstrong, unchecked passions; and if I wake, I seem to see my victims glaring at me through the gloom of my cell, or hear them shriek aloud for vengeance on my guilty head.

"The past is one great horror! The future one dread fear. A heavy, insupportable weight is on my heart, and I feel as if, did I not reveal its fearful secrets, I should go mad.

How awful is that hour, when conscience stings
  The hoary wretch, who on his death-bed hears,
Deep in his soul, the thundering voice, that rings,
  In one dark, damning moment, crimes of years,
  And screaming like a vulture in his ears,
Tells, one by one, his thoughts and deeds of shame;
  How wild the fury of his soul careers?
His swart eye flashes with intensest flame,
And like the tortures rack the wrestling of his frame.

"Violence done to the conscience, which is of the essence of sin, is a wrenching of the soul into a moral dislocation. It is a rupture of the bands which keep the moral fabric in its integrity, and from the consequent suffering there is no exemption. What matters the question of outward positive inflictions, when we have wrapped up within us the elements of unknown sorrows, from which we can no more escape than from our own consciousness!" *

If, then, such is the power of conscience to make the guilty wretched in the present life, despite our blunted perceptions and the hardening influence of sin, what will it be when every sin shall stand forth clear and distinct upon the enduring pages of memory, and the conscience that has so long slumbered or been but half awake, shall be roused to the fullest apprehension of its guilt, and to the keenest possible sense of its endless desert!

IV. We see that even here, notwithstanding all that may be done to deaden the sensibilities, and hush the voice of conscience in the soul of man, it has power to fill the mind with indescribable horrors, and to sting the immortal spirit with an agony that no language can depict.

"Now, how are we to account for such terrors of

* Bush on the Resurrection, p. 396.

conscience, and awful forebodings of futurity, if there be no existence beyond the grave? especially when we consider, that many of those who have been thus tormented have occupied stations of rank and power, which raised them above the fear of punishment from man? If they got their schemes accomplished, their passions gratified, and their persons and possessions secured from temporal danger, why did they feel compunction or alarm in the prospect of futurity? for every mental disquietude of this description implies a dread of something future. They had no great reason to be afraid even of the Almighty himself, if his vengeance do not extend beyond the present world. They beheld the physical and moral world moving onward according to certain fixed and immutable laws. They beheld no miracles of vengeance—no Almighty arm visibly hurling the thunderbolts of heaven against the workers of iniquity. They saw that one event happened to all, to the righteous as well as to the wicked, and that death was an evil to which they behooved sooner or later to submit. They encountered hostile armies with fortitude, and beheld all the dread apparatus of war without dismay. Yet, in their secret retirements, in their fortified retreats, where no eye but the eye of God was upon them, and when no hostile incursion was apprehended, they trembled at a shadow, and felt a thousand disquietudes from the reproaches of an inward monitor which they could not escape. These things appear altogether inexplicable if there be no retribution beyond the grave.

"We are, therefore, irresistibly led to the conclusion, that the voice of conscience, in such cases, is the voice of God declaring his abhorrence of wicked deeds and the punishment which they deserve, and that his providence presides over the actions of moral agents, and gives intimations of the future destiny of those haughty spirits who obstinately persist in their trespasses. And, consequently, as the peace and serenity of virtuous minds are preludes of nobler enjoyments in a future life, so those terrors which now assail the wicked may be considered as the beginnings of that misery and anguish which will be consummated in the world to come, in the case of those who add final impenitence to all their other crimes." *

* Future State, p. 76.

CHAPTER XX.

OUR CONTINUED LOVE FOR THE DEAD A PROOF OF IMMORTALITY.

If it be admitted that there is an all-wise and infinite Creator, it must also be admitted that except so far as we have induced discord and conflict by sin, all our powers and susceptibilities are in perfect harmony with the circumstances of our present being, and with the fact or otherwise of a future state of existence.

Fishes, whose home is in subterranean rivers, are found without eyes. As they are never wanted where no light ever comes, though their ancestors once possessed them, after a few generations nature causes them to be closed forever. If the bird were never to fly, no half-formed wings would be seen, while yet the birdlet is confined to the narrow limits of its shell.

And so of the soul of man: if she had not been predestinated by her Creator for another and an endless state, she would never have been invested with those wonderful powers and capabilities with which we find her so richly endowed, and which so eminently befit and adorn her as an accountable and immortal intelligence.

Look for example at the fact named at the head of this chapter—our continued remembrance of and love for the dead after they have passed from our earthly view forever, and their bodies have crumbled back to dust.

I. This passion or emotion of the soul is so common to all ages and lands that it might almost be called a universal instinct of the human heart. Why was it that the aborigines of our own country were wont to send messages of love by the wild forest birds, to their kindred in the spirit land? Why do some of the heathen kneel annually at the graves of their dead, and whisper "I love you still?" With what unearthly tenderness do we still cling to those whom we once knew and loved in this world, but who have passed from our society to return no more. The bereft mother still loves her darling babe, though its lifeless form reposes in the tomb, and she well knows it is but a mass of corruption. Nor is this all. If she scrutinize that tender tie that connects her aching heart with the departed object of her love, she is conscious that it is not the lifeless clod to which she so fondly clings, but that which thought, and knew, and smiled upon her though the little form it cast off at death—the *spirit babe* that has soared away to heaven! Hence she sings even amid her tears,

> "The great Jehovah from above,
> An angel bright did send,
> And took my little harmless dove,
> To joys that never end."

And still, though assured of its unalloyed happiness in another life, she can never forget it or cease to love it. From time to time I see her, looking over its playthings or garments long years after the body is dissolved in the tomb, and weeping with an affection as fresh and ardent as on the day when she imprinted the farewell kiss upon its cold and marble brow.

How touchingly is this continued love for the dead described in the following beautiful lines by Miss Priest:—

"Over the river they beckon to me,
Loved ones who've crossed to the further side;
The gleam of their snowy robes I see,
But their voices are lost in the rushing tide.
There's one with ringlets of sunny gold,
And eyes the reflection of heaven's own blue;
He crossed in the twilight gray and cold,
And the pale mist hid him from mortal view;
We saw not the angels that met him there,
The gates of the city we could not see—
Over the river, over the river,
My brother stands waiting to welcome me.

"Over the river the boatman pale,
Carried another, the household pet;
Her brown curls wave in the gentle gale,
Darling Minnie! I see her yet.
She crossed on her bosom her dimple hands,
And fearlessly entered the phantom bark;
We felt it glide from the silver sands,
And all our sunshine grew strangely dark;
We know she is safe on the further side,
Where all the ransomed and angels be—
Over the river, the mystic river,
My childhood's idol is waiting for me.

"For none return from those quiet shores,
Who cross with the boatman cold and pale,
We hear the dip of their golden oars,
And catch a glimpse of their snowy sail;

And lo, they have passed from our yearning hearts,
 They cross the stream and are lost for aye.
We may not sunder the vail apart,
 That hides from our vision the gates of day.
We only know that their barks no more,
 May sail with us o'er life's stormy sea;
Yet somewhere, I know, on the unseen shore,
 They watch, and beckon, and wait for me.

"And I sit and think where the sunset's gold,
 Is flushing river, and hill, and shore,
I shall one day stand by the waters cold,
 And list for the sound of the boatman's oar;
I shall watch for a gleam of the flapping sail,
 I shall hear the boat as it gains the strand,
I shall pass from sight with the boatman pale,
 To the better shore of the spirit land;
I shall know the loved that have gone before,
 And joyfully sweet will the meeting be,
When over the river, the peaceful river,
 The angel of death shall carry me."

A poor helpless girl, a cripple, who was doomed from childhood to pain and deformity, but who, nevertheless, felt all the warm impulses of an immortal nature, thus wrote and sung of "the loved and lost" who had gone before:

"Our buried friends can we forget,
 Although they've passed death's gloomy river?
They live within our memory yet,
 And in our love must live for ever.
And, though they've gone a while before,
 To join the ransomed hosts in heaven,
Our hearts will love them more and more,
 Till earthly chains at last be riven.

"I heard them bid the world adieu:
 I saw them on the rolling billow:
Their far-off home appeared in view,
 While yet they pressed a dying pillow.

I heard the parting pilgrim tell,
While passing Jordan's lonely river,—
Adieu to earth,—now all is well—
Now all is well with me forever.

"Oh! how I long to join their wing,
And range their fields of blooming flowers:
Come, holy watchers, come and bring
A mourner to your blissful bowers.
I'd speed with rapture on my way,
Nor would I pause at Jordan's river:
With songs I'd enter endless day,
And live with my loved friends forever."

II. Of the same general significance is the interest we all feel in whatever relates to the departed dead, and especially in the fond inquiry, "*shall we know our friends beyond the grave?*" We have no space for the consideration of this question here, and shall return to it in a future chapter; but as a fact needing little proof or illustration, we barely point to it now as an omen of our coming immortality. It is but a phase of the same love that adorns the cold pale corpse with flowers, and builds the monument, sculptures the marble with words of tenderest affection, and for long years afterward bedews the grave with tears.

III. Now we argue that the very existence of this continued love for the dead is in itself a proof of their continued being, and by parity of reasoning, of the immortality of all human spirits. If all souls perished at death, the infinite and all-merciful Creator would have so constituted us that the moment a parent or child or wife or husband was dead, we should cease to love them forever.

Take an illustration from the history of a recent scientific discovery.

For many years prèvious to 1845 it had been known

that the planet Uranus was subject to certain perturbations in its orbit; which could not be accounted for by the attraction of the sun, and of the other planetary bodies.* From the nature and amount of these perturbations, Le Verrier, a French mathematician, demonstrated the existence of an undiscovered planet, and so completely did he determine its place in the distant heavens, that when Dr. Galle of the Berlin Observatory pointed his telescope to the place designated by Le Verrier, he not only found the new planet, but found it within one degree of its computed location!

Here, then, we have not only an unknown planet casting the spell of its attraction upon those that are known and seen, and producing thereby its visible effects, but to the eye of reason these mysterious effects become the infallible proofs of the existence and direction of another world, hitherto undiscovered and unknown.† So with the human soul and its continued love for the dead. We follow them to the shores of the final river, and they recede from our

* It should be remembered, that in accordance with the Newtonian law of gravitation, every body in the Solar System attracts every other; that the attraction of each body is proportioned to its quantity of matter; and that in the same body the power of attraction varies inversely as the square of the distance. In order, therefore, to compute the exact place of a planet in its orbit about the sun, it is necessary not merely to regard the attraction of the central body, but also to allow for the influence of all the other bodies of the Solar system. To compute the exact orbit which a planet will describe, subject to the attractions of all the members of the solar system, is consequently one of the grandest problems of astronomy.

† For a full and accurate account of this wonderful discovery, see "Recent Progress of Astronomy," by Prof. Loomis, published by the Harpers.

view. No more do we listen to the music of their friendly voices, or behold the light of their smiling countenances. In all these respects they are hidden from our view by the vail of death, as from creation's morning Neptune had lain hidden from all mortal vision in the depths of immensity.

> The misty vail
> Of mortality blinds the eye,
> That we see not the hovering angel bands,
> On the shores of eternity.

But though distant and invisible we feel the spell of their celestial attraction. Yielding thereto our hearts are the subjects of tender perturbations, and sighs and tears are the witnesses of the susceptibility of our own natures to its distant and silent power.

Now we argue that the very existence of this continued love for the dead is, in itself, a proof of their continued and immortal existence. For if all souls perished at death, the infinite and all-merciful Creator would have so constituted us that the moment a parent, or child, or wife, or husband, was dead, all love for them would cease forever. Has the Creator so constituted the human soul that, despite itself, it remembers and still loves objects that have long ceased to exist? Has this palpable and tender effect no adequate cause? Comes this mysterious powerful attraction, that draws us so sweetly towards the unseen country, from the empty void of non-existence? To suppose this, is to impeach the Creator of the human heart, and to charge him with trifling with our most tender and most holy affections.

While, then, we follow our friends to the river of death, and after they have crossed wander sadly up and down its banks, still bound to them by the cords of a deathless love, every pang we feel when we realize that they are gone—every emotion of tenderness that thrills our hearts with its warm immortal glow—every tear that we shed, or sigh that we heave—each and all are but so many proofs in the soul herself that the dead, whose memory we so fondly cherish, still live immortal beyond the grave.

CHAPTER XXI.

NATURAL EMBLEMS OF THE SOUL'S DEPARTURE AT DEATH.

Among the rational evidences of a future state of existence, the natural world furnishes various phenomena strikingly illustrative of the departure of the soul from the body in the hour of death. To a few of these we shall now call attention.

I. The bursting of the shell in which the birdlet is confined, when the period of incubation is over, may not inaptly be said to represent and illustrate the emancipation of the soul when our mortal existence shall terminate.

Before this transition, though it had feet and eyes and mouth and wings, they could serve no appreciable purpose, unless it should be to indicate a coming existence under new and more favorable auspices. Like the latent or but half developed powers of the soul in the present world, they are a silent yet cogent prophecy of a more glorious state of being to come.

But at length the shell bursts and the prisoner is free! One by one the powers of taste and voice and eye and wing are disclosed, till the once hapless prisoner, is seen shooting through air and light, over forest and hill and plain,

Where nothing earthly bounds his sight,
Nor shadow dims his way.*

So of the great transition in the hour of death. It is but the breaking of the earthen vessel, that the soul may stretch her glad wings and soar beyond the stars.

How fitly, then, may the Christian be represented as saying to his friend who is weeping over his lifeless body,

The soul that thou hast loved,
Will not be there,
It will have plumed its wings,
And soared afar.
Then weep not o'er my change,
When I am free.
When I've left my cell and gained,
My liberty.

II. The pine tree, fresh and green amid the snows

* The following by Rev. Dr. Todd, though in language adapted to children, is a clear and attractive presentation of the same general idea:

"A little Robin lay curled up, unhatched in his small blue shell. Dim, very dim rays of light came through the small pores of the shell. He thus talked with himself: "Well, I'm a very, *very* small fellow, and I am in a narrow world. I seem to have parts and things about me which I cannot use. There is something that seems to be a mouth, but I have no food for it here; something that seems to be feet, but I cannot walk with them; something coiled up that seems like wings, but what can I do with them? This is a narrow place, and I can't use these things, and I can't understand why I have them. I am told, indeed, of another state, where the light is brighter and stronger, and where there is room, and where I can use all these things; but Oh dear! I can't now understand these sayings!" But in a few days his shell fell off, and his eyes opened, and his mouth received food, and feathers covered him, and his wings were complete, and his feet perfect, and he could run, and fly, and sing, as he rose up over houses, and passed over rivers and high trees. He could now see and enjoy this new, this higher, this better state. He was made for this and not for the egg state. He now saw why he had the things called wings, legs, and the like.

of winter, has been used as an emblem of the life of man beyond death, as in the following beautiful lines by E. C. Riggs. The author, a young man of delicate health, had, within a few years, followed a noble brother and two affectionate sisters to that sacred retreat of which he speaks.

When life's brief, changing scenes are o'er,
And I on earth shall dwell no more,
Then lay this mouldering form away
Beside the dust, the hallowed clay
Of friends and kindred loved so well,
Who sleep within the quiet dell,
Where rippling waters, dancing by,
Sing soft and sweet their lullaby.

When death unbars the door for me,
And lets the imprisoned spirit free
To roam through verdant fields above,
Where all is peace and joy and love—
Then lay my body 'neath the sod,
By mourners' feet so often trod,
Where brother's, sisters' dust is laid,
Beneath the pine-tree's soothing shade.

There lay the broken casket down;
'Twill useless be with jewels gone.
Let that sweet pine an emblem be
Of Life and Immortality;
And let the robins build their nest
Among its branches, o'er my breast;
There make their home and rear their young,
And cheer the day with joyous song.

And let the rootlets of that tree,
While creeping downward, twine round me;
And, from the dust that crumbles there,
Drink in the food they need, and bear
It upward to the topmost boughs,
To give them life through winter's snows,
And keep them green long as they wave—
A type of life beyond the grave.

While grows the pine, and upward shoots,
And downward sends its tender roots—
Defiance giving to the blast,
As through its leaves it rushes past—
Remember, friends, the soul shall live
In worlds on high. Then do not grieve;
For death is only a remove
From earth below to heaven above.

III. The opening flower of the water lily, as it reaches the surface of the lake in its upward progress, may illustrate the expansion of our immortal powers, when death is swallowed up of life. In the earlier stages of its growth it is but an unsightly stem and bulb, covered with slime and mud, and pressing its way slowly up from the bottom of the stagnant pool, through mud and decaying vegetation. There is no visible flower, no expansion, no beauty, no fragrance. At length it reaches the surface of the water, and instead of growing upward still, till it stands up above the water, it instinctively pauses at its surface, opens its calyx, lays down its overcoat upon the gentle water, as if to stand sentinel, and separate the world beneath from which it has just emerged from that above in which it is henceforth to dwell. Having thus reached a higher and purer element, it opens its spotless bosom, drinks in the light of heaven, lifts its anthers still upward toward the skies, and fills the air with its fragrance.

So with the soul of man. In the present life she grovels in darkness and sin, and at best can move but slowly upward, through ignorance, decay, and death, towards a more auspicious region. But when at length she shall reach the grave, lay aside there the outer vestments of the flesh, and inhale the atmosphere of immortality, she shall develope beauty and fragrance as yet scarce suspected, and wear a regalia befitting her higher and more glorious state of existence.

IV. The "seven year locust," as it is called, emerges from the earth at the end of its period, and crawls up upon the trees and shrubs, a rude, unsightly insect, without wings or voice, or power to eat. Fastening itself to a leaf or limb by the strong claws of its fore legs, it seems at first to fall into a stupor; and then bursts open on the back, from the head to the waist, whereupon the new insect crawls out, ascends to the topmost bough of the tree, stretches and dries its wings, sings its resurrection song, and at length soars from tree to tree unencumbered, free and joyful.*

V. Travelers tell us of a similar insect in Japan—a large *beetle*, which, at a certain period of its growth, bursts its unsightly casement, emerges from its ruins as an immense and gorgeous butterfly, and goes singing away towards the skies.† What a beautiful emblem of the putting off of our fleshly tabernacle at death, and the going forth of the glorified spirit to a better and an immortal life!

VI. The term *psyche*, says Dwight in his Grecian and Roman Mythology, signifies a *butterfly*, as well as the human soul. It is not unlikely, therefore,

* The author has some twenty of the abandoned coffins of this curious insect, obtained by him at Newark, N. J., in 1859. They were found still hanging to the lower limbs or leaves of the trees, while their former occupants were perched upon the topmost boughs, beyond all danger or annoyance, and were filling the air with their monotonous and piercing melodies.

† Payne's Geography, Vol. i. p. 20.

that such was its original import, as *pneuma* originally signified only *air* or *wind;* and that it was chosen to represent the immortal spirit of man, because the transition of that insect from its chrysalis to its butterfly state, was such a striking emblem of the emerging of the soul from the body at the hour of death.

Look at that curious insect in its caterpillar state. How active and voracious. How regular and healthful its growth. But at length it seems to fall sick and lose its appetite. Its skin becomes wrinkled, like that of an old man; its coat of hair becomes thin, and changed in color, and it seems about to die. But let no one be deceived by these appearances. Its youth will soon be renewed like the eagles. In a few days the gorgeous butterfly will emerge from that uncouth and sickening form, like a spirit bursting from the body, to flaunt its gay wings in the sunbeams, and drink in nectar from every opening flower.

What an exquisite emblem of the going forth of the soul from the body at the hour of death, to inhabit the regions of eternal day!

> Child of the sun! pursue thy rapturous flight,
> Mingling with her thou lov'st in fields of light,
> And where the flowers of Paradise unfold,
> Quaff fragrant nectar from their cups of gold.
> There shall thy wings, rich as an evening sky,
> Expand and shut, in silent ecstacy;—
> Yet wert thou once a worm,—a thing that crept
> On the bare earth, then wrought a tomb and slept.
> And such is man—soon from this cell of clay,
> To burst a seraph in the blaze of day.

Speaking of this wonderful transformation, an able writer says:—

"It seems like a resurrection from the tomb into a fresh life, with celestial destinations. It is so analogous to that which the human spirit is appointed to undergo, that the intellect cannot well avoid viewing the insect transformation as the emblem, the token, the natural herald and promise of our own. The ancients, without our Christian Revelation, thought so; for one of their most pleasing imaginations, yet visible on some of their grave-stones, which we dig up, is that of a butterfly over the name or the inscription whieh they record. They place the insect there as the representation of the Psyche—of the animating and surviving soul; as the intimation that it will re-appear in a new form and region of being. It is thus analogous to the word 'resurgam' on our hatchments. It beautifully and picturesquely declares, '*Non omnis moriar*—I shall not wholly die; but I hope yet to rise again.' The allusion and applicability are so striking that I cannot but believe that one of the great purposes of the Deity in creating his insect kingdom was to excite this sentiment in the human heart; and to raise by it the contemplative mind to look forward to a possible revival from the tomb, as the butterfly from its sepulchral chrysalis." *

"The transmutations," says Chalmers, "which take place in the state of other animals, as birds and insects, and yet with the subsistence of the living principle in each of the stages; warrant the conclusion, not that the soul *must*, but that the soul *may* survive the entire dissolution of that material frame-work wherewith it is now encompassed." †

* Professor Bush.

† Chalmers' Lectures on Butler's Analogy, Lecture I., Part I., Section 2.

"Like the insect, the human personality has three states, and changes, and forms of being, but continues indestructible through all. It emerges from its ovum into the figure and life of the present fleshly body; it rests in its earthly grave, unextinguished, though visible to mortal eye no longer; and it will emerge from that at its appointed time into its ethereal nature and immortalized capacities; always the same self in each transmutation; never dying or dissolving with its material investment; but surviving, to bloom in everlasting youth amid the most exquisite felicity—the spiritualized butterfly, with angel wings perhaps, and an imperishable vitality." *

We cite this extract as containing several beautiful ideas, and, on the whole, pertinent to our theme, but there is one point upon which we wish, in passing, to indicate our dissent; and that is, where the writer speaks of the "human personality" as resting in the grave unextinguished, to emerge therefrom at the resurrection. He *seems* here to imagine that the soul sleeps in the grave till the body is raised; and yet so contrary is this idea to what he had before said of the "*psyche*—the animating and surviving soul," that we rather attribute it to the confounding of the two ideas of the immortality of the soul, and the resurrection of the body, for the time being, in the mind of the writer; and to an overweening desire for the moment to make the analogy between the case of man and the butterfly as complete as possible. He had no idea after all of the sleep of the soul in the grave from death to the general resurrection.

We have thus seen that various facts and phe-

* Turner's Sacred History of the World, p. 354.

nomena in the natural world are strikingly adapted to shadow forth and illustrate the change of death, and the survivency of the spirit when the body dies. That such was the *design* of these arrangements on the part of the Creator, it might be too much to affirm; and yet what Christian can doubt that they were so intended? Who but man can become the observer and the student of these phenomena? And to what *can* he apply them, if not to the problem of immortality?

Man is not all of earth;
The glowing brightness of bright Fancy's fires,—
The boundlessness of all his soul's desires,—
Prove him of heavenly birth.

Look on his glorious face!
There the quick play of varied passions see!
Look on that brow of thought! Must it not be
A spirit's dwelling-place?

Behold that changing eye!
Does not that glance of tenderness and love,
That love of high resolve, or pity, prove
Something that will not die?

The grave can claim no part,
Save that on which there falleth our sad tears;
Clay cannot cover all those hopes and fears
Which swell each throbbing heart.

Would God a palace rear
For a frail being with no nobler life
Than that which closes with the dying strife?
A life that endeth here?

Ah, no? the tenant must
More glorious than its glorious mansion be;
Whose dome and columns soon, alas! we see
All crumbling into dust.

Dust may to dust return,
Ashes to kindred ashes fall again;
But thought dies not: of all the mind's bright train
None find a funeral urn.

Then, though thine eye grow dim,
And sluggish flow the current of thy blood,
Look up, O man! in steadfast faith, to God;
For thou shalt go to him.

CHAPTER XXII.

SUMMARY OF THE ARGUMENT AND PRACTICAL CONCLUSIONS.

We have now gone over the entire ground of the argument, noticing the principal evidences, natural and revealed, of the soul's immortality. Let us now recapitulate the various points established and considerations urged, and notice the bearing of the general doctrine upon several other minor questions in which we all have or should have a deep and abiding interest.

In the first ten chapters, devoted to the development of the Scripture doctrine of immortality, we have shown that matter and spirit are distinct essences—that man is a two-fold being, consisting of a spirit in a body—that souls are propagated and not immediately created—that as the life of Adam began with the *union* of the spirit with his body, so death is a *separation* of these two natures of man—that souls do not become extinct at death, or sleep in the grave with the body till the resurrection, but have a separate and conscious existence from death to the resurrection morning—that they do not at once enter upon their final abode, but remain in *Hades*, "Paradise," or "the intermediate state," till their bodies are raised in the last day—that immortal existence is not a result of redemption, hinging upon our faith in Christ; and that the supposed annihilation of the wicked at the day of judgment is both unscriptural and absurd.

In the last twenty-one chapters, Part Second, devoted to the Rational Evidences of a Future Life, we have explained the character and value of the Rational Argument; have cited various indications of another life in the structure and phenomena of the natural world; and have corroborated the infallible teaching of the Divine Oracles, by arguments drawn from the general belief of mankind—the relation of man to the lower animals—the exquisite structure of the human body—the dominion of the soul over the body—the unequal development of the mind and body—the energy of the soul in cases where physical organs are wanting—the completeness of our mental powers under bodily mutilations—the phenomena of reverie, sleep, dreaming and catalepsy; and the vigor and activity of the soul in the hour of death. We have also shown from natural analogies that the dissolution of the human body affords no ground for the presumption that the mind perishes with it; and have sustained the teachings of the Bible by arguments drawn from the indestructibility of matter,—the immateriality of the soul, and her powers of memory,—the rapidity of her mental process—her capabilities of improvement, and her vast achievements in know ledge and skill, the desire for posthumous remembrance and fame, our earthly discontent, the power of hope, and our longings for immortality.

To all this we have added an argument drawn from our forebodings of the future, and the power of conscience and remorse; and another drawn from our continued love for the dead, closing in the last chapter with the fragmentary gleanings of the field, under the head of natural emblems of the soul's departure at death.

We have thus seen that although nature and reason are incapable of satisfactorily revealing or discovering a future state of existence, yet, when once revealed, they fully respond to and corroborate this glorious truth. As earth echoed back the voice of God in the thunders of Sinai, so when a voice from heaven resounds in our ears the glad tidings—"Another life after death,"—the hills and vales of earth, the plants that grow, the beasts under our dominion, and the insect tribes—the moon and the stars, the human body and the deathless soul with all her powers, echo back the joyful pean—"another life!—*another life!!*—ANOTHER LIFE!!!"

> Oh, listen, man!
> A voice within us speaks that startling word,
> *Man, thou shalt never die!* Celestial voices
> Hymn it into our souls. According harps
> By angel fingers touched when the mild stars
> Of morning sang together, sound forth still,
> The song of our great *Immortality*.

And now, what is the *practical bearing* of the great and glorious truth that both heaven and earth have conspired to teach us? What lessons ought we to deduce from the survey of the evidences of an immortal, endless life after death, as developed in the preceding chapters? What should be the effect of the light of this great central truth, upon other and subordinate questions by which it is surrounded? We answer,

I. *That it discloses, in a strong and cheering light, the* IMPORTANCE, PERFECTION AND GLORY OF REVEALED RELIGION.

With all the light that "Reason and Nature" could shed upon the anxious problem, even with the aid of an early revelation, borne along the ages through the channels of tradition—the philosophers and sages of antiquity were utterly unable fully to assure themselves of another life beyond the grave. The best that Socrates could say, was, "I *hope* I am going to good men, though this I would not take upon me peremptorily to assert." Speaking of the two ideas, of immortality and of non-existence, Cicero could only affirm, "Which of these is true God only knows, and which is most probable a very great question." "When I read* I assent; but when I have laid down the book, all that assent vanishes." And such only was the faith of Seneca. "Immortality," said he, "however desirable, is rather promised than proved by those great men."†

Such is the light of "reason and nature." Not thus doubtful is the Christian believer. He *knows* that if his earthly house is dissolved, he has a building of God, eternal in the heavens; that to depart is to be with Christ, which is far better; and that beyond this transitory life there awaits him a conscious and joyful spiritual existence—a far more exceeding and eternal weight of glory.

Of the ages without revelation as compared with the present, it may well be said,

> Once star on star in kind succession rose,
> Now the great sun in healing splendor glows;

* The writings of Socrates and Plato. † Socrates and Plato.

And the man who rejects the *Bible*, and trusts to nature alone as his tutor, must ever wander in darkness and uncertainty, a prey to distressing doubts and anxious forebodings as to what awaits him when his change shall come. Look at Henry Kirk White first as a votary of natural religion, and then as a devout student of the Bible, as described in his own inimitable "Star of Bethlehem."

Once on the raging seas I rode,
  The storm was loud, the night was dark,
The ocean yawned, and rudely blowed
  The wind that tossed my foundering bark.
Deep horror then my vitals froze;
  Death struck, I ceased the tide to stem;
When suddenly a star arose,
  It was the Star of Bethlehem.

It was my guide, my light, my all;
  It bade my dark forebodings cease;
And through the storm and danger's thrall,
  It led me to the port of peace.
Now safely moored—my perils o'er,
  I'll sing, first in night's diadem,
Forever and forevermore,
  The Star! the Star of Bethlehem.

And it is only by the assurances of God's holy word that the soul ever can be "safely moored," or have her "dark forebodings" entirely cease.

How truthfully, also, has Beattie described the difference between natural and revealed religion, in his beautiful "Hermit."

'Twas thus by the glare of false science betray'd,
  That leads, to bewilder; and dazzles to blind;
My thoughts went to roam, from shade onward to shade,
  Destruction before me, and sorrow behind.

"Oh pity, great Father of light," then I cried,
"Thy creature who fain would not wander from thee;
So, humbly in dust I relinquish my pride:
From doubt and from darkness thou only canst free!

"And darkness and doubt are now fleeing away,
No longer I roam in conjecture forlorn,
So breaks on the traveler, faint, and astray,
The bright and the balmy effulgence of morn.
See Truth, Love, and Mercy in triumph descending,
And nature all glowing in Eden's first bloom!
On the cold cheek of Death smiles and roses are blending,
And beauty immortal awakes from the tomb."

Thus are life and immortality brought to light by the gospel.

Oh thou thrice blessed word of God!
Most wondrous book! bright candle of the Lord!
Star of eternity! the only star
By which the bark of man could navigate
The sea of life, and gain the coast of bliss
Securely;—only star which rose on time,
And, on its dark and troubled billows, still
As generation, drifting swiftly by,
Succeeded generation, threw a ray
Of heaven's own light, and to the hills of God,
The everlasting hills, pointed the sinner's eye.

By the anxious doubts and fears of the unbelieving heart, and by all the cherished joys that spring from the hope of a better and endless life after death, let us *love*, and *study*, and *believe*, and *obey* that holy volume the BIBLE, which alone is able to dispel all gloom and fear, and point the eager anxious spirit of man to the bright and open pathway of immortality!

II. *Though reason and nature are unable satisfactorily to reveal a future state*, YET ARE THEY NOT ON THAT ACCOUNT TO BE DESPISED OR UNDERVALUED.

As the ally and elucidator of revealed truth, natural theology has its legitimate office and its importance. Our complaint of the Deist is, not that he honors reason and nature, but that he lavishes upon them the attention and the homage due to revelation alone, and rejects the only guide that can make him truly wise. On the contrary, we should welcome to our vision the light from heaven, and let it variegate and beautify the whole realm of nature. With the Bible in our hands,

> Nature all o'er is consecrated ground,
> Teeming with growths immortal and divine.

Nature and revelation have a common Author, and are ever in harmony; hence, unless the judgment has been first perverted, and the reasoning faculties clouded by the dark shadows of scepticism, the most devout student of Nature will ever be found among the most humble and devout worshippers of the true and living God. As Christian believers, therefore, we have no quarrel with "natural religion," when properly interpreted and applied, and kept in its legitimate sphere as the ally and elucidator of the Bible.

III. *The years of our future and immortal existence stand* IN IMPRESSIVE CONTRAST WITH OUR PRESENT BRIEF AND RAPIDLY DEPARTING LIFE.

Well may it be called a "vapor," a "hand's breadth," a "tale that is told."

> Lo, on a narrow neck of land,
> 'Twixt two unbounded seas we stand.

Behind us are the numberless years of the past,

and before us roll the countless ages of eternity to come. "Life is a rapid moment, and it hastens to be gone; it gathers dimness and expires."* Like a bubble upon the wave it soon breaks and is seen no more.

With all its cares and anxieties, its days and nights and months and rolling years—its hopes and fears and joys and sorrows—what is this mortal life but the mere *beginning* of an endless existence?

> This is the bud of being, the dim dawn,
> The twilight of our day, the vestibule:
> Life's theater, as yet is shut; and Death,
> Strong death alone can heave the massy bar,
> This gross impediment of clay remove,
> And set us, embryos of existence, free.

As was said of a little girl whose pure spirit was early called away from earth, so it might also have been said of her had she lived and shone on earth for half a century.

> She sparkled, was exhaled, and went to heaven.

We step upon the stage of conscious being, cast a hasty glance around us, draw a few breaths, smile, shed a few tears, utter a groan of agony, and are gone! And, yet, we live, and shall live forever! Go count the leaves of all earth's forests, the drops of every sea and lake and stream, the sands of every shore, and all the stars of heaven—let each represent an age of the coming future, and when the last leaf and drop and star and grain of sand is told off in

* Rev. Dr. Dempster at a missionary meeting in Watertown, N. Y., in 1836, as he was about to embark for Buenos Ayres as a missionary.

registering the ongoing cycles of our immortal existence, even then we shall but have commenced to live; and the years of our conscious eternal life-time shall still go on, and on forever!*

IV. *The doctrine of the soul's immortality should enable us* THE BETTER TO UNDERSTAND THE INESTIMABLE VALUE OF THIS SHORT AND FLEETING LIFE.

As the years of childhood throw their influence forward upon the character and destiny and happiness of man as long as he lives in this world, and as the right improvement or neglect of spring-time determines the quality and the amount of the coming harvest, so this short life, brief and fleeting as it is, will throw forward its light or its shade upon all the years of our coming existence. As well expect the right eye of that little boy, that has been put out by the rebounding arrow from his cross-bow, to be restored when he reaches manhood, as to expect the soul to recover from the scars and bruises and dislocations of sin, in the world to which she goes. Whatsoever a man soweth that shall he also reap; and here only may we sow to the Spirit—to truth and virtue, and faith and holy living—that we may hereafter reap eternal life.

* What a very great sum is a billion! It is a million of millions. A million seems large enough; but a million of millions! how long do you suppose it would take you to count it? A mill which makes one hundred pins in a minute, if kept to work night and day, would only make fifty-two millions five hundred and ninety-six thousand pins a year; and at that rate the mill must work twenty thousand years without stopping a single moment, in order to turn out a billion of pins. What a vast sum, then, is a billion; it is beyond our reach to conceive of it. And yet, when a billion of years shall have passed, eternity will seem to have just begun. How important, then, is the question, "Where shall I spend eternity?"

How, then, can we squander these precious hours and days and years, in idle amusements and dissipation? How neglect from year to year the great salvation provided in Jesus Christ? Oh how unwise, how perilous, how suicidal!

> No room for mirth or trifling here,
> For worldly hope or worldly fear,
> If life so soon is gone.

Like the swift ships it is speeding away, and will soon be gone, to return no more.

> Our life as a dream; our time as a stream,
> Glides swiftly away,
> And the fugitive moment refuses to stay.
> The arrow is flown,—the moment is gone,
> The millennial year
> Rushes on to our view, and eternity's here.

As the generations that have preceded us like the successive waves of the sea are now all numbered with the dead, so we, dear reader, shall soon have done with all things earthly, and entered upon our eternal reward. Neglect not, then, the time and opportunities that you now enjoy.

> Seize, mortal! seize the transient hour,
> Improve each moment as it flies;
> Life's a short summer, man a flower;
> He dies, alas! how soon, he dies.

The Rabbins had a legend that when Methuselah was four hundred and sixty years old, the angel of the Lord appeared to him, told him that he was to live five centuries longer, and advised him to erect for himself a permanent dwelling-place. "Only five hundred years?" said the patriarch with a sigh; "if that is all I need no better dwelling. My old tent will answer till I leave the world."

Alas how few of us fully realize that this is not our home and live as strangers and pilgrims in the earth.

Oh for more of the spirit of this beautiful legend, even among the professed Christians and ministers of the land!

> The soul of man, a native of the skies,
> High-born, and free, her freedom should maintain,
> Unsold, unmortgaged for earth's little bribes.

V. *In view of the endless years before us, look at the* COMPARATIVE VALUE OF THINGS TEMPORAL AND THINGS ETERNAL.

The body needs food and raiment and shelter only for a few short years and yet how we struggle and toil and vex ourselves, and burden and enslave the immortal nature within us, to lay up much goods for many years. But of what account will it be to any of us a hundred years to come whether we were clad in coarse raiment, fed upon plain food and dwelt and died in a hovel, or were clothed in purple and fine linen, fared sumptuously every day, and lived and died in a palace? How little can our earthly condition in these respects, affect our destiny or our happiness in the world of spirits to which we go.

But not so with the immortal nature. If that has neglected to put on the wedding garment and to taste that bread of life of which if we eat we shall live forever, all is lost! True religion, and that alone, can prepare us either to live or die, or to be happy forever beyond the grave.

> Souls are her charge; to her 'tis given
> To train them for their native heaven.

While, therefore, as beings dwelling for a time in houses of clay, we give a portion of our attention and efforts to the satisfying of the demands of these dying natures, how unwise and unbecoming immortal beings to lavish all our time and powers upon the things of earth, as if we had no heaven to gain, and no hell to shun beyond the tomb!

Oh may we set our affections upon things above and not upon things on the earth! It is of little account how we are circumstanced here for a few brief years, whether rich or poor, honored or forgotten, if we are wise unto salvation, live for eternity, and lay hold upon everlasting life.

No matter which my thoughts employ;
A moment's misery or joy;
  But oh! when both shall end,
Where shall I find my destined place?
Shall I my everlasting days
  With fiends or angels spend?

Nothing is worth a thought beneath,
But how I may escape the death
  That never, never dies!
How make mine own election sure;
And when I fail on earth, secure
  A mansion in the skies.

Oh let us live, not for the body alone—for earth and time—but for the *soul*, for heaven and immortality! For what shall it profit a man if he shall gain the whole world, and lose his own soul? or what shall a man give in exchange for his soul?

VI. *In view of an immortal existence after death*, HOW REASONABLE AND SUBLIME AND GLORIOUS THE WORK OF REDEMPTION BY OUR LORD JESUS CHRIST.

To those who deny an immortal existence to man,

it is not strange that the glorious doctrine of redemption should seem a cunningly devised fable, and Jesus Christ as a root out of dry ground. If no hereafter awaits us, of what importance or real value can the redemption of the soul be? "Let us eat, and drink, for to-morrow we die." But if we are to live forever beyond the grave—if the curse of sin must either be removed by a sacrificial expiation, accepted by each individual spirit, or borne forever in the world to come, then the redemption of the soul becomes a theme that angels may well desire to look into. Well might the Father eternal give his only begotten Son to become the propitiation for our sins. Well might he wrap himself in the vestments of our humanity, that through death he might redeem us from the curse of the law, becoming a curse for us. Well might he bear our sins in his own body on the tree, that the blessings of pardon and holiness might light up all the ages of our endless existence. Such an object is worthy of God,—and of the infinite sacrifice of Calvary made to secure it.

And no wonder that heaven and earth, angels and devils, are enlisted in the solution of the problem of the character of our future existence—a problem that can only be measured by the agonies of the cross and the years of our coming eternity!

The soul of man—Jehovah's breath!
That keeps two worlds at strife;
Hell moves beneath to work its death,
Heaven stoops to give it life.

When we contemplate her powers—her capabilities of improvement, and of joy or sorrow—and her destination to endless being; then only do we rise to some just conception of her almost infinite value. Of what importance is a city, a fleet of ships, an empire, compared with one deathless soul of man?

Knowest thou the importance of a soul immortal?
Behold yon midnight glory! world on world!
Amazing pomp! redouble this amaze,
Ten thousand add, add twice ten thousand more,
Then weigh the whole! One soul outweighs them all,
And calls the astonishing magnificence
Of unintelligent creation poor!

CHAPTER XXIII.

CONSOLATION FOR THE BEREFT AND SORROWING.

A FIRM belief in the immortality of the soul is well calculated to mitigate our sorrow and dry our tears when those we love are removed from us by death.

I. *It is consoling to think as we see the once fair and lovely forms of friends and kindred consigned to the tomb, that they* STILL LIVE, AND MAY REMEMBER AND LOVE US STILL IN THE FAR OFF SPIRIT LAND.

Why, what is death but life
In other forms of being—life without
The coarser attributes of man, the dull
And momently decaying frame which holds
The eternal spirit in, and binds it down
To brotherhood with brutes? There's no such thing
As death! What's called so is but the beginning
Of a new existence; a fresh segment in
The eternal round of change.

Though we talk of them as *dead*, yet theirs alone is "the land of life."

"This is the desert, this the solitude:
How populous, how vital is the grave!"

Well may we write upon the tomb-stone, "*Not lost, but gone before.*" A beloved Christian friend has left us, but he has only emigrated to a "better country." We see beyond the stream the smoke of his cottage. Was the deceased a tender infant, a lovely little boy or girl? They have part in the great propitiation, without faith, without baptism, without "extreme unction," or any other ceremony. Christ the second Adam has for them fully retrieved the ruin brought upon them by the first. There is no place in hell for infant spirits; for "of such is the kingdom of heaven." Look up, then, bereft and weeping mother! Like flocks of snow-white doves, the souls of the early dead hover over the heavenly paradise, and dwell in the light of God's presence forever.

Even though you may not be a Christian, and therefore feel that you are not prepared to die, yet in respect to the babe that has been removed from you, all is safe. It had no knowledge of God, of his holy law, of the sin of Adam, or of Christ the Saviour, and could have none; and without repentance or faith its little robes are washed and made white in the blood of the Lamb. Think of it, then, not as in that tiny grave where you go to weep, but above the stars; not as while with you subject to sickness, pain, and death, but where none ever say I am sick, and where sickness, pain, and death, are unknown. Not as inhabiting a world of sin, but a citizen of that bright and holy land, where no clouds are seen, no tears flow, where flowers never fade, and where "sorrow and sighing shall flee away!"

II. *Do you weep for a pious brother, parent, child, or companion?* THEY LIVE AND ARE AT REST!

"Blessed are the dead who die in the Lord from henceforth: yea, saith the Spirit, that they may rest from their labors." Rev. xiv. 13.

I see a world of spirits bright,
  That taste the pleasure there;
They all are robed in spotless white,
  And conquering palms they bear.

"I shall go to him," said the heart-stricken David of his departed son. Oh how this thought has soothed the agonies of millions of bleeding hearts! "My brother, my wife, my gentle babe are gone, but they live immortal with the angels, where all tears are wiped away." Happy dwellers in that "better country."

Dreams may not picture a world so fair,
Sorrow and sin may not enter there,
Time doth not breathe on its fadeless bloom,
'Tis beyond the stars, and beyond the tomb.

Oh could they but speak to us from those realms of peace, how would they chide our sorrows, and bid us to weep no more. Methinks could we in this lower world but hear their joyful chorus—their song of triumph and rejoicing would be—

I shine in the light of God;
  His likeness stamps my brow;
Through the valley of death my feet have trod.
  And I reign in glory now.

No sin, no grief, no pain,
  Safe in my happy home,
My fears all fled, my doubts all slain,
  My hour of triumph's come.

I have reached the joys of heaven;
  I am one of the sainted band;
To my head a crown of gold is given,
  And a harp is in my hand.

Do you mourn when another star
  Shines out in the glittering sky?
Do you weep when the raging voice of war
  And the storms of conflict die?

> Then why do your tears run down,
> Why your hearts so sorely riven,
> For another gem in a Saviour's crown,
> And another soul in heaven?

Think of the scenes of glory that passed before the enraptured gaze of the Revelator. See that gorgeous city, with its gates of pearl, its twelve foundations, its streets of gold, its river and its trees of life! Do you see that joyful company in white robes? Mark those palms of victory! See those crowns of life adorning every brow! Mark how with harp and voice they pour forth their songs of everlasting joy unto God and the Lamb! Your departed kindred are there! Your friend is one of that joyful and immortal company.

> Oh their crowns! how bright they sparkle,
> Such as monarchs never wore:
> They are gone to richer pastures,
> Jesus is their Shepherd there:
>
> Hail! ye happy, happy spirits,
> Death no more shall make you fear,
> Grief nor sorrow, pain nor anguish,
> Shall no more distress you there.

Then wipe away those tears. Anoint thy head and wash thy face, that thou appear no more to sorrow. The land of darkness and tears, and the gates of death are passed; your kindred have entered heaven. Then weep no more till you too shall go, where all tears are wiped away.

III. *We may expect, if Christians,* TO MEET AND KNOW OUR PIOUS KINDRED, IN THE LAND BEYOND THE GRAVE.

We are not to know less but more hereafter. Now

we know in part, but then that which is perfect will have come. This is our childhood, that shall be our maturer life, when we shall have put away childish things. Now we see through a glass darkly, but then face to face, and knowing as we are known. Abraham, Dives, and Lazarus, knew each other. Moses and Elias are Moses and Elias still. The immortal whom John saw, Rev. xxii. 8, 9, introduced himself as a "fellow servant," and "of his brethren the prophets;" and the Jews are to see and know Abraham, Isaac, and Jacob, in the kingdom of God.

It cannot be that the saved shall not know each other in the heavenly land. Such an arrangement would detract indescribably from the bliss of that final state. "A stranger in heaven! The past all forgotten! Father, mother, wife, children and other kindred here, but I can never know them! I promised to meet some of them in heaven—they are here, I am here, I may have met them, sung with them, shouted with them, harped with them, walked the streets of the city and the sea of glass with them, bowed before the everlasting throne with them, but I do not, cannot know them! Earth was the grave of friendship—I can greet those I knew and loved on earth no more forever!" Ah no, heart-stricken mourner! No such soliloquy will ever be heard beyond the grave. Heaven is a land of purest social bliss, peopled with bright circles of deathless friends. *We shall know each other in heaven!*

Yes! oh, yes! in that land, that happy land,
They that meet shall know each other,
Far beyond the rolling river,
Meet to sing and love forever,
In that happy land.

How joyful the thought of such a meeting! How blissful the prospect of such a heaven! How fondly we dwell upon the tender theme of re-union with "the loved and lost" in the regions of eternal life! We stand and gaze across the river of death, we believe and hope, and yet we love to repeat the fond interrogatory—"*Shall I know my kindred in heaven?*"

When we hear the music ringing,
  Thro' the bright, celestial dome,
When sweet angel voices singing,
  Gladly bid us welcome home,
To the land of ancient story,
  Where the spirit knows no care,
In the land of light and glory,
  Shall we know each other there?

When the holy angels meet us,
  As we go to join their band,
Shall we know the friends that greet us
  In the glorious spirit land?
Shall we see their bright eyes shining
  On us, as in days of yore?
Shall we feel their dear arms twining,
  Fondly round us as before?

Yes! my earth-worn soul rejoices,
  And my weary heart grows light,
For the thrilling angel voices,
  And the angel faces bright,
That shall welcome me in heaven,
  Are the loved of long ago,
And to them 'tis kindly given,
  Thus their mortal friends to know.

Oh! ye weary ones and sad ones,
  Droop not, faint not by the way!
Ye shall join the loved and lost ones,
  In the land of perfect day!
Harp-strings touched by angel fingers,
  Murmur in my raptured ear,
Ever more their sweet tones linger,
  We shall know each other there!

Thus does the hope of another life after death become a solace to the wounded and bereft spirit, a balm for the aching and bleeding heart. Oh may all who weep on earth lay hold of its divine consolations, and weep no more!

CHAPTER XXIV.

GLORIOUS PROSPECTS BEFORE THE DYING CHRISTIAN.

Weep not, my Redeemer lives;
  Heavenward springing from the dust,
Clear-eyed Hope her comfort gives;
  Faith, Heaven's champion, bids us trust;
    Love eternal whispers nigh,
  "Child of God, fear not to die!"

In view of the doctrine of the soul's immortality, *how bright and glorious the prospect before the dying believer.*

O glorious hope of immortality!
At thought of thee, the coffin, and the tomb,
Affright no more; and even the monster Death
Loses his fearful form and seems a friend.

Death to the good man is but the dawning of an eternal day. Not till then does he enter upon a life unclogged by corruption. He ascends to be with Christ, which is far better. Then farewell earth—farewell toil and pain and tears and death! He goes to join the immortal company of heaven, who sing and shine in the presence of God forever.

And though the hills of death
  May hide the bright array,
The marshalled brotherhood of souls
  Still keeps its upward way;

Upward! forever upward!
I see their march sublime,
And hear the glorious music
Of the conquerors of time.

No doubts, no darkness, no fear! The two-leaved gates of eternity are gently opening before him, and the light of that brighter world is pouring forth upon the scene of his departure. Hark! He sings!

—What is this absorbs me quite,—
Steals my senses, shuts my sight,—
Drowns my spirit, draws my breath?
Tell me, my soul, can this be death?

The world recedes: it disappears;
Heaven opens on my eyes; my ears
With sounds seraphic ring.
Lend, lend your wings! I mount! I fly!
O grave, where is thy victory?
O death, where is thy sting?

See the dying Mozart, as he stands by the river of death, looks back upon the toils of the past, and forward to the joys of the immortal future. How appropriate the language of his "cygnean" song, the last he heard on earth.*

* Wolfgang Mozart, the great German composer, died at Vienna in the year 1791. There is something strikingly beautiful and touching in the circumstances of his death. His sweetest song was the last he sung —the Requiem. He had been employed upon this exquisite piece for several weeks, his soul filled with inspirations of richest melody, and already claiming kindred with immortality. After giving it its last touch, and breathing into it that undying spirit of song which was to consecrate it through all time, as his "cygnean strain," he fell into a gentle and quiet slumber. At length the light footsteps of his daughter Emilie awoke him. "Come hither," said he, "my Emilie— my task is done—the Requiem—*my* Requiem is finished." "Say not so, dear father," said the gentle girl, interrupting him as tears stood in her eyes. "You must be better—you look better, for even now your

Spirit! thy labor is o'er!
Thy term of probation is run,
Thy steps are now bound for the untrodden shore,
And the race of immortals begun.

Spirit! look not on the strife,
Or the pleasures of earth with regret—
Pause not on the threshold of limitless life
To mourn for the thing that is set.

Spirit! no fetters can bind,
No wicked have power to molest;
There the weary, like thee—the wretched shall find
A haven, a mansion of rest.

Spirit! how bright is the road
For which thou art now on the wing.
Thy home it will be with thy Saviour and God,
Their loud hallelujahs to sing.

In that better land "there shall be no more death, neither sorrow nor crying, neither shall there be any more pain, for the former things are passed away." There the wicked cease from troubling, and there the weary are forever at rest. There the Lamb that is in

cheek has a glow upon it. I am sure we will nurse you well again. Let me bring you something refreshing." "Do not deceive yourself, my love," said the dying father, "this wasted form can never be restored by human aid. From Heaven's mercy alone do I look for aid, in this my dying hour. You spoke of refreshment, my Emilie—take these my last notes—sit down to my piano here—sing with them the hymn of your sainted mother—let me once more hear those tones which have been so long my solacement and delight." Emilie obeyed, and with a voice enriched with tenderest emotion, sang the following stanzas:

Spirit! thy labor is o'er, &c.

as cited above.

As she concluded, she dwelt for a moment upon the low melancholy notes of the piece, and then turning from the instrument looked in silence for the approving smile of her father. It was the still passionless smile which the rapt and joyous spirit left—with the seal of death upon those features.

the midst of the throne shall lead us to fountains of living waters, and God shall wipe away all tears from our eyes.

No tear shall be in heaven, no gathering gloom,
Shall o'er that glorious landscape ever come,
No tears shall fall, in sadness o'er those flowers,
That breathe their fragrance through celestial bowers.

No tear shall be in heaven, no sorrows reign,
No secret anguish, no corporeal pain;
No shivering limbs, no burning fever there,
No soul's eclipse, no winter of despair.

No night shall be in heaven, but endless noon,
No fast declining sun, nor waning moon,
But there the Lamb shall yield perpetual light,
'Mid pastures green, and waters ever bright.

No tear shall be in heaven, no darkened room,
No bed of death, or silence of the tomb;
But breezes ever fresh with love and truth,
Shall brace the frame with an immortal youth.

In view of such a consummation, of what account are our momentary earthly sufferings, trials, disappointments, or persecutions? Are they worthy to be compared with the glory to be revealed? Should we not rather bless God for every pang we feel, knowing that our light affliction, which is but for a moment, worketh for us a far more exceeding and eternal weight of glory?

Then, oh my soul, despond no more,
The storm of life will soon be o'er,
And I shall find the peaceful shore
Of everlasting rest.
O happy day! Oh joyful hour,
When freed from earth my soul shall tower,
Beyond the reach of Satan's power,
To be forever blest.

Well might the dying Mrs. Osgood write, with her feet almost upon the eternal shore,

> I'm going through the eternal gates,
> Ere June's sweet roses blow;
> Death's lovely angel leads me there,
> And it is sweet to go.

Beloved reader! Does your bosom glow with this glorious hope of joys immortal beyond the grave? If so, let us rejoice together.

Blessed be the God and Father of our Lord Jesus Christ, who, according to his abundant mercy, hath begotten us again unto a lively hope by the resurrection of Jesus Christ from the dead, to an inheritance incorruptible, and undefiled, and that fadeth not away. May neither death, nor life, nor angels, nor principalities, nor powers, nor things present, nor things to come, nor height, nor depth, nor any other creature, ever separate us from the love of God which is in Christ Jesus our Lord. May this "good hope through grace," be our solace and strength through life, our support and consolation in death, and only cease to shine and glow within us, when mortality is swallowed up of life!

I said, "let us rejoice together." And yet the lines I now write will be read by some, when the hand that writes them has crumbled back to dust. But even then *let us rejoice together:*

> One army of the living God,
> To his command we bow;
> Part of his host have crossed the flood,
> And part are crossing now.

From beyond the stars we may exclaim, Rejoice

O earth! Cry out and shout ye inhabitants of Zion! ye heirs of glory on the way to these heavenly mansions! While from earth you may respond, Sing on! ye heavenly hosts, sing on! By faith we hear your melodies—we see your shining robes and sparkling crowns—we are treading the narrow way you trod—we have an earnest of our future inheritance,—we are fighting the good fight of faith, and expect to overcome by the blood of the Lamb, and to meet you ere long in heaven!"

> There all the ship's company meet,
> Who sailed with the Master beneath;
> With shouting each other they greet,
> And triumph o'er sorrow and death,
> The voyage of life's at an end,
> The mortal affliction is past;
> The age that in heaven they spend,
> Forever and ever shall last.

Cold and heat, hunger and thirst, weariness, sickness, pain, and death—all these are forever past.

> The mourner is blessed by his Saviour and God,
> The parted rejoin in that blest abode;
> 'Tis a mansion of beauty and glory and light,
> And the angels are there in their robes of white:
> Its walls are of onyx-stone, jasper and gold,
> But the half of its beauty can never be told—
> Our friends wait us there, and they beckon away,
> We hasten to join them in endless day.

But it will not be the everlasting rest—the robes and palms,—the harps and streets of gold—the river and trees of life—the society of the angels; the meeting again with those who have gone before, that will constitute the bliss of heaven.

Not all the harps above,
Can make a heavenly place,
If God his residence remove,
Or but conceal his face.

To THEE and THEE *alone*,
The angels owe their bliss;
They sit around the glorious throne
And dwell where JESUS is.

Well might a devout servant of God declare that he expected to gaze a thousand years upon him who bought him with his own blood, before he could notice any merely earthly friend or relative, however dear. Pure and holy and bright and enduring as are the heavenly mansions, they would be all clouds and darkness and gloom without the light of the Lamb.

When on my new-fledged wings I rise,
To tread those shores beyond the skies,
What object first shall strike my eyes?
And where shall I begin my joys?
I'll run through every golden street,
And ask each blissful soul I meet,
Where is the *God* whose praise ye sing?
Oh lead a stranger to your *King!*

But these pages may be read by some of the friends of our youth and early manhood,—fellow-Christians and fellow-laborers of other years,—who, like the writer begin to mark the lengthening shadows of life's declining day, and are looking for the welcome opening of the eternal gates.

To all such, who may look upon the memorial of our former earthly being, fronting the title page, when we are gone, or drop a tear over the spot where our ashes rest—to all such, kindred in the flesh, and beloved brethren in Christ, we would say,

The soul that thou hast loved
  Will not be there,
It will have plumed its wings,
  And soared afar.
Then weep not o'er my change,
  When I am free—
When I've left my cell and gained
  My liberty.

Afar in yonder sky,
  I'll find my home,
And wait in realms of light
  For thee to come.
Call me not back to earth,
  To leave my crown,
I have fought through sin and death,
  My victory's won.

Excuse, indulgent reader, these frank and unaffected disclosures of our personal hopes and prospects. They are the spontaneous outgushings of a heart still youthful and fresh in its friendships and Christian affections—a tribute to the memory of thousands of cherished earthly friends, scattered here and there over the fields of our itinerant labor, but whom we shall meet no more on earth. May we all meet in peace beyond the grave!

But of the prospect that opens before the good man in the hour of death,—

Who can paint the scenes of glory
Where the ransomed dwell on high?

Eye hath not seen, ear hath not heard, neither hath it entered into the heart of man fully to conceive of the glory that awaits the Christian beyond the vale of death.

No sickness there,
No weary wasting of the frame away,
No fearful shrinking from the midnight air,
No dread of summer's bright and fervid ray.

No hidden grief,
No wild and cheerless visions of despair,
No vain petition for a swift relief,
No tearful eye, no broken hearts are there.

Care has no home
Within that realm of ceaseless praise and song:
Its tossing billows break and melt in foam,
Far from the mansions of the spirit throng.

The storm's black wing
Is never spread athwart celestial skies:
Its wailings blend not with the voice of spring,
As some poor tender floweret fades and dies.

No night distils
Its chilling dews upon the tender frame:
No morn is needed there! the light which fills
That land of glory, from its Maker came.

No parting friends
O'er mournful recollections have to weep:
No bed of death enduring love attends
To watch the coming of a pulseless sleep.

No blasted flowers,
Or withered bud celestial gardens know:
No scorching blast, or fierce descending shower,
Scatters destruction like a ruthless foe.

No battle word
Alarms the sacred host with fear and dread:
The song of peace creation's morning heard,
Is sung wherever angel footsteps tread.

Let us depart,
If home like this await the weary soul:
Look up thou stricken one! thy wounded heart
Shall bleed no more at sorrow's stern control.

With faith our guide,
White-robed and innocent, to tread the way,
Why fear to plunge in Jordan's rolling tide,
And find the haven of eternal day?

Such is the prospect opened before the Christian as he passes the gates of death. No wonder he often shouts. No wonder he cries, "Victory! Victory! through the blood of the Lamb!"

Why should I shrink at pain or woe?
Or feel, at death, dismay?
I've Canaan's goodly land in view,
And realms of endless day.

Then welcome Death! welcome the tomb and the bright world beyond! Welcome ye angels immortal! Welcome ye blissful hosts, once of earth, and heirs of sorrow pain and death, but now forever free! Welcome my long-lost kindred who await my coming!

Welcome, thrice welcome, ye gates of day! thou city of my God! All hail *Immortality!* All hail ETERNAL LIFE!!

Forever with the Lord!
Amen, so let it be!
Life from the dead is in that word,
'Tis immortality.

Here in the body pent,
Absent from him I roam;
Yet nightly pitch my moving tent
A day's march nearer home.

Forever with the Lord!
Father, if 'tis thy will,
The promise of that faithful word,
E'en here to me fulfil.

So, when my latest breath
  Shall rend the veil in twain,
By death I shall escape from death,
  And life eternal gain.

Knowing as I am known,
  How shall I love that word,
And oft repeat before the throne,
  Forever with the Lord!

CHAPTER XXV.

CLOSING APPEAL TO THE UNCONVERTED.

'Tis not the whole of life to live,
Nor all of death to die.

AND now dear reader, our work draws to a close. A few more pages and our communion with you may end forever. To what additional theme ought those pages to be devoted? If you are to exist forever in another world—if the life that now is, is to determine our allotment in the world to come, and, especially if you are not a Christian, and have no good hope through grace of everlasting life in heaven, what *ought* I to say to you in closing the discussion of the momentous theme of the soul's immortality? Will you not expect an appeal in behalf of that undying spirit whose endless interests you have so long neglected? And will you not listen as a candidate for immortality, whose days are so soon to be accomplished as the days of an hireling?

I. *Have you a doubt in your own mind that your soul is immortal, and that you are to live in joy or woe forever?*

Is not this doctrine clearly revealed in the Holy Scriptures, and corroborated by all the facts and phenomena of reason and nature? Have you the remotest idea that when you die that is to be your end? You shudder at the thought. Every power and susceptibility of your undying nature cries out against the idea. You shrink back from the contemplation of the cold, dark, cheerless abyss of non-existence. You cannot, you *would* not shake off the conviction that that which thinks and knows and hopes and fears within you shall always exist.

> The sun is but a spark of fire,
> A transient meteor of the sky;
> The soul, immortal as its sire,
> Shall never die!

Whatever else, then, you may for the present believe or reject, let this great truth sink deep into your heart—I am to exist eternally! Believe it, ponder it, cherish it, till it shall permeate the whole soul and spirit, chasten your aspirations and relishes and hopes and mould your purposes for a life befitting your immortal destination.

II. *I beseech you to ponder the character of your past life.*

Are you not a sinner in the sight of God? Have you not often and long trampled upon his holy law, and done despite to the Spirit of grace? If they are cursed who continue not in all things written in the book of the law to do them, are you not under this curse? and does not the wrath of God abide upon you? Oh be candid and impartial with your own soul. You are alone with God, oh think as for eternity!

> 'Tis greatly wise to talk with our past hours,
> And ask them what report they bore to heaven.

Oh may the blessed Spirit of God seal upon the

conscience afresh a sense of the guilt and desert of sin, and of your need of pardon and reconciliation to God, before you go hence and are here no more!

III. *Remember the relation of the present life to the interminable future, as the seed-time of an immortal harvest.*

As we sow here so shall we reap hereafter. Beyond this fleeting life there is prepared for the righteous a crown of glory that fadeth not away. There is a heaven, a glorious heaven beyond the stars.

"And there shall in no wise enter into it anything that defileth, neither whatsoever worketh abomination, or maketh a lie; but they which are written in the Lamb's book of life." Rev. xxi. 27.

"And there shall be no more curse: but the throne of God and of the Lamb shall be in it; and his servants shall serve him: and they shall see his face; and his name shall be in their foreheads. And there shall be no night there; and they need no candle, neither light of the sun; for the Lord God giveth them light: and they shall reign forever and ever." Rev. xxii. 3–5.

"Blessed are they that do his commandments, that they may have right to the tree of life, and may enter in through the gates into the city." Rev. xxii. 15.

Yes, blessed be the Lord,

Beyond this vale of tears,
There is a life above,
Unmeasured by the flight of years;
And all that life is love.

Be assured also, that a miserable eternity awaits the unforgiven and unsanctified.

> There is a death whose pang,
> Outlasts the fleeting breath:
> Oh what eternal horrors hang,
> Around the second death!

The redeemed and blood-washed shall "see life" and enter heaven.

"Bnt the fearful, and unbelieving, and the abominable, and murderers, and whoremongers, and sorcerers, and idolaters, and all liars, shall have their part in the lake which burneth with fire and brimstone: which is the second death." Rev. xxi. 8.

"For without are dogs, and sorcerers, and whoremongers, and murderers, and idolaters, and whosoever loveth and maketh a lie." Rev. xxii. 15. "And these shall go away into everlasting punishment: but the righteous into life eternal." Matt. xxv. 46.

Oh do not be beguiled by the syren song of "no hell beyond the grave," to steer on without pardon or hope, till you are forever wrecked amid the dark rocks of error and the breakers of death! Trust not your endless destiny to a speculation that has no countenance in the word of God, and has failed its thousands when they most needed the girdings of truth and hope, and when it was too late to build on the Rock of Ages.

IV. *Remember that your only hope is in Jesus Christ, the Saviour of lost souls.*

Talk they of morals? O thou bleeding Love,
Thou Maker of new morals to mankind!
The grand morality is love to Thee.

"Other foundation can no man lay than that is laid, which is Jesus Christ." "We are all as an unclean thing, and all our righteousness as filthy rags." We are only forgiven "through the redemption that is in Christ Jesus," and "washed from our sins in his blood." There is "no other name given under heaven, or among men, whereby we must be saved." "Not by works of righteousness which we have done, but according to his mercy he saveth us, by the washing of regeneration, and the renewing of the Holy Ghost."

V. *Remember, also, that salvation from sin is through faith in the blood of Christ.*

"He that believeth and is baptized shall be saved." "He that believeth on the Son hath everlasting life." For "as Moses lifted up the serpent in the wilderness, even so was the Son of man lifted up, that whosoever believeth in him should not perish, but have everlasting life." He only becomes our personal propitiation "through faith in his blood;" for "with the heart man believeth unto righteousness; and with the mouth confession is made unto salvation."

VI. *Do not be deluded by the idea that because you cannot merit heaven, or wash away the guilt of sin, by a righteous life, that, therefore, you have nothing to do that you may be saved.*

We are workers together with God. Though salvation is of grace, still in an infinitely important sense is it true that,

We shape ourselves the joy or woe,
Of which the coming life is made,
And fill our future hemisphere,
With sunshine or with shade.

God has made us free, and has set life and death before us. Christ has died for us, the just for the unjust that he might bring us to God, and it is for us to believe on him and live, or reject him and perish.

Ages pass away,
Thrones fall, and nations disappear, and worlds
Grow old and go to wreck; the soul alone
Endures, and what she chooseth for herself,
The arbiter of her own destiny,
That only shall be permanent.

God has done all on his part that is necessary for your salvation, at least till you turn penitently to him: it now remains for you to settle your endless destiny. *If you will* you may be saved! You yet live, and,

Life is the hour that God has given
T' escape from hell and fly to heaven;
The day of grace—and mortals may
Secure the blessings of the day.

VII. Finally, brother immortal, candidate for heaven or hell, purchase of a Redeemer's blood, let me entreat you to *act at once, and neglect no longer the great salvation!*

Are you young? So much the more hope in your case if you now turn to God. Have you spent much of your short life in sin already? So much the greater need of immediate action. Time is flying; life is speeding away; we travel enchanted ground; and death and hell pursue! "Behold *now* is the accepted time; behold *now* is the day of salvation."

While God invites, how blest the day!
  How sweet the gospel's charming sound!
Come, sinner, haste, oh haste away,
  While yet a pardoning God is found.

A little longer and it may be *forever too late!* Why, then delay?

Hasten, sinner, to return!
  Stay not for the morrow's sun,
Lest thy lamp should fail to burn,
  Ere salvation's work is done.

PRAYER.

O GOD of infinite mercies! Look thou upon these pages with favor and compassion. Pardon their many errors and imperfections. Attend them with thy blessing, and shed thou upon the mind and heart of all who shall read them the light and precious guidance of thy Holy Spirit. May they be instrumental in thy hands in convincing the unbeliever of his immortal destination. May they strengthen the faith, brighten the prospects, and increase the joys of thy people. May they tend to bind the hearts of all who read them, to thy precious word, and to the cross of Christ. May they alleviate the sorrows of the bereft and broken-hearted; impress the soul of the reader with a deeper sense of the brevity and importance of this mortal life, the vanity of all things earthly, and the inestimable value of things spiritual and eternal. Above all, O Lord, we humbly beseech thee, so to follow with thy blessing this humble volume, wherever it may go, and by whomsoever it may be read, that as thy servant was brought to repentance and faith in thee through the instrumentality of a book,* so this book may be the means in thy hands of winning souls to Christ, who shall shine as the stars forever and ever.

Bless especially, we beseech thee, the unconverted reader as he may close this volume, and be about to turn his thoughts to other themes and pursuits. May he be persuaded by the brevity and uncertainty of life, the everlasting years before him after death, the joys of heaven, the pains of hell, the voice of conscience, the blood of Christ, and the strivings of the Holy Ghost, to GIVE THEE HIS HEART! And to Thy name shall be the everlasting praise!

And now unto the ever blessed and adorable TRINITY—the FATHER, SON, and HOLY GHOST—one God, world without end—be honor and

* The writer was convinced of sin and led to Christ, in December, 1834, through the instrumentality of "*The Course of Time,* a poem by ROBERT POLLOK."

Oh happy day that fixed my choice,
On Thee my Saviour and my God.

power, dominion and glory, forever and ever. *Amen.*

NOTE.—As stated in the Preface, so we here repeat, that it is the Author's purpose, should life and health permit, to prepare a similar volume soon upon *The Resurrection of the Dead;* to be followed by one devoted exclusively to *The Heavenly World,* and another upon the subject of *Future Punishment.* Should a gracious Providence favor this design, it is hoped that the entire four volumes may be issued, in uniform style, as early as January, 1867 at latest.

APPENDIX.

THE following excellent poems are so pertinent to the subject of Immortality, and yet so seldom to be met with, that we insert them here as well for the edification of the devout reader, as to prevent their falling into oblivion.

The first is by Mrs. S. K. Furman, but we are unable to give the author of the second.

THE OLD MAN'S VALEDICTORY.

Wayworn, infirm, and old,
Lo, on my pilgrim's trusty staff I bow;
While evening's gathering shadows, damp and cold,
Fall on my heart and brow.

The winds of time have swept,
Long since, my youth and manhood's prime away;
And through my frame a withering blight has crept—
The mildew of decay.

Along life's backward track
Sweet echoes float from out my cottage door;
And oft in solitude I wander back
To seek the loved once more.

My children, fair and bright
As golden sunbeams, gathered round me there;
Again I view the mother's fond delight
And list her trusting prayer.

Blest little ones that came
And caroled till their angel-plumes were given,
Perched in our hearts and lisped the parents' names,
Then flew away to heaven.

And long, lone years have flown
Since with her meek hands folded on her breast,
My gentle wife, o'er weary, laid her down
Beside her babes to rest.

O then, in that great grief,
God's loving chastenings I no longer spurned,
But sought the proffered balm of sweet relief
For which my spirit yearned.

Since then a rugged way
Ofttimes has led me through misfortune's vale;
Yet His sure word and grace have been my stay,
Whose promises ne'er fail.

Safe through the wilderness,
My home grows nearer in the realms of love;
Soon I shall join the sacred strains of bliss
Sung by the blest above.

In prayer and trust I wait
On life's dim threshold, free from doubt and fears,
Watching the opening of death's mystic gate
To the eternal years.

O 'twas a touching sight!
A toil-worn pilgrim on the golden strand,
With white locks waving in the mellow light
Of the soft Beulah Land:

That gentle interlude
Of second childhood's sweet simplicity,
A spring in autumn, tender and subdued,
Telling of life to be:

Flushing the weary heart
With loving pictures of life's early bowers,
Wreathing the spirit ere it doth depart
With sweet immortal flowers.

When came the Sabbath day
They bore him in with slow and muffled tread;
In hallowed rest before the altar lay,
White-robed, the sainted dead.

Earth's sorrows all are past;
On his mute lips the smile of joy we see,
And these his tender words, to us the last,
His valedictory.

IMMORTAL LONGINGS.

Christ, let me come to thee!
My heart is weary, and I long for rest;
Is not my earthly mission well-nigh done?
I cannot bear this burden on my breast—
It weighs my spirit downward like a stone.

My saddened life is ever vailed in clouds,
  And midnight darkness hath come o'er my soul.
My once bright hopes are wrapped away in shrouds,
  And sorrow's heavy surges round me roll.
    Sweet Christ, O may I come?

    Christ, let me come to thee!
Life hath a dark Sahara been to me!
  The few bright flowers that bloomed along my way
Were soon transplanted—each beloved tree
  To bloom perennial in the "perfect day."
My dear loved ones sit round thy golden throne,
  And wait—a broken circle till I come;
Let me not linger here on earth alone—
  O let me join them in their heavenly home!
    Sweet Christ, O may I come?

    Christ, let me come to thee!
Behind me roars the angry ocean tide;
  Each crested wave comes nearer, nearer still:
The muttering thunders in the billows hide;
  I shudder at their hoarse, loud voice so chill;
I cannot meet the fierce, wild storm of life!
  I have no strength to battle with it more!
Too long I've wrestled in the painful strife;
  I must lay down the burden that I bore.
    Sweet Christ, O may I come?

    Christ, let me come to thee!
In dreams I hear thy white-robed angels sing
  The golden glories of their beauteous land;
I hear the rustle of each snowy wing,
  And feel their touch upon my fevered hand.

Colder than ever seems the earth to me,
  When I awake and see them flit away;
I strain my eyes the last bright glimpse to see,
  And watch them vanish through the gates of day.
    Sweet Christ, O may I come?

    Christ, let me come to thee!
I watch my toiling breath grow faint and slow;
  I note the hectic deepening day by day,
And feel my life is like a wreath of snow,
  Which one kind breath of heaven would melt away.
A little longer in this world of vice—
  The wished-for boundary is almost passed—
I see the shining shore of Paradise,
  I know my pain is almost o'er at last.
    Sweet Christ, O let me come!

    Christ, let me come to thee!
I've seen the gates that guard thy holy clime;
  And often caught a gleam from far (within;)
I know they'll open in thine own good time,
  And let thy weary, wandering child come in.
I've had, all through this weary care and pain,
  One blessed hope, that ne'er has known despair—
It cheers me like the sunshine after rain!
  I know thou'lt hear my deep and heartfelt prayer,
    And let me come to thee!

INDEX OF SCRIPTURE QUOTATIONS.

INDEX OF POETIC QUOTATIONS.

GENERAL INDEX.

www.ingramcontent.com/pod-product-compliance
Lightning Source LLC
LaVergne TN
LVHW020115110826
845151LV00001B/162

* 9 7 8 1 4 2 5 5 4 2 8 3 2 *